D0759596

Albert Camus

Albert Camus

AND THE
LITERATURE OF REVOLT

JOHN CRUICKSHANK

*Il existe une bonne inquiétude, un
trouble salutaire.*

MAURIAC

GREENWOOD PRESS, PUBLISHERS
WESTPORT, CONNECTICUT

Library of Congress Cataloging in Publication Data

Cruickshank, John.
  Albert Camus and the literature of revolt.

  Reprint 6f the ed. published by Oxford University Press,
London, New York.
  Bibliography: p.
  Includes index.
  1. Camus, Albert, 1913-1960--Criticism and Interpreta-
tion. I. Title.
[PQ2605.A3734Z63 1978]   848'.9'1409   78-16380
ISBN 0-313-20580-9

For Kathleen

Note

I am very grateful to Professor C. A. Hackett, Head of the Department of Romance Languages and Literatures in the University of Southampton, for his constant interest and helpful advice during the writing of this book. I must also thank my friend and colleague Mr. A. R. Manser with whom I discussed, to my own advantage at least, the contents of Parts One and Two. The preparation of the manuscript owes much to the careful typing and intelligent checking of Miss Doreen Cross.

Some material in Chapters 7 and 8 reproduces, in modified form, two articles of mine first published in *French Studies* (Oxford, England) and *Symposium* (Syracuse, U.S.A.), and I am grateful to the editors of these periodicals for their co-operation. The extracts from Camus' own writings are published here by kind permission of the Librairie Gallimard, Paris, holders of the copyright.

J. C.

Southampton, July, 1958.

A TRIBUTE TO ALBERT CAMUS

*Delivered by John Cruickshank on 19 January 1960 at
the Institut Français, London*

I would count it an honour, in any circumstances, to be asked
to pay public tribute to Albert Camus. I am particularly honoured
by the invitation to do so here, in the Institut Français, before
this audience. At the same time, I know you will understand
completely when I say how deeply I regret this occasion—as
indeed we must all regret it. Camus' death, at the age of forty-six,
is a tragedy not only for France, but also for Europe and the
world. We must mourn him because he was a gifted and outstanding writer, but we also mourn him because of the kind of
man he had proved himself to be—one who, in his life and in his
work, embodied the French moral conscience at its most pure
and most persuasive. That is why France's loss is also our loss.
But to speak in sentimental terms of Camus' death would not be
to honour his memory. Sentimentality is the opposite of that
'virile reticence' of which he spoke and which he claimed as
part of his Mediterranean inheritance. And yet, not to mention
his personal qualities at all would be to do him less than justice.
What his intimate friends must have felt on learning of his death
one can only attempt to guess, but even simply to have lived
with his work for a number of years and to have corresponded
with him was sufficient to make one know real sorrow. One's
first thoughts now are less of his achievement as an artist than
of his qualities as a man. Various obituary notices have spoken
of Camus' simplicity, his kindness, his honesty, his outstanding
capacity for loyal friendship, his genuine modesty. That Camus
really possessed these qualities, that they are not the pious tributes
of the funeral orator, is clearly shown by the fact that they were
frequently referred to by those who knew him best while he was
still alive. Of his patience and friendliness I myself have proof.

As regards his modesty, this is the quality which made him mini-mize his own part in the Resistance just as it prompted him to speak quite genuinely of his 'bewilderment' and 'a kind of panic' on being awarded the Nobel Prize for Literature in 1957.

Characteristics such as these—simple, and yet perhaps not so very common—are the explanation of that intense humanity which Camus showed in deeds as well as in words. His concern for individuals, his hatred of cruelty, his fight against totalitarian-ism, his opposition to capital punishment—all these were atti-tudes which he found natural, which he could hardly help. But they were attitudes to which he gave a strong intellectual basis as well because he found, as others have found, that we live in an age when even elementary goodness must often be justified and defended in the face of ideological attack. It is important, then, that we should see Camus under a double aspect—as a man of conscience and integrity, and also as an intellectual whose mind could be subtle, ironic, incisive, yet grounded in common-sense. To see him in this way is to begin to understand both his direct descent from the great French *moralistes* and his importance for ourselves at the present time.

The fact is that whatever the reservations some critics may have expressed about particular works, Camus has generally been regarded by his contemporaries as the most significant writer of his generation for themselves; a writer who has been both a spokesman and a guide, yet without posturing or pretentiousness. In various surveys carried out in France since the war, and de-signed to discover what young Frenchmen have been reading, Camus has always been one of the first two names on the list, sharing the largest audience of readers under twenty-five with Sartre or Malraux. He constantly received letters from young people in many different parts of the world, as well as in Europe, letters testifying to the fact that his work expresses with unusual clarity the problems and aspirations of a whole generation. It is this aspect of his work—its importance for his contemporaries—that I shall try to explain and discuss in the remainder of this talk.

Camus himself described his writings as the outcome of an effort to understand the age into which he was born. The fact that he

grew to maturity in Algeria no doubt helped him in this undertaking, even though he always thought of himself, and rightly,
as a European. Algeria enabled him to gain a dispassionate and
comprehensive view of Europe before he himself settled in
France. In one of his post-war essays he wrote: 'From the shores
of Africa where I was born, helped by distance, we have a clearer
view of the face of Europe and we know it is not beautiful.'
Elsewhere he speaks of Europe as 'dark,' 'dreary,' 'sad' and even
'ignoble' because of the spectacle it has offered in our time of
wars and mass murder. In an essay of the same period he writes:

Do you know that over a period of twenty-five years, between 1922
and 1947, 70 million Europeans—men, women and children,—have
been uprooted, deported and killed?

It is within this context that Camus created his work as a writer.
This is the background of events which he witnessed, which
we have witnessed, and which he approached with a questioning
urgency. It is the subject of human suffering in our time. Faced
with such a spectacle Camus felt humility and inadequacy, but
he was not prepared to close his eyes to it. We all know, at least at
second hand, of torture and brainwashing, mass deportations
and scientifically controlled destruction, racial hatred and the
summary judgements of 'people's courts.' What is so particularly
alarming is that all these things have been defended, at one
time or another, in the name of ideologies claiming as their ultimate goal the greater happiness of human kind. The age for
which Camus wrote is thus one of moral and intellectual confusion and convulsion. The same values have apparently been
invoked on behalf of so many conflicting causes that these values
have lost all meaning. The story of our century has been the
story of increasingly terrible blows dealt against the traditional
humanist assumptions.

   Nihilism has therefore been the great temptation of our age.
For many, the only course open has been to proclaim the mean-
inglessnesss of everything and to adopt a comprehensive cynicism
which, in its negative form of indifference, encourages the
growth of its positive manifestation as political crime and moral
decay of the fascist or Stalinist type. We should note, I think,
that Camus does not speak self-righteously about these things.

He is careful to point out, as modern psychology—and perhaps even self-inspection—can confirm, that, as he puts it, 'we all carry within us our prisons, our crimes, our destructiveness'. 'But', he adds, 'to unleash them on the world is not our duty. Our duty consists in fighting them in ourselves and in others.' The whole problem is set out more fully in Camus' speech of acceptance on receiving the Nobel Prize. Speaking particularly for his own generation he says:

Those men who were born at the beginning of the first world war and were twenty at the time of Hitler's coming to power and the first revolutionary trials, who were then confronted, to complete their education, with the Spanish war, the second world war, the universal concentration camp, Europe ruled by the gaoler and the torturer, have now to bring up their sons and produce their works in a world threatened by nuclear destruction. Nobody, surely, can expect them to be optimists. And I believe, indeed, that we should understand, while continuing to oppose it, the mistaken attitude of those who, through excess of despair, have asserted the right to dishonour, and have rushed headlong into the nihilism of our day. None the less, the greater number of us, in my own country and throughout Europe, have rejected such nihilism and have tried to find some law to live by. They have had to forge for themselves an art of living through times of catastrophe, in order to be reborn, and then to fight openly against the death-instinct which is at work in our time.

The temptation of nihilism, and the eventual rejection of nihilism, to which Camus refers in this passage, comprise the double aspect of his own examination of his age—his rôle both as a symptom of his times and as an exemplary figure for them. His writings on 'the absurd', as he termed it, speak of his temptation by nihilism. His writings on 'revolt' show how he overcame this temptation in himself. These two related ideas—*l'absurde* and *la révolte*—are the two basic intellectual concepts behind his work. To speak of each of them in turn, and in more detail, will be to understand better his significance and his achievement.

Camus' first comments on the absurd treat it, characteristically, as an emotional experience rather than an intellectual idea. With an instinctive emphasis on individual experience, and referring to his own early life in Algeria, he describes what turns out to be a growing awareness of the absurd in his acute sense of contrast between the richness of physical existence and the inevitability of death. This is the dualism underlying his first published collection of essays, *L'Envers et l'endroit,* which appeared in 1937. The five essays contained in the book are written in elegant prose, an intense yet severe lyricism in which the intensity praises the profusion of the physical world while the severity recalls human transience seen against this physical background. The two aspects of existence, to which the French title refers, are summed up in Camus' conclusion that 'there is no love of life without despair about life'. This theme of the tragic ambivalence of human existence, the *nascentes morimur* of the ancients, is, of course, an old and familiar one in literature. What is striking, here, is the individual directness with which Camus expresses it and his personal need to maintain both terms of the dualism, refusing to suppress either of them in order to attain what would have been, for him, a dishonest peace of mind.

In the collection of four essays which he published two years later, under the title of *Noces,* Camus refers again to the dualism and, in particular, to the way in which each of the two terms intensifies his experience of the other and really raises the dualism to the status of a paradox. He writes: 'My horror of dying derives from my anxious appetite for life.' He adds: 'I want to maintain clearness of vision to the uttermost limit and face my end with all the wealth of my appetite for life and my horror of death.' In *Noces,* however, as the title implies, Camus is mainly concerned to celebrate those 'nuptials' with the earth which are the positive term of the paradox. He does so in pages describing the North African landscape which have done much to reinstate the lyrical essay as a striking literary form. As regards the negative term, which is at the basis of much contemporary nihilism, Camus examines this in a more widely known book, *Le Mythe de Sisyphe.*

Here again, the first hints of the absurd are linked with personal experience. Most of the time the repetitiveness of our lives does not disturb us. We are scarcely even conscious of it. We follow easily enough the ceaseless rhythm of 'getting up, taking the tram, four hours in an office or factory, a meal, the tram, four hours' work, a meal, sleep', and the same pattern is repeated week after week, month after month, year after year. (Incidentally, you will notice here that Camus seems to treat the deadening routine of most people's lives, particularly in an urbanized and highly industrialized society, as a modern embodiment of the Sisyphus myth.) But there are those who, one day or another, suddenly question the validity of this existence. They utter the simple word, 'why', and everything begins, says Camus, in this 'weariness tinged with surprise'. Everything begins, no doubt, because to have this experience is to receive what might be called the intimations of absurdity. A link in the chain of daily gesture has been broken irreparably. The temptation now is towards the brink, even the abyss, of nihilism as further evidences of the absurd present themselves. These other evidences may take various forms: the sudden awareness that time is carrying us away and will finally destroy our physical existence; an experience of the alien nature of the world outside us and a feeling that the strength and endurance of nature mock our frail mortality; a sense of a gap, which cannot be closed, between ourselves and other people, so that they even appear on occasion to exude a kind of inhuman essence; a sense of alienation from ourselves—that familiar and yet disquietingly unrecognizable person glimpsed in the mirror or an old photograph. Lastly, Camus speaks of death which he treats as perhaps the ultimate evidence of the absurd. In particular, elsewhere in his work, he emphasizes the terrible absurdity of arbitrary death and apparently needless suffering. In a lecture which he was invited to give to a group of Dominicans in 1948 he said:

As far as I am concerned I shall not try to present myself to you as a Christian. I share with you the same horror of evil. But I do not share your hope and I shall continue to fight against this universe in which children suffer and die.

But in the same year, when asked by an interviewer if the so-called 'problem of evil', in the sense of human pain and death, was what prevented him from accepting Christianity, Camus replied with typical honesty:

The insurmountable barrier does seem to me to be the problem of evil. But it is also a real obstacle for traditional humanism. There is the death of children, which means a divine reign of terror, but there is also the killing of children, which is an expression of a human reign of terror. We are wedged between two kinds of arbitrary law.

Camus goes on, after this, to speak of the absurd as a more purely intellectual concept. He sees our experience of the world as remaining beyond the reach of rational categories. The true history of human thought, indeed, is the story of its constant recantations and its failure to achieve any certainty. Camus says:

I can feel this heart inside me and I conclude that it exists. I can touch this world and I also conclude that it exists. All my knowledge ends at this point. The rest is hypothesis.

Our choice then, according to Camus, is between description which can be accurate but does not tell us anything significant about the world, and hypotheses of various kinds which claim to convey truth but are not demonstrably certain. It is on the basis of such an analysis that Christianity is rejected. Christian thinkers such as Pascal, Kierkegaard and certain modern existentialist theologians, have presented their beliefs as a way of escape from the absurd. Pascal urges us to *wager* in favour of God's existence, Kierkegaard accepts Christianity as being what he calls 'the supreme paradox'. But for Camus, existentialist theology, in its early or its latter-day forms, is an attempt to evade the absurd and not a direct elucidation of it. Christianity, he says at one point, is 'less genuine peace than tragic hope'.

The absurd is thus finally presented to us as something which arises from a confrontation between the human desire for coherence, for understanding, and the irrationality, the opacity, of the world. Camus' description of the absurd conforms to ancient, familiar mythic patterns used to represent the human condition. We have Tantalus tormented by water and by fruit-laden trees beyond his reach; we have Prometheus chained to a rock and become eternal food for the vulture; and we have Camus' own choice of myth in this particular book—Sisyphus pushing his boulder towards the hill-top from which it will always roll back. The absurd is denial by the gods of man's claim to parity with them, and Camus invests it with much of the intensity, the inevitability and the universality of classical tragedy.

The main moral consequence drawn by Camus from his analysis is that the absurd reduces all actions to ethical equality in so far as they cannot be referred to any *absolute* standard of right and wrong. The absurdist ethic does not positively recommend either what we normally regard as virtue or what we call crime. But neither can it totally exclude the one or the other. As Camus says ironically, speaking of virtue, one can, after all, be virtuous by caprice. It is this apparent lack of moral differentiation in nihilist theory which leads him, when he speaks of its ethical consequences, to stress quantity, not quality. The appetite for life which he discussed earlier, and which awareness of the absurd serves to sharpen, leads to concentration on the present moment and a desire to experience, in all its variety and to the greatest possible degree of intensity, the succession of present moments which constitutes one's life. In fact, we have here something very like the ethic of quantity and intensity advocated by Pater in the final chapter of *The Renaissance*. Having defined life as an interval between two voids—the void before birth and the void after death—Pater says: 'Our chance lies in expanding that interval, in getting as many pulsations as possible into the given time.' 'Multiplied consciousness', as Pater also calls it, is closely akin to the ethical position which, according to Camus, emerges logically as a possible way of living with the absurd.

At this stage, then, Camus derives from the absurd an attitude of acceptance expressed as an ethic of quantity. Yet within a few years he was advocating rebellion and preaching an ethic of quality. It is therefore of interest and importance to see how he made the transition from *l'absurde* to *la révolte*. There is one preliminary point which I should mention. Camus had made it quite clear in his brief preface to *Le Mythe de Sisyphe* that he was not elaborating an absurdist philosophy of his own in this book. His attitude to the absurd, he says, remains tentative and provisional. In fact, *Le Mythe de Sisyphe* is primarily a description of that experience of the absurd which he found widespread among his contemporaries, and an attempt to see as clearly as possible some of its logical consequences. Elsewhere, admitting that a part of him was undoubtedly attracted by contemporary nihilism, he adds that he never regarded the absurd as a point of rest; he saw it rather as a point of departure.

One of the most important factors which helped to take Camus

A Tribute

beyond the moral indifference of nihilism was undoubtedly the experience of the Occupation of France. He entered the Resistance in 1942, the year in which *Le Mythe de Sisyphe* was published, but two years after the book had largely been written. In the concrete situation of occupation and resistance an ethic of quantity, whatever its apparent logical coherence, could not be pursued by someone of Camus' integrity and humanity. For one thing, he now lived in circumstances where the making of moral choice and the acceptance of direct, personal responsibility could mean the difference between life and death for others, including close friends. This situation served to bring out what I myself think to be one of Camus' greatest virtues. Although an intellectual, he was neither prepared nor able to put ideology or rational demonstration above what human beings are actually experiencing in their daily lives. He could not live by an abstraction, he was sceptical towards ideology, he was too genuine a humanist and realist to try to bend and crack human nature in an effort to make it fit into some *a priori* intellectual framework. This, no doubt, is a considerable element in his appeal to the non-doctrinaire British, and the reason why his deep humanity, his practical sense and his feeling for the individual person have prompted some to compare him to Orwell and—surprisingly, though not unreasonably—to E. M. Forster. This characteristic is no doubt also at the basis of the much-discussed rupture with Sartre and the subsequent polemics in which Sartre appeared to be the victor on the level of dialectic and Camus the victor on the level of common moral experience.

Another effect of the war with Germany was to make Camus realize that Nazism, with its emphasis on violence and its contempt for individual human lives, was the moral and intellectual offspring of nihilism. This emerges clearly from the *Lettres à un ami allemand*, four letters to an imaginary German friend published in 1945 and written between 1943 and 1945. In the fourth letter Camus admits that he thought he agreed, at one stage, with the diagnosis of the absurdity of existence made by various German thinkers, and felt by the man in the street, in the 'thirties. He shared their scepticism towards moral absolutes and even now can understand, at least in an abstract way, their attempt to escape the apparent senselessness of existence by means of force, national self-aggrandisement and the practice of *Realpolitik*. Yet in the end, the Germans are fighting on one side and Camus on the other, despite something like a common intellectual starting-point. The only explanation he can offer of this situation is his inability to sacrifice human justice to philosophical theory and his conviction that the absurdity of life can only be affirmed by reference to some implied standard of coherence and sense. This desire for coherence, the frustration of which is what gives rise to the absurd in the first instance, is thus an important part of human experience. It cannot be ignored. It must be included, it must be accorded a real place, in any examination of nihilism and in any doctrine of nihilism. Thus Camus fought against Nazism in the conviction that, as he says, 'man himself possesses value and meaning precisely because he is the one creature whose desire for these things is constantly thwarted in the world'.

Lastly, Camus describes a more closely argued line of reasoning which led him from nihilism to rebellion against it. He points out that awareness of the absurd is already, in itself, a form of revolt—at least in a negative sense. To experience the absurd is, in essence, to experience a sense of scandal. The absurd scandalizes the reason and results, to this extent, from a revolt of the mind. Now once one begins to analyze this revolt it turns out to be a less wholly negative attitude than at first appeared. To claim experience of the absurd, as Camus had already pointed out, means that there is a value judgement, a value, involved when this claim is made. To speak of the absurd at all is to have rebelled, in the sense of having said 'no', to some state of affairs. But to do this is to say 'yes', by implication, to something which is not that state of affairs. This means, then, that to speak of the absurd is ultimately to affirm, within the individual who has spoken in this way, the presence of something against which the absurd is an offence. To say 'no' is to impose limits, and within these limits, we must conclude, values of some kind are still preserved despite the apparent destruction of all values by comprehensive nihilism. At this early stage the nature of such values may appear obscure, but their existence is no longer in doubt. And so Camus speaks with some confidence of three values ultimately derived from the apparently purely negative experience of the absurd itself. First, there is the individual's discovery of a part of himself which he holds to be important, which he identifies as his essence as a human being, in the name of which he confronts the absurdity of human existence—the value, we might say, of individual human worth. Second, the individual shares with other men this worth which he discovers in himself and this fact leads him to a second value—a common human nature. Third, this value takes him directly to the idea of a bond which links all men in face of the absurd—the value of human solidarity. Camus paraphrases Descartes and says: 'I rebel, therefore *we* are'. His conclusion is:

> Although apparently negative because it creates nothing, revolt is positive in a profound way since it reveals those elements in man which must always be defended.

And so Camus asserts the necessity of revolt, starting from nihilism, because of the inadequacy of a quantitative ethic in the midst of human suffering, because of the realization that a false assessment of the absurd can lead to terrible human disasters. and finally because closer scrutiny of the idea of absurdity reveals that germ of rebellion which it always contained.

Just as the whole concept of the absurd was mainly set out in a single work, *Le Mythe de Sisyphe,* so the concept of revolt is examined at length by Camus in *L'Homme révolté*—one of his books, translated under the title of *The Rebel,* which has been particularly admired in this country. He points out that revolt against the human condition has taken two main forms. Firstly, there is religion—the attempt to merit the kingdom of heaven, after our life on earth, through the operation of divine grace. Secondly, we have revolutionary politics—the attempt to change the *status quo* by force here and now in order to bring about a utopia on earth in the course of historical time. These two kinds of belief, religious conviction and political doctrine, are described respectively by Camus as representing vertical and horizontal transcendence. Vertical transcendence—the aspiration towards the kingdom of heaven—was criticized in *Le Mythe de Sisyphe.* But in any case, with the decline of religious conviction it has tended to be ousted by social and political doctrine. Indeed, there may seem to be a point at which, says Camus, 'the future (within history) has become the only transcendence of men without God'. This horizontal transcendence—a belief in the possibility of bringing about utopia by political means—found particularly dramatic expression in the French, and later in the Russian, revolutions. It becomes the main subject of criticism in *L'Homme révolté*.

Political revolution demands close scrutiny because of a fatal moral flaw which it seems to contain. The fact is that despite the idealism with which revolutions are undertaken, despite their initial declaration of human fraternity and, in many cases, their opposition to capital punishment, all resort sooner or later to the guillotine or the purge. In order to try to understand how this comes about Camus goes back to a study of those theorists who played an important rôle in promoting revolutionary ideas. Examining the writings of such thinkers as Saint-Just, Hegel, Nietzsche, Marx, he finds much that is admirable in their work. Nevertheless, he finds in the end that all made what he regards as a fatal mistake because all of them erected and defended false absolutes—concepts such as Reason, History, the Will to Power and Revolution itself. To such abstractions they sacrificed, or their followers sacrificed, human happiness in the here and now. The day arrives when, as Camus puts it, 'ideology comes into conflict with psychology' and the purest revolutionary ideals are contaminated as a result. It is considered permissible, even essential, that a real present be sacrificed to what must be, after all, a hypothetical future. Of the various attitudes just mentioned it is the deification of history, particularly by Hegel and Marx, that Camus considers to be most lethal in its effects. The result is that one of the most memorable features of *L'Homme révolté* is its remarkable analysis of Marxist theory and the related explanation of Stalinist practice. Camus goes on to suggest that the modern world, notably but not exclusively in Communist-controlled areas, has become a world of the *directive* handed down by higher officials rather than a world of the *dialogue*. The dialogue, which alone makes possible humane relationships between men, seems too expensive a luxury to those who are striving for the political realization of historical inevitability. This concept of the dialogue is an interesting one. It would be possible with more time, and perhaps more knowledge, to make illuminating comparisons between Camus' idea and the conception of the dialogue in Martin Buber's work, particularly in *I and Thou*. But even on a purely political level Camus gives the dialogue considerable importance. For example, he defines a democrat as 'one who allows his opponent to express his views and agrees to think about them'. Elsewhere he says, ironically, that the fact that he has not defamed those who disagree with him is his only originality. In general we may say that Camus' inquiry into the history and theory of political revolution reveals his humanity, his concern for the happiness of individuals, his refusal to make moral concessions to intellectual abstractions. Perhaps this emerges most clearly when he writes:

Justice is both a concept and a warmth of the soul. Let us ensure that we adopt it in its human aspect without transforming it into that terrible abstract passion which has mutilated so many men.

It is clear from all this that when Camus speaks of revolt he does not mean political revolution. Revolution he has shown to be on the side of a conception of history which has been dehumanized and has become a monstrosity. In the face of its abstract, formal demands human happiness is of no immediate account. Revolt, by contrast, is on the side of nature. It is centred on the idea of limitation, not absolutism; it preaches moderation, not extremism. In its social and political aspects it is a form of humility which recognizes that the fight against human suffering is inevitable and can have no end. And so Camus sees the decisive struggle of our times as one which must be waged not so much between Marxism and Christianity as between the deification of history and a return to nature. The Algerian in Camus, the man of the South, sees the fatal conflict as one between nordic intemperance and Mediterranean moderation. In his own words, we must choose between:

. . . nordic dreams and the Mediterranean tradition, eternally adolescent violence and mature strength, nostalgia, aggravated by learning and books, and courage tempered and enlightened by experience of life; in short, history and nature.

I have not found time, nor have I judged this occasion an appropriate one, to attempt to define and evaluate Camus' literary achievement. There is little doubt, however, that the great interest of his subject-matter is matched by the genuine skill of its imaginative presentation, particularly in the novels and short stories. Camus said that 'every authentic work of art is a gift offered to the future'. His death must prompt us to reflect how richly he himself endowed the future with his own literary work.

CONTENTS

1 INTRODUCTION

*Ce qui vient au monde pour ne rien troubler ne mérite
ni égards ni patience.*

RENÉ CHAR

It is not an easy task to present a living French writer satisfactorily
to an English audience. Quite apart from the obvious differences of
language and literary tradition, the French man of letters has a
special status in his own country which distinguishes him sharply
from his English counterpart. This status has two main aspects.
Firstly, a writer is the object of immense popular esteem in France
simply because he is a writer, an *intellectuel*. His relationship to his
public is such that his pronouncements on social and political questions receive widespread attention and respect. He is not only
encouraged to write newspaper columns, to sign manifestos or to
address meetings; he is positively expected to do so. He is given
considerable authority in spheres outside the business of writing
and this authority carries with it a public responsibility which seems
to have little connection with literature. Albert Camus, who has
been a notable repository of such confidence and an object of such
respect, himself says in *L'Été* that France is a nation which attributes an exaggerated importance to the profession of letters. In the
second place, the French writer normally lives and works on the
mainland of Europe. Unlike ourselves he has immediate land
frontiers with several foreign countries. As a result his thought is
more instinctively and more markedly European than that of most
English writers. It is largely on this account that certain contemporary French novels and plays appear remote or peculiar to some
English readers. Their authors have simply assumed in their public
the presence of experiences and attitudes which, though widespread
in France and Europe generally, may appear excessively dramatic
or gratuitously morbid in an English context.

Albert Camus

The operation of this dual status can be clearly seen in the case of Camus. His achievements as a novelist and playwright, for instance, contributed much to his influence and success as a newspaper editor. And in the years immediately following World War II his editorials in the French daily, *Combat,* had an authority equalled only by the articles of another leading novelist, François Mauriac, in *Le Figaro.* At one time Camus himself considered his journalistic responsibilities to be sufficiently important to justify his writing three editorials a week. Such authority and responsibility have been real factors in causing him, through the medium of the novel and the play as well as in his long essays on ideas, to choose to live mostly in that ill-defined no-man's-land between philosophy, politics and imaginative literature which is often merely the inevitable place of exile for second-rate *littérateurs* in England. Again, Camus' geographical position on the continent of Europe, together with his temperamental and intellectual remoteness from England, are emphasized by the most general consideration of his ideas. Among the themes which occur most frequently in his writings are the isolation of man in an alien universe, the insufficiency of certain traditional moral values, the estrangement of the individual from himself, the humanist failure of Marxism, the problem of evil, atheism, the pressing finality of death and the advocacy of a form of neo-paganism. Such subjects, particularly when treated by a gifted creative writer, are usually regarded as unfortunate aberrations by the practical English mind. They become objects of suspicion and are thought to be the undesirable products of humourlessness, excessive abstraction or mental and moral unhealth. Yet in Europe they have assured for Camus a serious and numerous following. In France particularly he has been one of the chief mentors of a new generation.

It is obvious that the extent of Camus' influence cannot be completely accounted for in terms of the sociology of French authorship. While it is true that his public status as a writer has created favourable conditions for the diffusion of his ideas, it is also clear that the essence of his influence lies in the nature of the ideas themselves. Although he has founded no literary 'school' and prefers a position apart from the more modish movements in politics and literature, his work is both a deeply-felt symptom of his times and a thoughtful commentary on them. In his choice of subjects he reflects many current intellectual attitudes and emphases. And in his treatment of these subjects he shows a humane and intelligent mind struggling to find an answer to some acute contemporary problems. He is essentially a witness—in the sense that Malraux, Sartre, or Graham Greene are witnesses—to the anxieties and aspirations of his age.

An honest witness to the contemporary world will have to speak at times in sombre tones. There may even seem to be more reasons for gloom than hope in a world dominated by two great wars and the threat of a third. There is no denying that Camus mostly writes about sombre subjects, yet it would be quite wrong to assume that he does so for perverse or ghoulish reasons. His books do not have that gratuitous savagery and sensational gloom which characterize products of the so-called *littérature noire,* and he attempts to avoid the two extremes of nihilistic pessimism and facile optimism. He is aware that the contemporary feeling of incoherence has become, in certain writers, as artificial an attitude as that optimistic nineteenth-century coherence against which it is a reaction. In a short essay written in 1950, and published with others under the title *L'Été*, Camus clearly defined his own attitude to the 'literature of despair' as it is sometimes called:

Real despair means death, the grave or the abyss. If despair prompts speech or reasoning, and above all if it results in writing, fraternity is established, natural objects are justified, love is born. A literature of despair is a contradiction in terms.

A certain kind of optimism, of course, is not my strong point. With the rest of my generation I grew up to the drumbeats of the First World War, and our history since then has continued the tale of murder, injustice or violence. But real pessimism, as we meet it today, consists in trading on all this cruelty and infamy. For my part, I have fought unceasingly against this degradation; I hate only those who are cruel. In the darkest depths of our nihilism I have sought only for the means to transcend nihilism.[1]*

Despite a genuine desire to transcend pessimism Camus has found himself writing repeatedly about violence, absurdity and death. Nicola Chiaromonte reports him as having said in the course of an interview:

* All translations from the French are my own, except where otherwise stated. The original French of all quotations of any length will be found in the appendix.

Albert Camus

I wish I could get rid of the theme of the extreme situation. When I was a boy my ambition was to write the story of a happy man. Even today, when I listen to Mozart, I can't help feeling that the ideal achievement for me would be to write the way Mozart composes. But the fact is that I have written a play for Jean-Louis Barrault, which is a variation on the theme of *The Plague*, and that I am writing another about Kaliaev, the terrorist who killed the Grand Duke Serge. After which, I tell myself, I shall write about happiness. The next moment, however, I wonder. We of the generation that has become mature from 1938 to 1945 have seen too many things. I don't mean too many horrors, but simply too many contradictory, irreconcilable things.*

These statements by Camus indicate two prominent characteristics of his mind: tenacious adherence to the truth of his own experience and the concern to avoid spineless pessimism. Intellectual tenacity is indeed apparent throughout his work. He proclaims a personal viewpoint with resolute insistence. Furthermore, his ideas are rooted in an impressive lucidity of mind and enhanced by a welcome clarity of expression. Such clarity has particular point at a time when so many French artist-philosophers not only turn to the more complex forms of German metaphysics but express themselves in a Germano-French syntax which doubles the difficulty of grasping their meaning. Camus happily possesses many of the virtues associated with the latin mind; on several occasions he has stressed his mediterranean origins and their clarifying consequences on his thought. This lucidity of mind is the real source of his qualified pessimism. Even the most depressing passages in *L'Étranger* or *Le Malentendu* are not simply the bitter fruit of invincible gloom. His work is dictated, rather, by a determination to avoid complacency and humbug, and by a conviction that happiness is not easily attained—if intellectual honesty is also to be preserved—by the majority of thoughtful human beings. The lure of easy optimism has no power over Camus. With Malraux he holds that the period of easy consolations is past. But he does believe that trustworthy hope may still be found by those who do not fear a certain feeling of despair. By means of what is more like tempered pessimism than qualified optimism, and by discussing the themes already mentioned, he leads his readers away from the relaxing

* Nicola Chiaromonte, 'Albert Camus and moderation', *Partisan Review*, X (Oct. 1948), pp. 1142–5. The two plays to which Camus refers are *L'État de siège* (1948) and *Les Justes* (1950). The English translation is by Chiaromonte.

climate of intellectual complacency towards the more bracing air of hope being rebuilt on the ruins of many traditionally held beliefs. In all this it is the idea of revolt, not consent, which provides him with a means of penetrating beyond the menacing to the promising.

The concept of revolt provides a key both to Camus' ideas themselves and to his significance for his times. The remainder of this book will be concerned with an examination of his ideas and their literary expression; at this point it may be useful, as an introduction to these ideas, to see Camus first in relation to the general background of revolt which has been such a prominent feature of recent literature. It is true, of course, that revolt in some form or other has often been a literary theme. Contemporary writers hold no exclusive monopoly in the subject. To go back no farther than the last century, we can point to the Romantics who produced a characteristic literature of revolt, and this revolt was a complex one with artistic, social and metaphysical aspects. The Romantic poets of England and France accepted an idealist tradition, however, in so far as they continued to believe in general and absolute values like Truth, Liberty, Nature, Intellectual Beauty, Pure Spirit. They were also traditional humanists in the sense that they accepted the reality of a Human Nature. The individual had a definite place in the order of things and his chief aim, even in revolt, was to embody within himself, as far as possible, a prior conception of Human Nature.

With the beginning of this century generally accepted values began noticeably to lose their power to evoke instinctive respect. Nineteenth-century absolutes such as Progress, Liberty and Science became increasingly bankrupt, or appeared as over-simplified and over-generalized terms being applied to extremely complex realities. This process of devaluation, and the distrust of capital letters which caused Romain Rolland to write: 'Je hais les mots à majuscules', engendered a new phase of revolt in France before and immediately after the First World War. The generation which includes Péguy, Valéry, Gide, Rolland and others still believed in some absolutes, but it did not accept them without question and was sharply aware of the frequent lack of correspondence between the theoretical nature of such ideals and their application in practice. Like the Romantics, these writers produced what might be called a normative revolt. That is to say they still held to certain absolutes, but they were also ready to scrutinize all absolutes closely, rejecting some. They considered the traditional humanist values to be at least severely threatened and they spoke more of the possibility of progress than of its certainty.

A new literature of revolt, less normative and more absolute, first arose in France with a new generation during the 1930s. It began, significantly if perhaps irresponsibly, with the nihilistic reaction of surrealism. It was fed by an acceleration in scientific and social change which inevitably brought intellectual convulsion and confusion. At the same time the political situation rapidly worsened and a second world conflict became certain. Political realities actually contributed to the decline of surrealism itself, but absolute revolt became increasingly common with the disappearance of more traditional humanist norms. The war which followed, from the bombing of Warsaw through the systematic degradation of Auschwitz to the scientifically controlled destruction of Hiroshima, dealt further blows against humanist assumptions. To the generation which came to maturity during this period—the post-1900 generation of Sartre, Malraux, Camus, Anouilh—absolute revolt often seemed an inevitable attitude. These writers had witnessed, at a crucial stage in their emotional and intellectual development, the failure of progress, of science, of democracy, of reason, and finally the failure of man. Malraux has characterized the situation by saying that ours is the first civilization in the world to be deprived of transcendence. This idea was admirably set out and discussed in a B.B.C. talk entitled 'A Society without a Metaphysics'.* The author, having described Dostoievsky's characters as being 'suspended between the absolutes of God and revolution', went on to say that our society, by separating theology and morals as well as rejecting the Marxian metaphysic, has cut itself off from a Dostoievskian existence and thereby lost its transcendence. One may say, I think, that Europe began to lose its transcendentalism with the general decline in Christian belief. This decline left behind it an uneasy nostalgia which the literature of revolt helped to turn from the worship of God to the worship

* See A. MacIntyre, 'A Society without a Metaphysics', *Listener*, 13 September 1956.

6

of man. With the advance of this century, however, humanism failed, individualism became increasingly ineffectual, and an ideal human nature took on the unreality of myth. Finally, in so far as Marxism turned out to be a god that failed, the possibility of historical, as distinct from theological, transcendence was also lost.

This loss of transcendence has affected contemporary revolt in various ways. There has been, for instance, a noticeable absence of those agreed standards from which earlier revolts derived their main emotional and intellectual force. For many modern writers meaning and purpose are not an integral part of the universe in which man finds himself; on the contrary, the world is characterized by lack of significance and coherence. Meaning has to be created, not found, and it has to be created by the individual out of the actual experience of revolt. The situation for writers like Malraux, Sartre, and Camus is summed up by the hero's remark in the second act of Gide's *Œdipe*: 'I am sprung from the unknown, without a past, without a model, without anything on which to rely . . . Oh Creon . . . not to know one's parents is a call to valour'.[2]

Such a situation clearly involves practical and logical difficulties. The doctrine of fundamental absurdity, of metaphysical incoherence, means for example that values can only be created in a very limited way. They will be subject to a particular historical situation, they will have a predominantly personal validity, they will not easily be given a broad basis. In other words it is difficult to derive a satisfactory ethic, satisfactory in the sense of being both generally acceptable and practically effective, from absolute revolt. There is also a logical difficulty. How can values really be created at all in a radically absurd universe? Is not absolute revolt obliged to accept, at least temporarily, the prior existence of some values in order to possess the very dynamic by which they are later rejected? These are problems of which writers like Malraux, Sartre, and Camus are of course aware. They are also problems, however, that they have only solved to widely differing degrees of satisfaction. The positive values of revolt, and the practical and logical difficulties to which they give rise, will have to be considered more closely when Camus' ideas are examined in detail.

In the meantime, it seems useful to point out that the absolute revolt apparent in recent and contemporary literature appears to have three main characteristics. Firstly, it has considerably blurred the traditional distinctions between good and evil, right and wrong. This is what one would expect from an attitude to life which stresses the fundamental incoherence of human experience. The heroes of many recent novels find that they cannot distinguish between right and wrong with any assurance. This, it may be noted, is as true of certain Catholic writers as it is of Camus or Sartre. Certain characters in the novels of Bernanos, or Arthur Rowe in Greene's *Ministry of Fear* who felt as though he 'had been sent on a journey with a wrong map', are as confused about moral standards as Camus' Meursault or Sartre's Roquentin. These Christian writers are not necessarily more concerned about such problems either, though their concern may take a different form. And they are at one with the non-Christian writers of revolt in creating a world of moral ambiguity and often placing their characters in situations where moral choice is imperative but where traditional standards seem to offer no satisfactory solution. Scobie, in *The Heart of the Matter*, is a case in point. In the conversation between Louise Scobie and Father Rank at the end of the novel Greene shows Scobie to be a man whose suicide escapes the certainties of moral classification :

'For goodness' sake, Mrs. Scobie, don't imagine you—or I—know a thing about God's mercy.'
'The Church says . . .'
'I know the Church says. The Church knows all the rules. But it doesn't know what goes on in a single human heart.'

Secondly, absolute revolt has meant an emphasis on concrete situations rather than abstract attitudes. The writers of revolt show a determination not to be tempted by traditional abstractions. They maintain an obstinate loyalty to the immediate facts of their own experience. This is the attitude of Fowler in Greene's *The Quiet American*—an attitude summed up in the remark: 'I laugh at anyone who spends so much time writing about what doesn't exist—mental concepts.' Meursault is a typical fictional embodiment of this point of view and it is noticeable that Camus himself, in a radio comment on *L'Étranger*, saw Meursault's main virtue as a refusal ever to say more than he feels. It is this same emphasis on the concrete and the immediate which has been a contributory men women

factor in the anti-rhetorical style of writing which marks the work of such differently endowed authors as Hemingway, Greene, Camus and Sartre. Their dislike and distrust of abstractions has inclined them towards economical and unadorned prose. All of them are so consciously anti-rhetorical, however, that they have really produced what amounts to a laconic counter-rhetoric of their own. Obviously this kind of writing, and the general attitude behind it, are to be expected in the case of Existentialism which, as its very name suggests, emphasizes the priority of existence over essence and the concrete over the abstract. But most writers of revolt, even when like Camus they reject the existentialist label, still maintain what may at least be called an existential (as distinct from existentialist) bias in their approach to experience. A concern then with things, with material objects rather than ideal essences, is a noticeable feature of recent French literature. It is by no means confined to the novels of Sartre or Simone de Beauvoir, nor is it only a fashion carried over from the immediate post-war popularity in France of the school of 'tough' American writers. It appears without demonstrable American influence in writers like Michaux, Ponge, Cayrol, Beckett and Robbe-Grillet. At the same time, its expression in France offers various intellectual refinements of what is the basically similar attitude rather sentimentally expressed in Hemingway's *A Farewell to Arms*:

There were many words that you could not stand to hear and finally only the names of places had dignity . . . . Abstract words such as glory, honour, courage or hallow were obscene beside the concrete names of villages, the numbers of roads, the names of rivers.

Generally speaking, then, the writers of revolt have reacted strongly against such abstract concepts as Glory, Honour, Beauty, Truth, Goodness. Their attitude reflects the doubt cast on such concepts by changed moral beliefs, by new psychological doctrines, by revolutions in the scientific criteria of reality. Quite apart from these considerations it is clear that absolutes have lost meaning and prestige, particularly during two world wars, because of the contradictory or hypocritical interpretations to which they have repeatedly been subject. There are always unscrupulous statesmen ready to appeal to some abstract 'right' in order to conceal selfish motives. Individuals are not lacking who will readily invoke some absolute 'truth' in support of irrational or partisan opinions. Every time this happens the words 'right' and 'truth' lose further meaning and prestige. In the end they are added to the number of those 'sterile myths' to which Camus referred when he wrote in 1938 in *Noces:*

The most repellent form of materialism is not what is usually thought of as such but the kind that wants to make dead ideas masquerade as living realities and to divert towards sterile myths that obstinate and lucid concern which we have with what is mortal in ourselves.[3]

For atheist thinkers like Camus this situation has raised a particular problem. They hold, with Nietzsche, that 'God is dead', and they consequently believe in the 'death' of those intermediary values between God and men which brought some security to the earlier humanist and normative revolt. They are not content simply to suggest that certain values have become threadbare; they are much more inclined to reject the possibility of values existing in any absolute form at all. One of their problems is therefore to try to create new values in an incoherent universe without restoring at the same time a deity who might be interpreted as giving absolute sanction to these values, or as embodying a principle of coherence. In an incoherent universe deprived of transcendence it is difficult to establish any values without beginning by making incoherence itself a value. We shall see later that this is, in effect, what Camus does. His attempts to give logical satisfaction in the process are not very satisfactory. What these writers find, at best, is a series of values which perhaps satisfies their own demands but which can only be commended to others on particular, not universal, grounds.

This 'death' of God and humanist values, which has been such a common feature of recent French literature, leads directly to the third main characteristic of absolute revolt: a continual insistence on the fact of human responsibility. The picture that emerges is one in which the individual is bereft of all metaphysical aids. There is no supernatural authority to which he can appeal. There are no inherited values on which he can rely. He must fashion his own destiny in complete isolation. The literature of absolute revolt presents life not as an established order but as an order to be established. This is the experience of human existence which Sartre calls anguish, and the responsibility of each individual which he terms freedom. It is also Malraux's picture of the human condition, the basis of what he calls destiny. It is a view of the world which, if not fully shared by Christian writers like Greene and Bernanos, nevertheless produces a similar atmosphere of alienation and individual responsibility in their novels. It has fashioned Greene's outcast heroes just as it prompted Bernanos to write, in *Sous le soleil de Satan*, that everything must always be begun all over again. Not least of all, this is the world of Camus. It is a world inhabited by Meursault, the outsider, and by Dr. Rieux fighting against a plague whose nature and origins remain obscure. It is a world symbolized by images of the prison, medical quarantine, a state of siege. It is also a world in which the individual is perpetually condemned, like Sisyphus, to roll the stone of his absurdity up a steep slope which always sends it rumbling back. Yet although Camus does not shrink from the evidence of incoherence which he calls the absurd, neither is he content with apathy and resignation. The open sea, as well as the prison, is a major symbol in his work. The dynamic of revolt which is produced by the absurd possesses sufficient force to carry him beyond negation to affirmation. This evolution in ideas and attitude is not easily achieved, and Camus' development has been hesitant, tentative and exploratory at many points. It has, I think, its unconvincing aspects, but it still represents a remarkable intellectual odyssey through our times. And it is the odyssey of a writer of great literary gifts who has really lived the life of his age while adorning it with his artistic achievements.

Before considering in more detail the development of Camus' thought it may be useful to give a brief biographical account of the man himself. Camus has never encouraged public myth-making or journalistic curiosity about his life and personality. He has taken the very reasonable view that what is of relevance for the public is to be found in his published writings. Nevertheless, in certain letters, conversations and essays which have been published, he has given details worth recalling here concerning his life and the composition of some of his works.

Albert Camus was born on 7 November 1913 at Mondovi in the Constantine department of Algeria. His father, an agricultural worker of Alsatian origin, was killed within a year of Camus' birth during the first battle of the Marne. His mother was of Spanish descent and he gives evidence several times of deriving a certain romantic satisfaction from this indirect Spanish ancestry. After his father's death the family moved to a poor and over-crowded district of Algiers. Here, in a two-roomed apartment, he lived with his mother, his maternal grandmother, his uncle and his elder brother. His mother worked as a charwoman to help keep the home together. The general atmosphere of this home is described by Camus in some pages of *L'Envers et l'endroit,* a collection of five essays printed at Algiers in a limited edition in 1937 and not republished until 1958. This descriptive passage is typical :

I am thinking of a child who lived in a poor district. What a district, what a home! There was only a first storey and the staircase was unlit. Even today, after the lapse of so many long years, he could find his way back there on the darkest night. He knows that he would run up those stairs without stumbling once. His very body is pervaded by that house. His legs still retain an exact sense of the distance between each step. His hand still has an instinctive and invincible horror of banister rails —all because of the cockroaches.[4]

In addition to apparently reliable descriptions of Camus' home, his mother, his grandmother and his uncle, *L'Envers et l'endroit* contains, as we shall see later, details of his early mental development and the first published formulation of some of his most characteristic attitudes.

Camus attended a local primary school from 1918 to 1923. Here he attracted the attention of a teacher, Louis Germain, who helped him, by encouragement and extra tuition, to win a scholarship to the *lycée*. In the late 1920s, while still a *lycéen*, he began to read some of the French writers who were taken as examples and guides by his generation. He appears to have been particularly impressed by Gide and to have read the works of Malraux and Montherlant as they appeared. He continued to read these and other writers (Proust, Jean Grenier, André de Richaud, etc.) after becoming a philosophy student at the University of Algiers. During this time Camus also developed further that enthusiasm for sport which he still retains. Like Montherlant, whose *Bestiaires* he had read in 1926, he is a celebrated French writer who has also been a regular club goal-keeper. He has said of his student days: 'Sport was the main occupation of all of us and continued to be mine for a long time. That is where I had my only lessons in ethics . . .'[5] To this active participation in sport was added great enthusiasm for the theatre in all its aspects. Clamence, the main character in Camus' novel *La Chute*, seems to reflect very faithfully the attitude of his creator when he says:

I was only really sincere and enthusiastic during the period when I played games, and also in the army when I acted in plays which we put on for our own enjoyment . . . . Even today, the stadium crammed full of spectators for a Sunday match, and the theatre which I loved with unequalled intensity, are the only places in the world where I feel innocent.[6]

Camus' active participation in games was interrupted in 1930 when he was found to be tubercular. He also had to leave home for reasons of health. After a short stay with an uncle he began to lead a much more independent life. He supported himself by various jobs including selling spare parts for cars, working in a marine broker's office, acting as a clerk at the *préfecture* and taking a post in a meteorological office. He also had some brief experience as a political propagandist for the Communist Party. Like so many young European intellectuals of the period he joined the party at the age of twenty-one, but left it within a matter of months following Laval's mission to Moscow in 1935 and the consequent modification of the party line on the question of the Algerian moslems. Camus has never been able to accept expediency as an adequate basis for political action and the generous social idealism which drove him into the Communist Party was bound to drive him out again before long. During these varied experiences in employment and politics he managed to continue his university studies on a part-time basis. Having obtained his *licence* he went on, in 1936, to complete a dissertation, a *diplôme d'études supérieures*, on the relations between Greek and Christian thought in Plotinus and Saint Augustine. In 1937 a renewed attack of tuberculosis prevented him from taking the *agrégation* and his university career ended at this point.

By 1937, however, Camus had behind him more than a year's experience of the avant-garde theatre in Algiers. His passion for the theatre has already been mentioned, and in 1935 he had founded the Théâtre du Travail. This was a theatre group composed mainly of young amateurs whose aim was to bring good plays both to the working population and to a progressive intellectual élite. This experiment in theatrical revolt shows, in the wording of its manifesto, the spirit of idealism current at the time in theatrical circles. At this early stage there is little sign of absolute revolt, in the sense used earlier in this chapter, in Camus' theatrical activities. Social and political considerations are still dominant and cause him to conceive of the theatre as a 'school of values' somewhat in the way Romain Rolland had done in his *Théâtre du Peuple*. The manifesto of Camus and his friends proclaims that collective efforts and social responsibility are to be combined with high artistic standards:

Thanks to disinterested and collective efforts a Théâtre du Travail is being organized in Algiers. This theatre is conscious of the artistic value inherent in all popular literature. It wishes to show that art sometimes gains by leaving the ivory tower and it believes that a feeling for beauty is inseparable from a certain feeling for humanity . . . . It will attempt to restore a number of human values rather than produce new ideas.[7]

If the Théâtre du Travail felt unable to promise new ideas, it nevertheless began its active existence with a new play. It is said that Camus wrote most of *La Révolte dans les Asturies*, but he himself still likes to think of it as the product of creative teamwork. The subject of the play was of contemporary political significance. It dealt with the revolt of the Spanish miners of the Asturias in 1934, their capture of Oviedo and their subsequent defeat and execution. *La Révolte dans les Asturies* was published in 1936 by the Éditions Charlot in Algiers but the authorities refused to allow it to be produced on the stage. It was somewhere around this time that the Théâtre du Travail was reorganized as the Théâtre de l'Équipe. Camus continued, however, to be the dominant figure in the newly named collective enterprise. A number of plays and adaptations of novels were performed including Malraux's *Le Temps du mépris*, Gide's *Le Retour de l'Enfant Prodigue*, Vildrac's *Le Paquebot 'Tenacity'*, Pushkin's *The Stone Guest*, Ben Jonson's *Epicene, or The Silent Woman*, the *Prometheus* of Aeschylus and Copeau's adaptation of *The Brothers*

Karamazov. This was both an exhilarating period in Camus' life and an important one for his own future development as a dramatist. The collectivist character of the company meant that he was able to learn a great deal about writing and staging plays as well as about acting in them. His stage rôles with the company included Ivan in *The Brothers Karamazov* and the Prodigal Son in Gide's play, while it was his own adaptation of *Prometheus* that the group performed. Also, within a year, he had written his first play, *Caligula,* though this was not to be published until 1944, and was not performed in Paris until 1945.

The period from the founding of the Théâtre du Travail to the outbreak of war in 1939 is one of remarkable energy in Camus' life, particularly in view of the fact that his health was so precarious. Apart from his theatrical activities he travelled a good deal, visiting France, Italy, Czechoslovakia, and the Balearic Islands. In the summer of 1939 he was about to embark for Greece when the international situation forced him to give up the idea. He read a great deal also, clarifying his own ideas further by contact with the writings of Pascal, Kierkegaard, Nietzsche, Sorel, Spengler and the more recent works of Gide and Malraux. Between 1937 and 1939 he also served his apprenticeship as a journalist with *Alger-Républicain.* He performed a variety of functions under the guidance of Pascal Pia and the experience he gained was to prove most useful six years later when, again in collaboration with Pia, he took over the editorship of the Parisian daily, *Combat.* His activities with *Alger-Républicain* included at different times reviewing, reporting, leader-writing and sub-editing. One of his most important pieces of reporting was a survey of social conditions in the Kabylia district of Algeria. Among the books he reviewed were Sartre's *La Nausée* and *Le Mur.* Even at this early stage Camus expressed a critical attitude towards Sartre's ideas which is significant in view of their later quarrel. He considered, for example, that the pessimism of *La Nausée* leaned too heavily on an exaggerated reaction to the ugliness of the world. He found the short stories of *Le Mur* too negative, saying that to assert the absurdity of existence should not be an end in itself but rather should provide a point of departure for positive reconstruction. Both these judgments are partial and, I think, premature judgements of Sartre. Something similar might be said of Camus' own early work. But they are of interest because they emphasize Camus' early opposition to a pessimism which he suspected of being entirely negative. They are also significant in so far as Camus began at this time (i.e. from 1938 onwards) to make notes for a novel, *L'Étranger* (completed in May 1940), and for his essay on the absurd, *Le Mythe de Sisyphe* (completed in February 1941).

With the outbreak of war Camus volunteered for military service. Having been rejected on the grounds of his health he travelled about North Africa in search of employment. His anti-colonialism made him *persona non grata* with the government, however, and the failure to find a job in Algeria eventually sent him to France in March 1940. In Paris he joined the staff of *Paris-Soir* on the recommendation of Pascal Pia. His association with this evening paper was cut short by the German invasion in May and the subsequent occupation of the north of France. He returned to North Africa in January 1941, taught for a short time in a private institution in Oran, completed *Le Mythe de Sisyphe* and began writing the first draft of *La Peste* which was not finished until 1947. The original conception of this novel owes a good deal to Camus' reading of Melville's *Moby Dick*, particularly its interpretation as an allegory of man's fight against the radical evil of the universe. Shortly afterwards Defoe and Cervantes also exercised an influence on Camus' treatment of the plague theme, and it was during this relatively inactive period that he read such authors as Marcus Aurelius, Spinoza, Madame de Lafayette, Sade, Vigny, Balzac and Tolstoy.

In 1942 Camus returned to France and joined a southern Resistance network calling itself 'Combat'. He operated chiefly in Lyon and St. Étienne until, towards the end of 1943, the 'Combat' organization sent him to Paris where he continued his underground activities. During the Occupation he wrote his second play, *Le Malentendu*, and two of the four *Lettres à un ami allemand* published together in 1945. His work with the Resistance brought him into contact with Malraux and Claude Bourdet as well as involving a new kind of association with Pascal Pia. In particular, Camus formed a close friendship with the young poet René Leynaud who was executed by the Germans in 1944. After the war he wrote a preface to the posthumously published poems of

Leynaud whom he describes as combining profound poetic sensibility with deep, if unorthodox, Christian convictions. The preface recalls some of their conversations together, including discussions on boxing, swimming and camping, and adds:

... far from making me a better person in the way that edifying books describe, his death intensified my revolt. I can say with more nobility, where he is concerned, that he would not have joined me in this revolt.[8]

After the liberation of Paris in August 1944 Camus took over the editorship of *Combat*, which had first appeared clandestinely during the Resistance with the general support of the 'Combat' organization. Shortly after this he had a play produced in Paris for the first time. The Mathurins theatre put on *Le Malentendu*, his second play in order of composition, with Maria Casarès and Marcel Herrand in the main parts. It was not well received, but one feels that this was due in part to the fact that its disturbing aspects were not understood by the theatre-going public and most of the critics. Many articles on the play produced little more than that mocking, sometimes witty and intentional, misunderstanding in which so many Parisian dramatic critics excel. Within a year, however, the Hébertot had presented his first play, *Caligula*, with Gérard Philipe causing a sensation in the title rôle. This time the attitude of the critics was generally very favourable and Camus gained a position of some importance in the post-war French theatre.

During 1945 Camus also published his 'Remarque sur la révolte' in a collection of essays by various hands which Jean Grenier edited for Gallimard. It turned out to be a preliminary statement of certain general themes developed more fully later in *L'Homme révolté* (published in 1951). It was towards the end of 1945 also that he went on a lecture tour of the U.S.A. About this same period he discovered the writings of Simone Weil—another unorthodox Christian who, like Leynaud, made a considerable impression on him.

Camus had continued his work with *Combat* since 1945, though not without various difficulties. He maintained a resolutely independent left-wing line and an attitude of high moral fervour in his political commentaries. Eventually, after disagreements over the policy of the paper, he relinquished the editorship to Claude

Bourdet. He visited Algeria again shortly afterwards in 1948. In October of the same year his new play, *L'État de siège*, was produced at the Marigny with a brilliant cast which included Barrault, Madeleine Renaud, Maria Casarès, Pierre Brasseur and Pierre Bertin. Again the critical reaction was very mixed, though Barrault's restlessly choreographic production seems to have provoked more unfavourable comment than Camus' actual play. Fourteen months later, in December 1949, the Hébertot gave a performance of what is probably Camus' best play to date, *Les Justes*. Maria Casarès and Serge Reggiani played the main parts; audiences and critics alike gave the play an enthusiastic reception.

It was during the summer of 1949 that Camus visited South America, and on his return to Paris he became seriously ill again. For two years he retired almost completely from public life though he did publish *Actuelles* in 1950—mainly a collection of his most important political articles written between 1944 and 1948. Then, during his convalescence, he completed *L'Homme révolté*, his long essay on the idea of revolt published in 1951. In the following year he visited Algeria again, but 1952 is chiefly notable for another reason. The publication of *L'Homme révolté* had given rise to a great deal of controversy in French intellectual circles, mainly about the political views expressed. The chief opposition to Camus came from the communists and Sartrians of the extreme left, and at the centre of the controversy was a sharply critical review of the book written by Francis Jeanson for Sartre's monthly, *Les Temps modernes*. Soon Camus and Sartre were themselves drawn into severe polemics in this periodical. What had been for some time an uneasy friendship between them came to an end as a result. (Incidentally, something very like a fictional transposition of this quarrel is excellently described and argued in Simone de Beauvoir's *Les Mandarins*.) The Sartre/Camus quarrel was fascinating for many reasons, and not least because of the contrast it revealed between the former's intellectual rigour and the latter's moral fervour. It also produced, of course, some necessary clarification of the political ideas of both men. A political gesture by Camus in November of this same year was his resignation from UNESCO following the admission of Spain to membership.

In 1953, at the Angers festival in June, Camus renewed his theatrical activities with adaptations of Calderón's *La devoción de*

Introduction

la Cruz and *Les Esprits* by the sixteenth-century French comic dramatist, Larivey. Maria Casarès played with Serge Reggiani in the Calderón play and with Paul Œttly in *Les Esprits*. Camus has not completed any plays of his own since *Les Justes*, but he is said to be working on a version of the Don Juan theme. In 1955 he published *Un cas intéressant*, a French version of Buzzati's *Un caso clínico*. It was produced at the La Bruyère theatre. More recently, in 1956, the Mathurins put on his stage adaptation of Faulkner's *Requiem for a Nun* with Catherine Sellers and Michel Auclair as Temple and Gowan Stevens. In 1957 he published a French version of Lope de Vega's *El caballero de Olmedo*. Apart from such adaptations Camus has published a limited amount of work since 1953. He has collected in book form more political commentaries, *Actuelles II,* and various articles and essays written between 1939 and 1953, *L'Été.* He has also written prefaces to more than a dozen books, including the 'Pléiade' edition of Roger Martin du Gard's *Œuvres complètes,* and in 1956 he published a third novel, *La Chute,* which shows that his creative powers are still active and considerable. This impression is confirmed by the artistic virtuosity of his collected short stories, *L'Exil et le royaume,* published in 1957. Late in 1957, at the remarkably early age of 44, Camus was awarded the Nobel Prize for literature. His speech of acceptance was published in 1958 under the title: *Discours de Suède.*

Camus has only reached his middle forties, yet already he has produced an impressive body of imaginative and journalistic work. He has written original and distinctive novels and plays which embody a disturbing, yet often compelling, response to contemporary life. He has helped to give the shorter essay new scope and authority. He has shown himself to be a political theorist who commands wide attention. Apart from these things his own life has also been an influence and an example. One naturally assumes that more literary activity and further personal development lie before him, and this must mean that the assessment of his work at this stage is even more provisional than all literary criticism must in any case be. Some judgements arrived at now will certainly have to be modified in the course of his future evolution. Yet a writer who so consciously reflects, and reflects upon, the problems of his age demands immediate, though provisional, commentary and assessment. Since he has opinions to express which are particularly addressed to his contemporaries and their problems it is obviously desirable to make some attempt to explain and discuss these opinions now. It is true that greater critical objectivity should be attained when a writer's work has been completed and is removed to some temporal distance from the critic. Nevertheless it would be a betrayal of the outlook and purpose of a witness like Camus to venture no judgement on his work until it could be embalmed in some literary pantheon. His published work urgently addresses his contemporaries. It is reasonable that these contemporaries should adopt an attitude to it here and now by reacting as sensitively as possible to its immediate significance.

Part One

REVOLT AS AN ATTITUDE TO LIFE

2 THE QUEST FOR HAPPINESS

Tout intellectuel a forcément l'idée d'un Paradis Perdu.

JEAN GRENIER

Many of Camus' dominant ideas bear the clear stamp of his mediterranean origins. Like Grenier or Montherlant—writers who have had a distinct influence on certain aspects of his thought—he expresses in much of his work an attitude to life that one associates with countries like North Africa, Greece and Italy which possessed well-developed pre-Christian civilizations. North Africa in particular was never significantly touched by medieval strictures on physical pleasure or on sensualism generally, and these ideas have persisted there to a remarkable degree. Camus particularly emphasizes the value of spontaneous sensualism in his earliest works. In an interview which he gave some years ago he still described himself as being conscious of bearing a special responsibility because he was born, during the Christian era, in a land of strongly surviving pagan traditions. He said that the circumstances of his birth made him feel a closer affinity with the values of the ancient world than with Christian values.* This aspect of his early formation has remained important. Foreign travel and his continued residence in France since 1942 have increased his awareness of the pagan/Christian and southern/northern dichotomy. It is interesting to see the same distinction made in similar terms by a European approaching it from the opposite direction :

... in Algiers itself, far more after crossing the Atlas into the desert, the traveller is conscious of having left Europe far behind, not the mere geographical entity, but all the complex edifice of Christianity, social, moral, intellectual, legal organization and custom, the civiliza-

* See Camus' interview with G. d'Aubarède published in *Les Nouvelles littéraires* of 10 May 1951.

22

tion of the centuries. In entering a world so different, so remote, to which one has so little direct access, and in which one's familiar personality has so little place or meaning, one has the sense of being in a vacuum, free—if that be the word—to create, *ab ovo*, thought, religion, laws, an ethic for oneself.*

These words were written by Professor Bisson in the course of some comments on the enthusiastic though somewhat synthetic neo-paganism of Gide. They throw considerable light on the more spontaneous, if still slightly synthetic, neo-paganism of Camus.

Next to North Africa itself Camus has a particularly strong feeling for Greece. This is of course the country where those mediterranean virtues which he most admires have traditionally found, and perhaps still find, their most perfect expression. In an essay on Greece, 'L'Exil d'Hélène', written in 1948 and later collected in *L'Été*, he contrasts the pastoral civilization of ancient Greece with the ugly urban disquiet of modern Europe. He also praises the sceptical moderation of ancient Greek thought, as he interprets it, at the expense of what he calls modern intellectual absolutism. This particular form of historical nostalgia is in itself by no means new. It has often been expressed in much the same terms. Camus' case is not so common, however, since he makes these points from the much less usual angle of an articulate mediterranean who speaks *en connaissance de cause*. Furthermore, he insists that the most important features of his mediterranean inheritance, which have to do primarily with ways of thinking and only indirectly with methods of social organization, could become valuable and effective in the modern world. Eventually he proposes what we may conveniently call the Greek way of life, rather than the later Christian inheritance, as the best hope for Europe today. This is a contention which will have to be discussed later, but for the moment we are concerned only with the early expression of these ideas in his first published works.

The early essays of Camus reveal two main features: an instinctive atheism and continual emphasis on the individual's physical experience of his environment. At this stage Camus mainly discusses the two extremes of intellectual frustration and physical enjoyment. He mentions again and again the relation of opposi-

* L. A. Bisson, *André Gide* (1859–1951): *a memorial lecture*, Belfast, Boyd (for Queen's University), 1951, p. 12.

tion existing between his 'horreur de mourir' and his 'jalousie de vivre'; he searches for a means of reconciliation between these two experiences, for some middle way between extravagant positions in thought and action. This awareness of the sharp duality of life was strongly felt by the Greeks, while they also evolved ways of thought which helped to lessen its tragic ambivalence. It is to the Greeks that Camus turns, then, both for confirmation of the reality of his problem and possible guidance as to its solution. In the interview previously mentioned he is quoted as saying: 'Greece is shadow and light. We men of the South know perfectly well that the sun has its dark side.' [1] He adds that Greek thought always defined itself by reference to opposing limits and thus provided this clear awareness of contrasting extremes with an ideal of moderation which could include them both and reduce, if not remove, the conflict between them. It is this Greek attitude, brought to bear on his early North African experiences, which introduces into Camus' first essays a continual alternation, which is also the search for a mean, between desire for life and horror of death, sensual exaltation and severity of mind, lyricism and asceticism. The resulting combination of exultancy and despair ultimately provided Camus with the basis of revolt, but at first it led rather to a provisional attitude of acceptance and stoical detachment. The wisdom emerging from the early essays is a doctrine of proud and somewhat bitter isolation and independence. Such bitter pride is the outcome of what is, in essence, a frustrated quest for happiness. It represents the early discovery that happiness is not easily achieved by a certain lucid type of mind. It is important to note, however, that the search for happiness is not simply abandoned, nor is a belief in the ultimate possibility of happiness ever wholly dismissed. Many of Camus' readers have insisted too much on the rigour of his pessimism. One of its most distinctive features is the fact that it is continually formulated against a background of mediterranean sunshine. Incidentally, this is one of the ways in which it differs profoundly from the German-inspired pessimism of Sartre. Camus has, I think, rightly insisted that a personal response to happiness is a central theme in his work. He said in the same interview of 1951: 'When I seek to discover what is most fundamental in myself it is a taste for happiness that I find. . . . There is invincible sunshine at the heart of my work.' [2]

The Quest for Happiness

The mediterranean duality at the basis of Camus' thought strikes one immediately in his earliest published work, *L'Envers et l'endroit*. The title itself suggests a dualism with its reference to the right and the wrong sides of a piece of material. This image also emphasizes the close relatedness of the two terms of his experience. In this book Camus presents a dualism in which the riches of sun and sea emphasize human poverty; joyful indulgence of the senses makes death more tragic and horrible; the flowering of tenderness and desire uncovers the fact of human loneliness; an exclusive pleasure in the immediate and the physical is contrasted with the spectacle of inadequate and unconsoling religious observances. In each instance happiness and suffering intensify one another. The acuteness of Camus' reaction to each is due to the fact of their contrasting coexistence. Today Camus is very much aware of the artistic shortcomings in his account of these experiences, but he still holds that it contains in embryo the essence of his conclusions about human experience.* There is a good deal in this view, yet to re-read *L'Envers et l'endroit*, particularly in the light of Camus' subsequent writings, is to realize just how formless and vague much of its content is. There is clear evidence of a strong individuality behind the book, but the book itself remains an essentially immature statement of ideas. It describes with a certain originality the instinctive desire of a young man for pleasure without giving any very clear content to this desire itself. The emphasis on poverty, loneliness and death is little more than the by-product of an apparently threatened or frustrated quest for happiness. The two contrasting emphases are loosely held together by a pride which recognizes the fact of the dualism without having fully assimilated either of its terms.

L'Envers et l'endroit contains a mere sixty pages of prose and consists of five parts which are a mixture of autobiography and more generalized meditation. Each of the five parts hovers indecisively between the essay and the short story. The first, entitled 'L'Ironie', is a study of the contrast between youth and age embodied in a series of observations on religion, human loneliness and the fact of death. The atmosphere and characters described appear

---

* See his preface to the 1958 edition. Because of his dissatisfaction with the literary quality of these essays Camus refused to republish them between 1937 and 1958.

to be those of Camus' own home and family although there is no explicit statement to this effect. An old woman—probably modelled on his grandmother—fears the near approach of death; an old man—resembling his uncle—is puzzled and disappointed by modern youth; a young man and his friends prefer to spend an evening at the cinema rather than remain in the company of the old people. The old woman is religious through fear, not love. Camus, in an ironic re-phrasing of Pascal's phrase, describes her as being caught up in 'la misère de l'homme en Dieu'. Her religion is a last resort, an act of desperation, a final attempt to soften the bitter reality of death. Its value is to be measured by the fact that if she could be sure of recovery from her present illness she would readily turn from devotion to the stucco Virgin to human contacts and activities. When the young people go to the cinema and only her daughter remains she feels more acutely the horror of her solitariness. She is afraid, her *tête-à-tête* with God has brought no comfort, she clings desperately to her daughter's hand. Camus comments: 'God did nothing for her except deprive her of human companionship and make her lonely. She did not want to leave the world of men.'[3]

The old man, for his part, talks incessantly about his youth and the failure of the new generation to enjoy itself in the right way. He tries very hard to hold the young people's attention, embroidering his stories to make them more interesting and impressive. And yet, all the time, he knows, and they know, that he is old, useless and a bore. The young people soon cease to listen. They find their relief from the deadening routine of a dull job not in an old man's tales but in billiards, cards and the cinema. Later, the old woman's death occurs and we have a description of the young man's failure to feel genuine sorrow and loss which recalls the attitude of Meursault to his mother some years later in *L'Étranger*. The contrast between youth and age, life and death, pleasure and fear is maintained throughout 'L'Ironie'. This contrast between different age-groups is also the irony with which each individual's life is eventually marked. Camus makes a final comment which acknowledges this and then turns determinedly away from it:

A woman whom one leaves alone in order to visit the cinema, an old man to whom one no longer listens, a death which redeems nothing, and then, on the other hand, all the brightness of the world. What does it matter if one accepts all these things? Three similar and yet distinct destinies are involved. Death comes to everyone, but to each his own death. After all, the sun warms our bones despite everything.[4]

These lines express the bitter acceptance of the tragic dualism which Camus adopted at this time. It is an acceptance in which youthful harshness comes to the aid of youthful vulnerability. Loneliness, old age and death, experienced in their immediate human reality, are at once a stimulus and a menace to the young man's pursuit of enjoyment. They emphasize the urgency of seeking happiness but they also emphasize its frailty and relatively short duration.

In the next section, 'Entre Oui et Non', the title again refers to the ambivalence of human life. Camus writes further about his home in Algiers. He describes at some length its poverty and gloom, and makes a sharp comparison between the disturbing silence of his deaf mother and the angry cries of his tyrannical grandmother. The son's attitude to his mother, whose silences remind one of those of Rieux's mother in *La Peste*, is an uneasy compound of love, fear, pity, duty and a sense of the gulf between them. The nature of their relationship makes him conscious of himself, aware of his separate individuality, in a way he had not experienced before. A heightened sense of the otherness of people gives him a certain detachment both from himself and from the world around him. Once again Camus ends on a note of acceptance, but on this second occasion his acceptance is more reflective, less instinctive and less selfish, than in 'L'Ironie'. It is a provisional attitude to be adopted until life has been experienced further and thought about more fully: 'Since this moment is like an interval between affirmation and negation I shall leave to other moments the hope or despair of living. . . .'[5]

The third and fourth of these pieces, 'La Mort dans l'âme' and 'Amour de vivre', contain reflections by Camus on his travels in Czechoslovakia, Italy and the Balearic Islands. He finds that the most striking thing about travel is its power to induce in him a continual questioning of himself and of the outside world. Here, then, the consciousness of his own separate individuality discussed

27

in 'Entre Oui et Non' is further emphasized. The value of travel, he says, is its power to disturb the individual by removing him from the shelter of familiar and comforting routines. Travel takes away, at least temporarily, those masks and disguises behind which we normally hide. It provides us, or at least it can provide us in certain circumstances, with a new and startling revelation of our fundamental loneliness and unfamiliarity to ourselves. It lifts the curtain of habit to reveal the pale features of disquiet. One is confronted with an unfamiliar self through contact with an unfamiliar outside world. In Prague and Palma Camus had a particularly acute feeling of being a stranger. In Prague he did not know how to get from one place to another, he was ignorant about the city transport system, and everything was further obscured by his inability to speak the language of the country. It is true that all such problems can soon be met, if not fully solved, by common sense and some ingenuity. But there is an initial period of alienation. An alien self, abandoned in an alien milieu, experiences something resembling the anxiety and dread of the metaphysical stranger— the outsider. A sensation not unlike the 'nausée' of Sartre's Roquentin arises from the traveller's sense of 'un grand désaccord . . . entre lui et les choses'. Camus finds in the experience of travel one of those intimations of absurdity, as we might call them, which he later scrutinizes in *Le Mythe de Sisyphe*.

When he moves from Czechoslovakia to Italy this 'man of the South' is much more at home. He responds more readily and naturally to the sun and the Italian landscape. And yet, even in Italy, a feeling of anxiety is present although warmth and beauty surround him. The landscape is beautiful, but its beauty contains a disturbingly impersonal quality. Even the clear brightness of the sky contains the colour of indifference. As he gazes at the scene before him he can find in the landscape no promise of immortality for himself. On the contrary, the enduring features of the natural scene are a reminder of the brevity of his existence. Yet on this occasion he accepts more readily the dualism of which he is so continually aware. The intense beauty of the Italian countryside arouses in him such passionate attachment to the life of the senses that he shrinks from the prospect of that incorporeal existence which immortality of the soul would imply:

What use had I for life re-lived in the soul if it meant no eyes with which to see Vicenza, no hands with which to touch the grapes of Vicenza, no skin with which to feel the caress of night on the road from Monte Berico to the villa Valmarana? [6]

The sense of physical mortality barely concealed by these words explains that 'iron in the soul' to which the first of these two travel pieces, 'La Mort dans l'âme', refers. And yet the bounty of Italy is such that it eventually brings some consolation as well as unmistakable warning. From an impersonal landscape which is also beautiful, from an indifferent sky which is also bright and clear, the traveller somehow receives power to accept both the enduring splendour of the natural world and his own transitoriness. This ability to recognize the given calmly remains difficult to acquire. The passage of time does not make it any more easy to accept time's destructive power over the individual. The struggle involved is severe and the necessity for it is bitter. Nevertheless, the revelation of Italy is important for Camus because it emphasizes the need to combine lucidity with courage. This type of courage will later prove to be an essential quality in the kind of revolt he practises himself and commends to others.

The second travel piece, 'Amour de vivre', contains reflections on a visit to the Balearic Islands. Here again the tragic ambivalence compounded of the desirable intensity and inevitable brevity of physical life is stressed. The spontaneous enjoyment of life at Palma and the natural beauty of Ibiza and San Francisco underline the individual's status as being inscribed for a brief moment on the world's timelessness. In this section the experience of the gulf between the individual and the natural world prompts Camus to relate the two terms of the dualism again in tragic interdependence: 'There is no love of life without despair about life.' [7] This might be taken as Camus' own explanation of the fact that pessimism and the tragic sense always haunt his search for happiness.

The general title of the book, *L'Envers et l'endroit*, is also the title of its fifth and last section. Sun, sky, stars and landscape on the one hand, and human beings on the other, are interpreted as the *envers* and *endroit* of a total existence which contains them both. Camus stresses once again the contrast between the apparently eternal and the demonstrably mortal. What seems an unbreakable bond links the timeless and the temporal, joy and death, 'les hommes et leur absurdité'. He does not renounce the doctrine of acceptance in these last pages, but he returns again to an insistence on the importance of enjoying the brief exaltation of the senses which life makes possible. Life is short, he says, and to sin means to waste one's opportunities for enjoyment. In conscious opposition to the Christian ethic he adds that his kingdom is entirely of this world ('A cette heure tout mon royaume est de ce monde'). The essay closes with what is ultimately a counsel of despair:

If I listen to the irony which lies hidden at the heart of things she slowly reveals herself. Winking her small bright eye she says: 'Live as if . . .' Despite much searching this is the sum of my wisdom.[8]

It should be clear from this summary of *L'Envers et l'endroit* that the book contains no really unified argument. In each of the five essays emotional attitudes are vividly expressed but there is little attempt to justify them adequately in the light of further thought. There is a good deal of vagueness, too, in the way Camus arrives at his conclusions, and these conclusions themselves do not form a coherent whole but alternate uncertainly between the positive and negative poles of *carpe diem* and stoic withdrawal. These features of the book make it easy to imagine why Camus now finds his first work unsatisfactory from a formal point of view. It is true that *L'Envers et l'endroit* contains the basic themes of much of his later work, but the presentation of the themes at this stage is inadequate and disjointed. At the same time one cannot read even these early essays without being impressed by that austere poetry which has remained a striking and highly individual feature of much of his prose.

Camus' second book, four essays collected under the title *Noces*, was published in 1939 after the actual writing had been done during the previous year. *Noces* is, of course, still close in time to *L'Envers et l'endroit* and the two books have many points of similarity as regards their subject-matter. In *Noces* Camus again discusses those same ancient and obstinate problems of human existence and individual transience, but they are more fully developed here than in the earlier book. They are presented in terms of more rigorous thought and yet at the same time they are invested with even more striking poetic intensity. The lyrical exaltation is combined with a more precise notation and detailed description of the North African landscape. Running through the four essays there is evidence of a conscious symbolism of sun and wind, sea and desert. The themes of joy and despair first enunciated in *L'Envers et l'endroit* are now subjected to more careful and more thorough meditation. However, although both themes remain present in *Noces*, the emphasis is on the rapture of physical existence. The positive term of the dualism in *L'Envers et l'endroit* is singled out for special attention. Three years later, in *Le Mythe de Sisyphe*, the emphases will be reversed with the stress being placed on the absurdity of human existence. In this later and much longer essay it is the negative term of the dualism in *L'Envers et l'endroit* which, in its turn, receives particular consideration.

Noces is again a relatively short work of about eighty pages. It begins with a prefatory quotation from Stendhal which might suggest, contrary to what has just been said, that Camus will concentrate here on the negative and pessimistic side of *L'Envers et l'endroit*. The quotation from 'La duchesse de Palliano', in Stendhal's *Chroniques italiennes*, reads: 'The executioner strangled Cardinal Carrafa with a silk cord which broke: twice he had to try again. The Cardinal watched the executioner without deigning to utter a word.' [9] It is true that Camus uses this quotation as a violent symbol for the condition of mortal man in a malevolent universe. It is also true that it carries the suggestion, at the very beginning of *Noces*, that in this book we shall find Camus' sense of human tragedy given intensified expression. We should not forget, however, his earlier statement that heightened despair about life is related to heightened passion for life. Consequently, although *Noces* begins with a quotation suggesting a deeply pessimistic symbolic interpretation, and although pessimism remains behind many of its pages, there is no contradiction involved, within the context of Camus' emotional and intellectual world, in the fact that these essays go on to stress the joy of life in the flesh. Reservations are made at various points, of course, and Camus realizes for instance that such joy can only be experienced for a short time within the life-span of each individual. When such qualifications have been made, however, *Noces* is still a remarkably sustained paean of praise to immediate physical existence. It amply confirms, in the author's response to what he calls 'le grand libertinage de la nature', his own claim that happiness is a central preoccupation of his work.

The physical exaltation of *Noces* begins with an intense and colourful evocation of the assault made by the Algerian countryside on the senses. The landscape is drenched by the sun to become a tumult of light and colour. The air is heavily perfumed by a vivid profusion of flowers—purple and rose-coloured bougainvilleas, red hibiscus, blue irises and tea-roses as thick as cream. The sea is laced with silver and white and the sky is a flaxen blue. The countryside is crossed by buses painted a buttercup yellow. Occasionally one sees against the landscape the bright red cart of a butcher on his rounds. Such is the profusion of the many sense impressions that they release on the transparent air 'un alcool généreux qui fait vaciller le ciel'. This is an ideal place both for sun-bathing and sea-bathing. The Algerian beaches, says Camus, resound with the laughter of young people whose magnificent physique recalls that of the athletes of Delos. On the sea itself canoes are filled with the nut-brown cargoes of young gods and goddesses with whom he feels a deep, fraternal bond. The senses are quickened, the blood is stirred and he must give the name of imbecile to anyone who is afraid to enjoy himself in such conditions. Shame would be a meaningless word on the Algerian beaches; there can be nothing shameful in being happy. Camus adds: '. . . if there is a sin against life it is perhaps not so much despair about this life as hope in another which evades the inexorable grandeur of the here and now.' [10] Sin, in so far as the word has meaning, should be thought of as a turning away from the richness of physical existence rather than as a full and spontaneous embracing of it. Camus feels that he will never be able to have enough contact, or sufficiently close contact, with the natural world. This desire for close and constant intimacy with nature—indeed for those 'nuptials' with nature to which the collective title of these essays refers—emerges over and over again in passages of sensual lyricism. He exults in the sensation of being fashioned by wind and sun to the pattern of the burning countryside stretching before him. He feels his blood throb in rhythm to the pulsations

of the sun at the zenith. As he stands by the ancient ruins of
Djemila he becomes completely detached from himself and is conscious only of identification with the scene before his eyes: '. . . I
am this wind, these pillars and this archway in the wind, these
flagstones which give off heat and these pale mountains surround-
ing the ruined town.'[11]

At first sight these lines may suggest an attitude of pantheistic
rapture—something similar to that earth-worship and identification of the individual with natural objects which constitutes the
lyrical essence of, for example, Richard Jefferies' *The Story of my
Heart*. In fact, however, Camus' view of the Algerian landscape is
essentially unsentimental and unspiritual despite the lyrical vocabulary by which he often describes it. An excess of exaltation in the
lines just quoted causes him to make a verbal identification between
man and nature. What he emphasizes, however, elsewhere in
Noces, is the correspondence between man and nature which is
momentarily, but wrongly, experienced as identification. This
correspondence leaves intact the otherness of nature. However
available for the pleasures of physical enjoyment nature may be,
it remains alien and material. Camus does not play the pantheist's
game of making mountains and fields assume some life of the spirit.
This remains true even when he allows himself to slip into the
poetic language of identification. What gives him satisfaction is not
spiritualization of the landscape but a feeling of correspondence
between this landscape and his own mood. Whereas the pantheist
seeks escape from himself through identification with a spiritual-
ized nature, Camus is at pains to emphasize the strictly physical
reality of natural objects and of his own presence in nature. The
searing beauty of Algeria, he says, teaches no spiritual lessons. It
offers rich indulgence to the senses but has nothing to give to those
who seek from it food for the soul or comfort for the mind. Algeria
can be described, and it ought to be enjoyed, but it does not resemble those more 'humanized' landscapes in Europe where men
are tempted to flee their own humanity, their own mortality, by
seeking, and apparently finding, deliverance from themselves in
the consolations of nature. The burning skies of North Africa carry
no message of hope or redemption. Of the sky above Algiers
Camus says:

Albert Camus

Between this sky and the faces turned towards it there is no means of introducing mythology, literature, ethics or a religion; there are only rocks, the flesh, stars and those truths which the hand can touch.[12]

Camus sees perfectly clearly the tragic implications of this resolutely non-spiritual exaltation of the natural world. In the midst of sensual delight he is as aware as ever of that self-perpetuating dualism which was the dominant theme of *L'Envers et l'endroit* and which prompts him to say here in *Noces* that what exalts life also intensifies its absurdity. He has described in lyrical terms the life of the senses and rejoiced in its perfection. The very perfection and intensity of his experience, however, involve a double limitation. Firstly, the life he describes can only be temporarily enjoyed by the individual. Its splendour need not be diminished while it lasts, but it cannot last for long. Those who stake all on the flesh know that they must lose all in old age and death. The fact of death is therefore particularly present in the rich and abundant Algerian landscape which invites fulfilment of the senses. Camus expresses his dilemma in a brief phrase already referred to: 'Mon horreur de mourir tient dans ma jalousie de vivre.' A second limitation, related to the first, arises from this 'jalousie de vivre'. The essence of physical pleasure is its immediacy. To stake everything on the flesh is to stake everything on what is immediately present. But the immediate, as Camus interprets it here, is experienced as a contrast with that continuing landscape, those eternal mountains and sky, from which it is itself derived. We can only seek pleasure from nature because we are human, not vegetal, and consciousness of our humanity involves consciousness of our mortality. Nature, on the contrary, is not mortal but self-perpetuating. The Algerian summers succeed one another in an unending procession; the sea and the coast carry on their eternal love-making; the wind still fashions mountains as old as time. This is the second flaw in the experience of sensual delight. Camus finds natural joy in sun and sea, mountain and wind, but these objects of his delight will outlast him, will outlast his capacity to experience them, as they have outlasted all the mortal creatures of all the centuries. He writes: 'Je sais seulement que ce ciel durera plus que moi', and in this aspect of his own mortality he finds that happiness is again disfigured.

The Quest for Happiness

This recognition of human transience, emphasized by the permanence of earth and sky, is a familiar theme. One readily associates it with sentiments of self-pity, with expressions of melancholy pride, with the search for some consoling spiritual solution. I think that Camus manages, however, to bring fresh accents to his theme. Not only does he bring to it a youthful intransigence; he rejects the conventional attitudes by making the inevitable acceptance of his lot lose nothing of the uncomfortable features which this lot contains. In other words, acceptance for Camus does not involve any conscious or unconscious stratagem by which the human dilemma is mitigated. In the interests of what he believes to be lucidity and honesty of mind he insists on an insoluble conflict between desire for life and the fact of death, between the here and now which he knows and the hereafter of which he knows nothing. He regards temporal, mortal life as the only reality and the only happiness of which he has certainty. He sees this attitude as loyalty to his human condition. He regards any form of consolation as being at best a pure hypothesis allowing of no verification. In this youthful world of sensual certainty and spiritual distrust belief is based only on sight: '... je vois équivaut à je crois.' He declares:

If I obstinately reject all the 'hereafters' of the world it is because I am also not prepared to renounce my immediate riches. I do not choose to believe that death opens on to another life. For me it is a closed door .... Everything that is suggested to me is an attempt to take from man the burden of his own life.[13]

Camus states specifically here what was really apparent in any case: his decision to stake everything on immediate physical life is the result of arbitrary choice. The fact that such a choice comes more naturally to the North African does not make it any less arbitrary in essence. Having faced a dilemma similar to part of the dilemma outlined by Pascal, Camus wagers in the opposite direction. This refusal to consider the possibility of an after-life is an aspect of that general rejection of absolutes and abstractions which he learns from the Algerian landscape. He embraces what is present to his senses and treats everything else as gratuitous construction. The natural world is beautiful; beyond it, or apart from it, there is no salvation. Such direct and unhesitating disbelief is striking and unusual in a writer of Camus' stature and reputation. He expresses in *Noces* what might be called 'naïve atheism' since it occupies a place in religious speculation analogous to that of 'naïve realism' in the theory of perception. It is markedly uncomplicated compared with the atheism of a Malraux or a Sartre and serves to underline again the effect of his mediterranean origins on Camus. It is true that he has since claimed confirmation for his attitude in discussion of the problem of evil or of the shortcomings of the Church and individual Christians, but the atheism which he presents here is unreflective in origin. He expresses the outlook—held consciously or unconsciously—by a people whom he describes as being primitive and uncomplicated. For these North Africans, he claims, words such as 'sin', 'virtue' and 'repentance' have no absolute meaning although they do, of course, practise a certain day-to-day morality—which he calls an automatic 'code de la rue'. They take their unreflecting pleasure mostly in groups and in public places, and their ethics are based on the elementary rules of such communal living: consideration should be shown to pregnant women; you must not steal your friend's girl, etc. Apart from this elementary morality, which is supported by social rather than religious sanctions, he claims that: 'These people, given over completely to their present life, live without myths, without consolation.' [14] It is from such 'barbares', as he calls them, who find their pleasure on the beaches of North Africa, that most may be expected for the future. Theirs is a direct and healthy attitude to life which can, albeit all unconsciously, create a culture in which human dignity would receive adequate expression.

We have here, of course, something approaching the myth of the happy savage in which sophisticated minds occasionally indulge. It is obvious that these people who themselves have no need of myths supply Camus, by the same token, with a myth and a symbol. Although he was born in the same pagan atmosphere he is essentially different from these people by virtue of his education, his travel, his reading. Much as he admires them, understands them and has at certain points shared their life, he is separated from them by the fact of his own reflective mind. What is an instinctive attitude in them is not instinctive in him either in the same way or to the same degree. The consciousness which prompts him to speak of them as 'ce peuple enfant' and 'ces barbares' is a consciousness of his difference from them. He is placed outside their world in so far as he realizes, and they do not, their absence of any need of myths. Within the terms of their own world of unreflecting physical exaltation he justifiably disapproves of the cerebration in Gide's *Nourritures terrestres*,* but this disapproval is itself the result of cerebration by Camus at another level. Such cerebration is as inevitable in him as it is alien, on his own showing, to the people whose attitude to life he praises and admires. It is only fair to add, however, that although Camus accepts these points he insists that something in him remains closely identified with this 'peuple enfant'. Indeed he claims, in a recent letter, that this is why sophisticated Paris has never accepted him unreservedly and why he cannot, on his side, give allegiance to the Parisian social and literary world.

This conscious cult of the 'average sensual man' now suggests, therefore, that even Camus' 'naïve atheism' is something less spontaneous than at first appeared. The very fact of *describing* his unbelief as instinctive removes it to some extent from the sphere of the spontaneous. What is presented throughout eighty pages as an uncomplicated attitude on his part presupposes more reflection, and a greater element of choice, than he is ready to admit. It can be argued at this point that Camus' attitude is still spontaneous in the sense that he genuinely fails to see what the Christian sees and cannot make any contact with the Christian consciousness. There is, I think, a good deal of justification in this view, at least in the early stage of his development represented by *Noces*. But it remains a fact that he had contact with the Christian religion, however unsatisfactorily it may have been practised by people he met, from an early age. Therefore his own attitude must remain a refusal of transcendence as distinct from that unawareness of the very idea of transcendence which he sometimes seems to attribute to the youth of Algeria brought up in an entirely pagan atmosphere. The kind of atheism which Camus reveals in himself is still comparatively simple and uncomplicated, taking its main strength from love of life and horror of death, but it does contain an arbitrary element. In fact, what he presents in *Noces* is an early form of that 'passionate disbelief' which he was to describe ten years

* See Camus' footnote on Gide in *Noces*, pp. 47–8.

Albert Camus

later as the distinguishing feature of contemporary atheism.* His atheism is not a denial of religion in the name of science, in the nineteenth-century manner; it is a disbelief which rejects all absolutes, scientific and religious alike. Just as there is religious belief which contains certain twentieth-century features, so there is an essentially contemporary disbelief, and Camus' atheism is of this kind. It is not militant assault, it does not fight battles; it is, rather, steady refusal whose self-sufficiency normally steers clear of polemics. There is an underlying tolerance to be felt in this atheism which sees human solutions as the natural answer to human problems. One final feature of this early atheistic attitude is the fact that it is based on a very concrete conception of reality. This is implied, of course, in the rejection of absolutes just mentioned. What is real, for the author of *Noces*, is what can be experienced by the senses. Not all forms of atheism are necessarily materialistic, but Camus' atheism here does result from the determination to trace everything back to a solid physical basis.

By resolutely adopting what he calls 'lucid attention' to the fact of human mortality, and by refusing at the same time the consolation and solution offered by religion, Camus deprives himself of hope—at least in the usual meaning of the word. And yet, at the same time, he will not accept the term 'resignation' as a correct description of his attitude. He does not hold a refusal of religious belief to be resignation. On the contrary, he understands by resignation a giving up of the world in exchange for what he regards as illusory spiritual values. The Greeks, he says, produced hope last of all from Pandora's box as the greatest of human ills. He finds in this a moving symbol of the fact that it is indeed hope, contrary to the usual belief, which means resignation. To live without hope, to accept the transience of the physical rather than to reject it in favour of an immaterial permanence placed outside this life—this is precisely to refuse resignation.

In the closing pages of *Noces* Camus uses this conception of non-resignation in order to support his contention that to renounce hope is not necessarily to destroy the possibility of happiness. He defines happiness as a simple harmony relating the individual to

* See Camus' article in *La Vie intellectuelle*, 1949, p. 349, which includes this statement: 'Contemporary disbelief no longer relies on science as it did at the end of the last century. It denies both science and religion. It is no longer a sceptical reaction to miracles. It is passionate disbelief.'

his existence. What more sure basis can there be for happiness, then, than recognition by the individual of that insoluble paradox which constitutes his position in the world? Happiness will follow from a relationship in which the individual accepts the eternal antagonism between his desire for life and the inevitability of his death. We have here one of several instances in which Camus presents a crucial point in his thinking by means of something very like a play on words. His argument relies on the rather formal application, to the situation he has been describing throughout most of the book, of his definition of happiness as a relationship. Also, his rhetorically effective reversal of the usual applications of hope and resignation depends precariously on the virtually unexamined assumption that spiritual consolation is a delusion. Once more it seems clear that what Camus puts forward here as a coherent argument is essentially an arbitrary decision. Having made this decision, however, he is in no doubt about the value of the position to which it leads. He claims to have attained by lucid acceptance of his lot a happiness which makes the popular conception of happiness appear futile. This supra-happiness is not easily explained and seems to escape adequate formulation. It is something like the stoical serenity which may come from a recognition of the impossibility of happiness. He says: 'une certaine continuité dans le désespoir peut engendrer la joie', and one is reminded of a phrase from Graham Greene's *The Heart of the Matter*: '. . . one is left alone with the worst and it's like peace'. Such happiness, according to Camus, gives a satisfaction in no way inferior to the more usual interpretations of the word.

This attitude might seem at first to deny the whole tenor of the previous argument in *Noces* by offering stoicism as a substitute for brief sensual pleasure. What Camus does, however, is to place the roots of his stoical supra-happiness in the physical. He reaffirms the value of physical happiness by making it the only possible source of supra-happiness. The very brevity of physical pleasure gives true human dimensions to this stoical attitude by making its truth and value of the same perishable quality as man himself: 'What have I to do with an imperishable truth, even were I to desire such a thing? It is not made to my measure. To desire it would be to deceive myself.' [15]

It should finally be borne in mind that Camus does not separate this form of stoicism from revolt any more than from indulgence of the senses. Revolt of this type, and at this stage, is still a vague and negative concept, but one can see, I think, that the rejection of absolutes, even within the generalized terms of these four essays, has its defiant and rebellious aspect. We may say, therefore, that the quest for happiness which forms a constant thread through *L'Envers et l'endroit* and *Noces* ultimately reaches its goal by accepting both joy in what is physical and revolt against anything that would tend to mask the physical tragedy of man's condition. *Noces* ends with a neat expression of Camus' formula for happiness which is also a play on words: '. . . how can harmony between love and revolt be consecrated? By the earth! In this great temple abandoned by the gods all my idols have feet of clay.' [16]

3 THE NATURE OF THE ABSURD

*Il est au cœur de monde occidental un conflit sans
espoir . . . il apprend à la conscience à disparaître et
nous prépare aux royaumes métalliques de l'absurdité.*
ANDRÉ MALRAUX

There is a special quality about Camus' lyricism in *Noces*. The
distinctive tone of this book, and to a lesser degree of *L'Envers et
l'endroit*, is partly explained by the fact that even when it cele-
brates the abundance of physical life it does so with a lyrical intensity achieved by restraint rather than profusion. The vocabulary
used by Camus has an almost anti-lyrical rigour and clarity. The
lyricism of the book suggests a hard, clear flame, not a soft and
warm radiance. Although Camus is preaching sensual indulgence
he does so with a mind that impresses by its precision and orderly
functioning. These mental qualities with which the neo-paganism
of *Noces* is formulated are still more clearly seen—and no doubt
more appropriately used—in *Le Mythe de Sisyphe*. This work,
published in 1942, marks a sharp transition from the lyrical expression of an attitude to life to the intellectual investigation of the
same attitude. It is an essay on the absurd, and by the absurd
Camus generally means the absence of correspondence or congruity
between the mind's need for coherence and the incoherence of the
world which the mind experiences. *Le Mythe de Sisyphe* follows
in a direct line from *L'Envers et l'endroit* and *Noces*. Like the
earlier essays it possesses originality of tone, but in this case the
passionate assertions are mainly moral, not sensual. The tension
running throughout the whole book arises from a combination of
moral frustration and intellectual analysis. The neat and orderly
intelligence behind *Le Mythe de Sisyphe* gives it an appearance of
simplicity and definiteness. It contains a greater directness of statement than do the earlier essays. And yet the book is certainly less
clear and less simple than at first appears. The more obvious

intellectualism cannot always conceal continuing lyrical under-
tones. If there is more clarification, there are also more difficulties,
and the argument is sometimes conducted so tersely or expressed
with such intensity that it is difficult to follow. Whereas the
lyricism of *Noces* was enhanced by intellectual order, the intellectual order of *Le Mythe de Sisyphe* is sometimes impaired by
lyricism.

Readers and critics alike are often quick to find some label by
means of which they can characterize or summarize an original
writer and thereby render him less disturbing. Once the formula
has been found the actual work itself can be largely ignored. Camus
was subjected to such a labelling process at an early stage and soon
came to be generally regarded as a 'philosopher of the absurd'. In
a brief preliminary note to *Le Mythe de Sisyphe*, however, he
states clearly that he is not elaborating a 'philosophie absurde' but
describing the 'sensibilité absurde'. He adds that his attitude
towards the absurd is a provisional one. Nevertheless, the majority
of readers have taken no notice of these remarks. They have continued to equate the various—and sometimes conflicting—ideas of
L'Étranger, Caligula or *Le Malentendu* with Camus' own private
beliefs. The result is that he is still most widely known as the
author of *L'Étranger* and *Le Mythe de Sisyphe*. He continues to
be described as a writer or philosopher of the absurd. The com-
plexities of his own attitude to this question, together with his
development since 1942, are too often ignored.

Camus was sufficiently incensed by this situation to write an
essay about it in 1950.* He describes as 'one of the puerile notions
of Romanticism' the belief that an author necessarily writes about
himself and reveals himself accurately in his books. A writer's
work, he says, is more often the history of his temptations and
nostalgias. While admitting that a part of him was tempted by
the absurd, and still responds to it, he claims that what he primarily
did in *Le Mythe de Sisyphe* was to examine the logical basis and
intellectual justification of that 'sensibilité absurde' which he found
expressed in various forms by so many of his contemporaries. We
shall see in the next chapter that Camus goes on, in *Le Mythe de
Sisyphe*, to draw ethical conclusions from the absurd which make
his own account of his relationship to it unsatisfactory in some

* See 'L'Énigme', collected in *L'Été*, pp. 123–38.

ways. At this stage, however, it is necessary to realize that he did not apply the moral implications of absurdism to his own life. He does not advocate them for others either, except in very general terms relating to their form, not their content. Indeed, this book is more concerned with public stocktaking than with public advocacy. I use the word 'public' advisedly, for Camus attempts in this essay a kind of dialogue and discussion with his readers. *L'Envers et l'endroit* and *Noces* were essentially literary works in which artistic considerations were very important. As such they sought the reader's aesthetic interest, and if they roused this without compelling his agreement they would still be far from having failed. In *Le Mythe de Sisyphe*, on the contrary, Camus clearly aims at a full exchange of views, if not complete agreement, between his readers and himself. The essay is a serious attempt to define and assess attitudes and reactions contained in the earlier works.

Le Mythe de Sisyphe, then, is the fruit of further reflection and more disciplined thought about the content of *Noces*. It attempts a rational investigation and formulation of an earlier emotional experience. It moves forward from a predominantly physical to a predominantly intellectual response to existence. The added thought brings new emphases as well as new problems. In particular, the contrast between physical exaltation and the certainty of death, which remained a dualism in *Noces*, becomes so intensified in *Le Mythe de Sisyphe* as to be one of those insoluble paradoxes giving rise to a sense of the absurd. This intensification is also the source of more acute and comprehensive scepticism—a scepticism which nevertheless prepares the way ultimately for a series of affirmations. One is indeed tempted to describe *Le Mythe de Sisyphe* as Camus' *Discours de la méthode*. It is founded on a doubt that extends to the evidence of both sense and mind. It derives its own particular kind of *cogito* from this doubt. It produces a provisional morality also, though the provisional morality of Camus would be much less generally approved—if perhaps more widely practised—than that of Descartes.

The sensibility examined here by Camus is one that can make no contact with absolute truths and values. The kind of man described —and he is presented as a common contemporary figure—is one who instinctively wishes to be happy, who wants his life to continue indefinitely, who seeks close contact with other human beings and with the natural world, but who finds these desires frustrated by the nature of existence. It is Camus' contention that such desires cannot be satisfied by human life as it is. Thus his purpose is to discuss what the individual should do when, consciously or unconsciously, he experiences anxiety, disappointment, a sense of estrangement and horror of death. At the very outset Camus insists that a man who experiences the absurd in this way must first of all face the situation lucidly and accept the painful paradox that it entails. The existence of the dilemma must be realized, and also the fact that no system or creed can eradicate it. The absurd both makes direct knowledge of the world impossible and cuts the individual off from supra-rational knowledge.

It may seem at first as though there are at least two possible ways of solving the dilemma—suicide or the leap of faith. Nearly half of Camus' argument is concerned to show that neither reaction is in fact a solution. He attempts to show that the only coherent position is to preserve the paradox, to live the tensions and conflicts which it involves and to refuse alleged solutions that turn out to be nothing more than evasions. We must learn not to make unrealistic demands of life but to accept it as our minds experience it. The lucid contemplation of the absurd may even prove, in itself, a partial release. It will at any rate require a certain kind of lucidity and imply a certain kind of innocence that may make life more liveable without necessarily making it more rational.

It will be clear from what has been said so far that much of the analysis in *Le Mythe de Sisyphe* covers familiar ground. Indeed, we have already seen that Camus claimed his subject to be a contemporary commonplace. Whatever the special character of Camus' conclusions, the absurd itself remains a contemporary manifestation of a scepticism as old at least as the Book of Ecclesiastes. *Le Mythe de Sisyphe* is yet another contribution to the centuries-old debate carried on around such problems as the one and the many, the relative and the absolute, essence and existence, experience and the experiencing mind, etc. Camus' treatment of these questions, however, is individual in tone and in keeping with certain present-day trends. That is to say, he approaches the absurd from an existential—though not existentialist—standpoint. He comes to his subject from a practical and human angle. He generally avoids abstraction and speaks more as an involved individual than as an objective philosopher. He argues from what appears to be personal experience, and does so as a thoughtful human being, not as a professional metaphysician. As a result we find in *Le Mythe de Sisyphe* that private emotion and logical thought are sometimes at variance with one another. The term 'absurd' itself is emotional as Camus uses it, and one notices that he employs it differently from Sartre. It is also significant, I think, that the word occurs much less often in the writings of Sartre who is much more a professionally trained philosopher than Camus.*

Apart from this personal note, *Le Mythe de Sisyphe* shows another distinctive quality. In it the North African Camus discusses the solution of experiences similar to his own in such writers and thinkers as Kierkegaard, Nietzsche, Dostoievsky, Chestov, Jaspers, Heidegger and Husserl. As a result we have the interesting spectacle of mediterranean reason and clarity examining a shadowy and often anti-rational nordic and slav world of thought. This encounter gives added individuality to the book. Camus criticizes the attempts by these different writers to suppress the absurd by rejecting reason and cultivating their own individual forms of what he holds to be irrationality.† At the same time, however, he remains on his guard against that deification of reason to which his own tradition is prone. Complete faith in reason or absolute rejection of reason are both, he holds, betrayals of man's situation in the world and only serve to promote harmful delirium. Camus' concern is to find a way of living which accepts the absurd instead of veiling it behind either rationalism or irrationalism.

---

* Sartre has commented as follows on the different meanings he and Camus give to the term 'absurd': 'Camus' philosophy is a philosophy of the absurd. For him the absurd arises from the relation between man and the world, between man's rational demands and the world's irrationality. The themes which he derives from it are those of classical pessimism. I do not recognize the absurd in the sense of scandal and disillusionment that Camus attributes to it. What I call the absurd is something very different: it is the universal contingency of being which is, but which is not the basis of its being; the absurd is the given, unjustifiable, primordial quality of existence', *Paru*, December, 1945.

† There is, I think, rather less similarity between these different thinkers than Camus admits. In some cases their conclusions take on a different character when put back into the context of a complete individual system of thought. Camus' account of Kierkegaard, for instance, might be challenged at several points. He also shows little understanding of phenomenology and Husserl's conception of essences.

I have already said that *Le Mythe de Sisyphe* sharpens the dualism of *Noces* to such an extent that this dualism takes on all the discordancy of a paradox. Now it is clear that one can live less easily with a paradox than with a dualism. A dualism presumably allows of some kind of accommodation, but a paradox can cast doubt on the possibility or value of living at all. It is not surprising, then, that *Le Mythe de Sisyphe* begins with the question as to whether or not one's life should not be voluntarily terminated. It opens with a discussion of suicide. Again, mention has been made above of the greater degree of reflective thought in this essay than in *Noces*. Camus himself says that increased thought leads to increased disquiet: 'Commencer à penser, c'est commencer d'être miné.' The result is that recognition of a paradox, together with persistent thinking about it, gives to *Le Mythe de Sisyphe* some sort of double tension so that the book opens on a note of anxious inquiry far removed from that stoical detachment with which *Noces* came to an end. The first chapter considers the question of suicide; the first sentence of the book states unequivocally that suicide is the only serious philosophical problem. At the very outset, therefore, Camus gives to his reflections a markedly practical tone. His criterion for judging the importance of a question is: what actions does it involve? Judged by this criterion a question which, if answered in a certain way can lead to suicide, is clearly an important one. People do not die for the ontological argument, but men and women continue to kill themselves because they fail to find sufficient reasons for living.

In so far as suicide means that a particular individual no longer considers his life to be worth living it involves the decision to break an established set of habits. The pattern and daily repetition which make up an ordinary life are felt to be without meaning or value. Not only so; they eventually become wholly unbearable and are consequently destroyed. In other words, some kind of divorce has arisen between the individual and his day-by-day existence. This feeling of estrangement between a man and his life, which sometimes ends in suicide, is the most elementary way of experiencing the absurd. It seems therefore as if suicide in general, apart from specialized forms like *hara-kiri*, is a product of the absurd. It must be pointed out, however, that no simple reciprocal relation exists between the two things. Suicide normally involves recognition of the absurd at some level, but recognition of the absurd by no means automatically results in suicide. Indeed, *intellectual* recognition of the absurd seldom does so. Camus himself points out that Schopenhauer, for example, who wrote much about the meaninglessness of life and theorized about suicide, did not put his theories into practice to the extent of killing himself.

This last point gives rise to a new question: does intellectual recognition of the absurd *logically* entail suicide? Schopenhauer did not do away with himself, but was he required by logic to do so? Camus puts this question in a compressed form by saying: '. . . y a-t-il une logique jusqu'à la mort?' Behind this terse question, at least as put by Camus, there lurks, I suspect, some kind of tautology or circular argument. In the immediately preceding sentences he speaks, not of thinking logically, but of being logical. In particular he raises the problem of being logical to the utmost limit. Indeed, in the whole of the argument up to this point, it is clear that he means by logic a rigorous measure of consistency between thought and action. This being so, Camus' question, at least as he puts it, ceases to be a meaningful one. His use of the term 'logical' prior to this point means that when he asks whether the absurd logically entails suicide he is in effect asking whether consistency of thought and action is entailed by consistency of thought and action. What we appear to have here, early in the book, is an example of failure to separate clear thinking from an emotional attitude; it is something which takes away much of the substance from Camus' argument even though it leaves the formal neatness and orderliness of the argument intact. The question which he has asked, at least in the way he puts it, may be emotionally understandable but it is philosophically unsound. Of course Camus claims at most to be a moralist, not a philosopher. He states specifically that he wishes to discuss the feeling of the absurd, not a philosophy of the absurd. Clearly one must accept this position, but in doing so one must realize that what we primarily have in *Le Mythe de Sisyphe* is a testimony to a certain widespread state of mind rather than a strict philosophical scrutiny of it. Nevertheless, the confusion which arises above from a particular interpretation of what logic is will be important for much of the subsequent argument since a large part of the essay is devoted to a discussion and attempted solution of the question in which this confusion occurs. Therefore, if one is to treat the essay seriously, some way must be found of getting round the tautology. The most obvious way seems to be to accept, at least provisionally, the fact of a certain discrepancy between Camus' feeling and his thought. It may still be that his feeling that a problem exists is correct even though he has not expressed the problem in a way that would satisfy the requirements of formal logic. Indeed, we know already that later in the book he does present the absurd as being, among other things, a divorce between thought and experience or between what the feelings demand and what the mind can achieve. It could thus be argued that Camus' question illustrates the nature of the absurd and requires further discussion; the content corresponds to human experience while the logically unsatisfactory formulation shows the limitation of the mind in dealing with such experience.

Having raised the problem of suicide and its relation to the absurd, Camus leaves it temporarily on one side and makes a further preliminary point. He has already said that experience of the absurd results in some people annihilating their bodies by physical suicide. He now points out that recognition of the absurd may alternatively lead to annihilation of the intellect by a kind of mental suicide. Later, particularly in connection with certain Christian existentialists, he calls this 'le suicide philosophique'. He does not actually mention Tertullian, but no doubt the latter's 'credo quia absurdum est' is the *locus classicus* of philosophical suicide in this sense of the term. The mention of this second form of suicide brings the first chapter to a close and we may say that so far Camus has set forth three main ideas: the absurd, physical suicide and philosophical suicide. The absurd can prompt both self-destruction (through physical suicide) and self-preservation (through philosophical suicide). Camus' investigations now branch out in three different directions and he attempts to answer three main questions in this order: (i) what is the nature of the absurd? (ii) does the absurd justify philosophical suicide? (iii) does the absurd justify physical suicide?

The history of the word 'absurde', used in French in this metaphysical sense, is no doubt an interesting one. I am not aware of this history having been written, but there are various isolated examples of its use early in this century (e.g. by Loti in 1917), and the story of its origins could probably be traced back at least to a growing reaction against science already under way in the second half of the nineteenth century. For our immediate purpose, however, what is so striking is its ubiquitousness in contemporary or very recent French writing. Malraux, for example, in his first major work, *La Tentation de l'Occident*, speaks several times of a metaphysical absurdity dominating the western world in the twentieth century. This concept of the absurd is also prominent in such novels as *Les Conquérants* and *La Voie Royale*. Sartre uses the term more sparingly, but he gives a full account of what he means by it in Roquentin's reflections on the chestnut tree in *La Nausée*. Various other writers have used the term, but its most recent and fullest investigation is that contained in *Le Mythe de Sisyphe*. Malraux, Sartre and Camus differ about the precise content which they give to the term, but all agree in relating it in some way to the apparent irreducibility of the world to satisfactory rational categories. They also agree in attributing to the absurd considerable contemporary relevance and importance.

This discussion of the absurd by leading men of letters points, I think, to certain prior philosophical origins. The notion as treated by European writers at the present time suggests either disillusioned Hegelianism or possibly a crisis within Hegelianism itself. Concern about the absurd as currently expressed indicates some kind of continuing nostalgia for the panlogism of Hegel. Intellectual awareness of the absurd is the experience of a person who has expected—no doubt on the basis of Hegel's assurances—a rationally ordered *cosmos*, but who finds instead—on the basis of his own immediate experience—a *chaos* impervious to reason. The absurd is the conclusion arrived at by those who had assumed the possibility of a total explanation of existence by the mind but who discover instead an unbridgeable gulf between rationality and experience.

Incidentally, it is significant that two of the thinkers whose negative attitudes Camus has assimilated very fully—Pascal and Kierkegaard—both opposed what they considered to be excessive claims on behalf of reason in their own day. Pascal rejected the sweeping rationalist claims of Descartes, just as Kierkegaard was later to react vigorously against the system of Hegel. It will be noticed that Camus' intellectual lineage in this sphere is associated with moralists and theologians rather than with philosophers in the strictest sense of the term. Indeed, we shall shortly see that his discussion of the absurd is open to various philosophical objections. Nevertheless, there is no doubt that his preoccupation with the absurd reflects a prominent feature of the current intellectual climate in Europe. It translates something of that sense of crisis which seems to characterize contemporary European metaphysics.

Within a historical context, then, the notion of the absurd appears as a particularly intense form of anti-rationalism. It may be so intense as to differ from this anti-rationalism in kind as well as degree, but a rejection of the claims of classical rationalism obviously prepared the ground for it. This is as much the case in France as elsewhere. There are those, of course, who continue to find it curious and surprising that writers about the absurd should be so numerous and prominent in France with her Cartesian tradition. And yet, quite apart from considerations of an 'inevitable reaction' or a 'swing of the pendulum', the plain fact of the matter is that there has always been in France, alongside Cartesianism, an anti-rational tradition. This tradition came very much to the forefront in France at the end of the last century and the beginning of this. Among the professional philosophers and teachers of philosophy, men like Bergson, Meyerson and Brunschvicg denied the efficacy of reason and doubted the mind's capacity to make more than very limited contact with experience and the external world. Bergson criticized the concept as failing to make contact with concrete reality. Meyerson held that when the mind tries to make experience conform to its own categories it leaves untouched a considerable irrational residue. Brunschvicg emphasized the fact that the mind is constantly coming up against radical unintelligibility and must frequently offer description and classification as a substitute for comprehension. One finds what is of course a less strictly argued presentation of such ideas in the imaginative literature of the period. Julien Benda said somewhat sharply, in 1913, that Bergson's anti-rationalism told his contemporaries exactly what they wanted to hear. There is confirmation of this not only in the general emphases of Symbolism and Impressionism, but in such writers as Proust, Péguy, Rolland, and in the literary criticism of Thibaudet and Charles Du Bos.

A notable feature of Bergson's anti-rationalism is its continuing belief in the inherent intelligibility of existence. To say that existence is intelligible means for Bergson both that it *can* be known and that it *is* known. It is true that he claims that the mind cannot of itself encompass reality, but he does not deny that reality can be known by other means. Indeed, Bergson's doctrine of intuition asserts the existence and explores the possibility of a method of contact between the individual and experience. It is at this point that the greater rigidity and absolutism of contemporary views of the absurd emerges. Contemporary 'philosophers of the absurd' not only claim that reality is unknown, but that it is unknowable. They refuse to admit the existence of an intelligibility with which contact can ultimately be made either by reason, intuition or any other means. For Camus the absurd takes on an irremediable character that is certainly different in degree, and perhaps in kind, from the anti-rationalism which preceded it and helped to make it possible. Whereas most earlier thinkers stressed the shortcomings of reason partly out of enthusiasm for an alternative means of knowledge (intuition), Camus claims that reason is powerless and he offers no comparable alternative avenue to truth.

Although the conventions of ordinary linguistic usage often oblige Camus to employ a noun and speak of 'l'absurde', he is not in fact unwittingly substituting another absolute for those absolutes which he denies in its name. It is quite clear from what he says that although an existing object may make the absurd manifest, the absurd itself is not an existing object. In one particular passage quoted below he stresses that the absurd is a relationship, a relationship of nonconformity between the individual and the world. The absurd is not a 'thing-in-itself' but the confrontation of two things other than itself—existence and an individual mind. Now, because the absurd is a relationship with an experiencing mind as one of its terms, it follows that the absurd cannot strictly be presented as something absolute and universal. The fact of its being a relationship, and the nature of that relationship, only justifies the statement: 'this appears absurd to *me*'; it does not permit one to say: 'this *is* absurd'. Therefore, although Camus goes the length of saying that what he does not understand is unintelligible, he is only justified in meaning by this that what he does not understand is unknowable for him. Yet his actual phrase suggests that he regards what he does not understand as being unknowable in an absolute sense. This is something that he can obviously neither demonstrate nor verify, but it is an interpretation to which several passages lend themselves. In fact, the whole discussion of the absurd in *Le Mythe de Sisyphe* is made confusing and debatable by a failure to distinguish clearly between 'unknown' and 'unknowable'. Thus in the passage in question Camus writes:

> I said the world is absurd, but I was being too hasty. All one can say of the world is that it is not amenable to reason. The absurd, however, is the confrontation of this non-rational world by that desperate desire for clarity which is one of man's deepest needs. The absurd depends as much on man as on the world for its existence.[1]

More particularly in the first two sentences of this passage Camus appears to imply a distinction between 'unknown' and 'unknowable'. He rightly says that the world is not necessarily absurd, but simply not reducible to rational categories. In other words the world is unknown, but he is not claiming it to be unknowable. The way is still left open, presumably, for some such hypothesis as Bergsonian intuition. In a later passage, however, Camus ignores the legitimate and, I think, necessary distinction made above. He presents us instead with the view that the absurd is wholly irremediable. Man is radically different from the rest of the creation. His consciousness as a human being seals him off from the world and from his standpoint the world is not simply unknown but unknowable. A gulf is fixed which no knowledge can bridge; knowledge of the world would only be possible for man if he ceased to be man and became part of the external, physical creation which he experiences: 'If I were a tree among trees, a cat among the animals, this life would have meaning, or rather this problem would be without meaning because I would be part of this world'.[2]

This passage, taken in conjunction with the one previously quoted, illustrates the kind of confusion to which I have referred: between regarding the world as not known but possibly knowable and holding it to be inherently unknowable. Apart from this, however, Camus also seems to go too far when he claims that the absurd is an absolute and universal relationship. The necessarily subjective human factor in this relationship only permits him to claim confirmation of his own experience in the similar experiences of others. To do this then requires recognition of the fact that this experience is no more universally valid, in the absence of absolutes or divine revelation, than that of a very much larger number of thinkers who hold the contrary or a different view. Here one is inclined to suspect, as on several other occasions in *Le Mythe de Sisyphe*, that Camus is insisting with some perversity on the impossibility of knowledge of the world in order to conserve intact his notion of the absurd. There is never far from these pages a strongly emotional attitude, a clear predisposition in favour of the absurd, that always threatens and sometimes falsifies their logic. Camus insists on the necessity for 'l'absence totale d'espoir', 'le refus continuel', 'l'insatisfaction consciente', and he adds:

Anything that destroys these demands, that stifles them or refines them out of existence (and above all consent which demolishes difference) ruins the absurd and devalues the attitude to be derived from it.[3]

Camus justified this assertion on the grounds that he must preserve whatever he judges to be true. Yet he also admits shortly afterwards that the world is not completely alien. He rightly says: '. . . nous pouvons comprendre et expliquer beaucoup de choses.' It is indeed this partial efficacy of reason that ultimately causes it to posit the absurd and enables it to witness to its own limitations. The gulf between man and the world is not as radical and absolute as some of his other statements suggest. In view of his principle that he must preserve what truth he finds this last point should not be ignored by him. It would form an equally legitimate—and perhaps a more sensible—basis of behaviour. Yet this would divert attention from the absurd, it could lessen drastically the value of revolt, and, at least at the stage represented by *Le Mythe de Sisyphe,* Camus will have none of it.

   This discussion of the absurd so far emphasizes the fact that it is often a highly intellectual notion. But Camus also makes the point that whatever name we may give it the absurd is also a widespread emotional experience. It is felt by many people who do not develop it to the stage of intellectual apprehension. In fact, he asserts that it is first experienced as feeling and only subsequently formulated in intellectual terms. In the second chapter of *Le Mythe de Sisyphe* he begins with an account of emotional experience of the absurd— what it is like and how it arises. Later in the same chapter he goes on to discuss it as a rationalized attitude to the world.

Albert Camus

Camus claims that this feeling of the absurd is something of which we find evidence not only in literature but in daily conversation and ordinary contacts with other people. The absurd may be experienced quite spontaneously without preparation of the mind or senses. Its revelation of itself to certain individuals is as arbitrary as the operation of divine grace for a believer in predestination. Generally, however, a sense of the absurd is most likely to arise in one or more of four different ways. Firstly, the mechanical nature of many individuals' lives, the deadening routine that marks them, may one day cause some of these individuals to question the value and purpose of their existence. Such questioning is an intimation of absurdity. (We may notice, incidentally, that Camus seems to regard the deadening repetition of most people's lives, particularly in a highly urbanized society, as a contemporary form of the Sisyphus myth.) Awareness of the absurd finds its second possible source in an acute sense of time passing—a sense of time as the destructive element. We may link with this experience a realization of the inevitable and ineluctable character of death. Thirdly, the absurd arises from that sense of dereliction in an alien world which people feel in varying degrees. This sense of dereliction may be produced by a feeling for the contingency and arbitrariness of our existence, a feeling to be found in Pascal and Kierkegaard as well as among modern Existentialists. It may also result—and this is an instance examined by Sartre in *La Nausée*—from sudden awareness of the radically alien nature of those natural objects that are normally domesticated and rendered familiar by the names of 'stone', 'tree', 'bench' etc. We may have an intense feeling of what Camus calls 'l'hostilité primitive du monde'. Lastly, we may possibly experience the absurd through an acute sense of our fundamental isolation from other human beings. Human beings, Camus says, have a capacity for exuding a kind of inhuman essence. During certain moments of vision we are struck by the apparently mechanical and senseless gestures that make up the normal behaviour of people. The feeling is similar to that which we sometimes get from watching a man have a telephone conversation but being unable to hear what he says. The impression is of a non-human puppet. Another simile for this intimation of the absurd might be, I think, that feeling of vague uneasiness that sometimes comes from the inhuman quality of human figures performing actions in silent films. Under this same heading Camus also adds the sense of alienation from ourselves that we may experience by seeing a familiar and yet disquieting brother, who is ourself, in a mirror or a photograph.

Turning to intellectual apprehension of the absurd, Camus is concerned to show the inability of the mind to give a satisfactory account of experience. The primary operation of the mind, he says, is to distinguish truth from falsehood and certainty from supposition. But as soon as thought reflects on its own activity it finds itself powerless to make such distinctions really effective. To illustrate his point Camus considers in turn what he claims to be the failure of logic to attain truth and the failure of science to achieve a rational explanation of the world. On the question of logic he refers to Aristotle's demonstration that to assume everything is true or to assume everything is false leads in either case to a logical impasse. This is the old problem about the Cretan who said all Cretans were invariably liars and who, if he told the truth, was speaking a lie since he was himself a Cretan. The full form of the argument goes as follows: If we state the proposition that all propositions are true, then we are affirming, among others, the contrary proposition that all propositions are false (i.e. if all propositions are true then the proposition that all propositions are false is true), therefore our first proposition cannot be true. Conversely, if we state the proposition that all propositions are false, then this proposition itself must also be false, therefore at least one proposition must be true. In addition, if we state that only the contrary proposition to our own is false, or that only our own proposition is not false, we commit ourselves to the existence of an infinite number of judgments concerning truth and falsehood. Here Camus is guilty, I think, of somewhat misrepresenting Aristotle who did accept the possibility of logical demonstrations. The fact that Aristotle is quoted out of context is suggested by the first sentence in the passage cited by Camus (*Le Mythe de Sisyphe*, p. 31). Furthermore, modern logicians do not find this paradox to be insoluble in the way Camus suggests although he uses it to support his claim that the mind's demand for unified and absolute truth must always be frustrated.

The criticism of physics offered by Camus has been made before. Goethe is only one of several thinkers who anticipated what Whitehead was to call the fallacy of 'misplaced concreteness'. Such 'misplaced concreteness' confuses the scientist's picture of reality at any historical moment with reality as it really is. Camus is aware of this confusion and at pains to point it out. Science, he says, begins by enumerating various physical laws. We accept these laws in our desire for further knowledge. The scientist then proceeds to dismantle the mechanism of the physical world, and our hopes increase. He isolates various component parts, he reduces each part to atoms, each atom to electrons, and so on. But a point comes where, if asked to continue, he speaks of an invisible planetary system gravitating round a nucleus. This, for Camus is the moment of supreme disillusion. What set out to be a rational account of reality ends in a poetic metaphor. Because of recent scientific developments this metaphor replaces earlier ones (e.g. the watch or clock metaphor of the eighteenth century) but it will be replaced in its turn. The most that science can offer by such images and hypotheses is efficacity, not knowledge. Camus considers that science leaves us with a choice between a description of the physical world which may be exact but will tell us very little, and hypotheses that claim to give us knowledge but are continually changing and must therefore be inexact. And so he concludes that as logic ends in relativity, physics ends in poetry. He says: 'L'intelligence aussi me dit donc à sa manière que ce monde est absurde'. It should be noted, incidentally, that Camus, in speaking of science, does not invoke the conclusions of modern astronomy to emphasize human dereliction and contingency. To do so could be held to be inconsistent with his views on physics, and in any case he shows no taste for certain modish forms of astronomical intimidation.

Camus' views on both logic and science are clearly open to various objections. As regards his difficulties over logic I need only point out that they have been met by modern logicians who have relegated such terms as true and false to the realm of semantics and established quite different logical categories for propositions. His strictures on science also remain narrow in conception. For example, they ignore any discussion of how far efficacity can be taken as confirmation of genuine, if not formally demonstrable, knowledge. There is one overriding respect, however, in which Camus' position would appear to be impregnable, though whether he meant it to be so in this particular way is doubtful. In *Le Mythe de Sisyphe* Camus is really asking for a world that is logically necessary *in itself*. Being made up of matters of fact, however, the world could never be so. Facts must always be arbitrary or unintelligible since it is always possible, *a priori*, that they might have been different. The world that he demands could never appear intelligible in his sense to an experiencing mind. The impregnable character of his position follows from the fact that in making his claim that there can be no rational account of the world Camus interprets a rational account of the world in such a way that his claim must really be accepted almost before it is made. Yet his observations on the absurd serve usefully to remind us, in common with all forms of existential thinking, that existence cannot be grasped conceptually and that the abstractions of thought will always fail to pin down the particularity and concreteness of things.

Camus' description of the absurd conforms to ancient and familiar mythic patterns representing man's condition. The absurd stands for a situation similar to that of Tantalus tormented by water and fruit-laden trees beyond his reach, of Prometheus chained and become eternal food for the vulture, of Sisyphus pushing his rock to the hill-top from which it must always roll back. In this basic form the absurd recalls the denial by the gods of man's claim to parity with them. Indeed, Camus invests the absurd with much of the intensity, inevitability and universality of classical tragedy. And yet he is not prepared to accept the absurd without question. He presents it as a fusion of passion and desiccation that cannot be borne by human beings and must be overcome in some way. Valéry once wrote ironically that Sisyphus at least got something—well-developed muscles—out of his absurd task, but Camus wants much more than this. He wants to discover whether some kind of spiritual muscularity can be obtained, and if so, to what positive use it may be put. Before exploring the positive possibilities of the absurd, however, he first considers whether it can simply be negated. The traditional methods of negating the absurd are two. Since it is basically a relationship, the most obvious way to dispose of it is to destroy one or other of the two terms on which it is founded. For example, one might negate the world that the mind experiences as absurd by discarding reason, by directing one's activity into spiritual channels and by putting one's faith in an after-life in which divine intelligibility must prevail. This is, of course, the leap of faith, with the absurd as its springboard, advocated in different ways by Tertullian, Pascal, Kierkegaard and others. Camus calls this philosophical suicide. The other traditional procedure, more irremediable than the first in its consequences and hence less frequently carried out, is to negate the second term of the relationship—to suppress the absurd by suppressing the individual who experiences the irrationality of the world. Physical suicide is the one certain and expeditious way of doing this. Through suicide the individual destroys his only medium for experience of the absurd—i.e. himself—by an act that hardly seems inconsistent with that experience.

Camus now considers these alternatives in more detail, beginning with philosophical suicide. We have seen that he has a special place in the anti-rational tradition, yet he begins his consideration of philosophical suicide with an attack on anti-rationalism. There is no real contradiction here, however, because he is attacking that anti-rationalism mentioned earlier which, having discovered the limitations of reason, rejects these limitations by accepting faith or intuition as the means to absolute knowledge. Camus' doctrine of the absurd also recognizes the limitations of reason but then reacts in a quite different direction by accepting them and holding to reason as man's only link, though of course an extremely tenuous one, with reality. And so in a certain sense Camus' insistence on the fact of the absurd is bound up with a kind of extreme rationalism. The anti-rationalism which he rejects he calls 'la pensée humiliée'.

Acute awareness of the absurd is claimed by Camus to be a common feature of such different thinkers as Kierkegaard and Chestov, Heidegger and Jaspers, Husserl and Scheler. As Camus interprets them—and his interpretations would certainly cause much disagreement among historians of philosophy—all found that the royal highroad of reason was blocked and chose to advance instead along the narrow and perilous mountain-tracks of irrationality or religion. In the last pages of the second chapter he briefly summarizes the testimony of each to the absurd. In the third chapter he goes on to choose Chestov and Kierkegaard for more detailed discussion as his main examples of how recognition of the absurd comes to be followed by the leap of faith which he himself regards as a leap into gratuitous supposition. He also refers more briefly to Jaspers, and this reference will show us most conveniently and succinctly the nature of that philosophical suicide which he rejects. Jaspers is quoted as saying that the failure of reason to comprehend existence 'surely displays, beyond all possible explanation and interpretation, not nothingness but the existence of transcendence'. Jaspers affirms transcendence and a purposive pattern in existence by appealing, on his own admission here, to a transforming process 'beyond all possible explanation and interpretation'. This is a straightforward instance of the *credo quia absurdum est* type of argument which Camus refuses to accept and which he discusses in its more complicated formulation in the writings of Kierkegaard and Chestov. Later, in the same chapter, he criticizes the phenomenology of Husserl, starting from the latter's concept of intention in perception. He mentions the phenomenologists because, although they do not make the leap of faith in the manner of the Christian Existentialists, they evade the facts of the absurd, so he claims, by what turn out to be formally similar methods. Thus Husserl, after allowing that thought is description, not explanation, introduces the idea of an infinity of extra-temporal essences that impart significance to an infinity of objects. By means of this 'polythéisme abstrait', as gratuitous from Camus' viewpoint as the theism of Chestov or Kierkegaard, Husserl makes what might be described as a leap of faith into the realm of absolute reason. The example of Husserl, considered after Chestov and Kierkegaard, is meant to show us that thought can be betrayed by 'la raison triomphante' as well as by 'la raison humiliée'. This happens because the will to reach a positive conclusion overrides adequate consideration of the method employed. In this respect Husserl is as guilty as Kierkegaard. What he calls absolute reason is ultimately a form of irrationality. Both Husserl the abstract philosopher and Kierkegaard the religious thinker have attempted to overcome the absurd by denying the very thing —severely limited human reason—that made them aware of it in the first place. Such a procedure is unacceptable to Camus, who wants to deal with the absurd while still retaining and recognizing the means by which he became aware of it.

The objections to physical suicide are derived from the same basic attitude. On the physical level, as on the level of thought, suicide involves some measure of contradiction and is ultimately an avoidance of the problem and not a solution of it. It clearly destroys the individual's vision of the absurd when it destroys the individual who is a necessary term in the relationship by which the absurd is manifested. But this does nothing to alter the absurd as an actual or potential experience for everyone else. At best it can only be a private answer devoid of general validity. If it is accepted as a method of negating the absurd it is certainly not a means of refuting it. Now we shall see in the next chapter, as Camus had already tentatively suggested in *Noces*, that a distinction can be made between the judgment that life has no meaning and the decision that it is not worth living. There is after all some logical force—in Camus' sense of logic—in saying that life can only be judged to be absurd in the light of action that attempts to find meaning in existence. Suicide implies consent to the absurd, acceptance of the absurd, but this attitude is inconsistent with that scandalized resistance and objection that produced awareness of the absurd in the first instance. This means that suicide can only be an instance of collusion with the absurd and not a solution of it. It may even be argued that suicide, far from negating the absurd, actually confirms and intensifies it. Death, as we have already seen, is one of the features of the absurd. Now suicide means a voluntary moving forward and anticipation of death in time. On the other hand the impulse to revolt which the absurd arouses in the individual is partly revolt against the fact of death. It is not consistent with this revolt that one should deliberately connive at death by suicide. The natural impulse of the man condemned to death is to desire life all the more intensely. And it is not logical that a man, metaphysically condemned for an unknown crime, should contribute himself to his own disaster. This seems to be Camus' meaning when he writes that the man who commits suicide and the man who is condemned to death are complete opposites: 'Le contraire du suicidé, précisément, c'est le condamné à mort'.

In the opening pages of a later book, *L'Homme révolté,* Camus makes two further points, based presumably on more reflection, against suicide. Firstly, suicide can only be justified by denying the first premises of the notion of the absurd. If the world is irremediably absurd, and if one is a stranger to oneself as well as to other people and to material things, then to commit suicide is to behave as though such action itself could have value or meaning in a meaningless existence. By attempting to give meaning to suicide one denies the total nature of the absurd that prompted it. This can still mean that suicide is a possible action within the context of total absurdity, but it destroys any logical link between the two and involves the conclusion that to decide against suicide is neither more nor less logical than to decide for it. A second point follows. Suicide is not the absolute negation of everything which it is often assumed to be. Like the judgment that life is absurd, it implies an appeal to some value. It is positive if limited assertion beneath an appearance of thorough-going negation. Suicide implies that the absurd was not total, yet by its very nature it prevents one from using, in a positive attack on the absurd, the value or meaning to which it testified.

In the ways just outlined Camus rejects both philosophical and physical suicide as coherent attitudes for a man to adopt towards the absurd. These various arguments now lead him to the conclusion that the absurd cannot be 'elided', as he puts it, without violence being done both to the evidence of our reason and our desire for consistent behaviour. It follows that Camus has left himself only one possible position—acceptance of the absurd as his mind and body give evidence of it. He allows himself no other choice and seems to be back where he started. As he now presents this position, however, he gives it a quite different emphasis. The situation appears to be the original one, but his attitude to it has changed. The exploration of the alleged solutions of irrational flight or physical annihilation, which he calls his 'raisonnement absurde', leads him to the conclusion that the absurd is not unacceptable in the way he first supposed. He now argues that the absurd is at any rate the source of one important value—truth—since he holds it to be true. The frustrated search for truth, which made him conscious of the absurd, is at least satisfied on one point in that it attains the truth of the absurd itself. Now this same desire for truth demands, he claims, that one should maintain and defend any truth that one discovers. Thus he concludes that the fact of the absurd should be preserved, not evaded. In the nature of things the absurd cannot be resolved; in the light of his arguments it cannot be dismissed; it can now be more readily accepted since it establishes a truth. By rejecting both physical and philosophical suicide he preserves the truth of the absurd, and the more fully this attitude is understood the more positive it becomes. In describing the absurd as a relationship between the intellect and the material world Camus emphasized its character of conflict and refusal, calling it 'une confrontation et une lutte sans repos'. In order to retain awareness of the absurd and thus preserve the truth that it establishes, we must constantly tread a 'vertiginous ridge' by refusing all the suggested ways of escape. Camus calls this attitude of refusal revolt. By such revolt we wager in the opposite direction to Pascal; we assert 'the marvellous and harrowing wager of the absurd' ('. . . le pari déchirant et merveilleux de l'absurde'). This wager solves no intellectual problems; it simply rejects the two forms of suicide and keeps faith with the primary reality of the senses:

The body, compassion, the created world, action, human nobility will then resume their place in this insane world. Man will find again the wine of absurdity and the bread of indifference which nourish his greatness.[4]

A revolt that involves these consequences satisfies both the stoic and the sensualist in Camus.

What we have here is, in effect, Camus' *cogito*. His inquiry, which set out to discover how the absurd paradox might either be solved or destroyed, ends by making this paradox itself a basis for positive action. As Descartes derived the certainty of his existence from prior doubt concerning it (I doubt, therefore I think, therefore I am), so Camus derives meaning for his existence from an original denial of the possibility of meaning. Both these arguments are open to various common objections, quite apart from the special criticism of assumptions to be made in Descartes' case. Without pressing the Cartesian analogy any farther, however, I should like to make three brief critical comments on Camus' conclusion. In the first place, the whole enterprise of making the absurd intelligible, of using it as a source of values, seems to involve a *petitio principii*. This becomes quite explicit on occasions, as in the verbal contradiction of: *'L'absurde* n'a de *sens* que dans la mesure où l'on n'y consent pas'.* There is here an emotional attitude which works against the interests of logic. Camus is determined from the start to have his revolt, and he must therefore reject suicide. Yet within the general context of the absurd one can only opt arbitrarily either for suicide or revolt and the attempt to give revolt an air of logical inevitability is bound to be unsatisfactory. Secondly, Camus gives the notion of the absurd three different meanings during the demonstration of his *cogito*: (i) it is the whole tragic paradox of the human condition and a subject of scandal and complaint; (ii) it is a situation that we are called upon to maintain as fully as we can; (iii) it is an attitude of revolt (the wager of the absurd) which somehow requires us to use the absurd in sense (ii) above against the absurd in sense (i) above. These different meanings of the term 'absurd' involve three different kinds of relationship and are both confused and confusing. I think they explain why Camus, shortly after asking us to reject suicide because it connives at the absurd (in sense (i)), advocates revolt and thereby asks us to connive at the absurd (in sense (ii)). Throughout the whole argument there is a disturbing lack of clarification or definition of terms. Lastly, it is difficult not to feel that Camus' enthusiasm for the absurd, on the basis that it testifies to the truth of its own existence and that this truth must be preserved, is rather too formal an argument. This impression is felt all the more strongly against a background of discussion which set out to treat the pros and cons of suicide as the only really serious philosophical question. I imagine that some such objection lies behind Blanchot's complaint that *Le Mythe de Sisyphe* leaves him with an uneasy feeling because of the way it transforms the tragedy and malediction of the absurd into something with which compromise is not only possible but desirable.† A sudden twist in the argument changes the absurd into a solution, a rule of life, a kind of salvation. Camus takes as his key to existence the very fact of not having a key. By giving different meanings to the term 'absurd' he appears to extricate it marvellously from its own implacable logic. It is difficult not to regard this as an arbitrary decision, not a logical deduction, despite the arguments with which Camus covers it. In the end it looks as though he has simply performed his own particular kind of leap

* My italics (see *Le Mythe de Sisyphe*, p. 50).
† See Maurice Blanchot, *Faux pas*, Paris, Gallimard, 1943, p. 75.

with the absurd again acting as his spring-board. Indeed, he seems to give the game away by speaking of a 'marvellous and harrowing *wager*'.

Camus' 'solution' appears to confirm Malraux's claim, made as early as 1928 in *Les Conquérants*, that one cannot continue to live in awareness of the absurd without having made some concessions to it. The rejection of suicide by Camus, his desire for life, must be a compromise with the absurd to some extent. However, once we are clear that this is a question of choice, not logical necessity, it becomes much more acceptable. A choice of this kind can be defended on various grounds. It may even be shown to contain a certain necessity. But this necessity is of a different kind from the formal inevitability that Camus claims on its behalf. Again, it seems fair to say that an act of choice, in this sense, is more consistent than purely formal logic could be with Camus' existential approach and his determination to deal with problems in concrete, human terms. Elsewhere, he does sometimes express his reaction to the absurd as a practical attitude based on a sensible choice. For example, he writes in the fourth of his *Lettres à un ami allemand*:

I have chosen justice . . . so as to keep faith with the earth. I continue to believe that this world has no supernatural meaning. But I know that something in the world has meaning—man—because he is the only being who demands meaning for himself. This world at least contains the truth of man, and our task is to justify him in the face of destiny itself.[5]

In statements such as this we have an expression of reasoned choice which is more convincing than the attempt at complete logical inevitability contained in *Le Mythe de Sisyphe*. The choice made in this passage is supported by an argument much more in keeping with Camus' general approach to questions of decision and action. No doubt it is in the end a sentimental choice, but it is also a moral choice, and Camus always convinces us more when speaking as a moralist than when speaking as a logician.

4 THE EMERGENCE OF REVOLT

Ce qui rend la vie finalement si passionnante c'est donc que l'antagonisme entre le sens profond de la vie et son non-sens soit justement laissé sans réponse.

RAYMOND GUÉRIN

The last quotation mentioned in the previous chapter was included there simply to show that Camus' 'solution' of the absurd seems more acceptable expressed as a deliberate choice than as a logical deduction. His plea for what he calls in this quotation 'the truth of man' is, however, part of a quite different and later stage in the development of his thought. For the present we must return again to the passage in *Le Mythe de Sisyphe* where he advocates wagering in favour of the absurd. The refusal of both suicide and transcendence automatically re-affirms the absurd and this means that the wager represents a turning-point in the whole argument of the book. Up to the wager Camus used a predominantly negative method, but it now begins to appear that the effect of methodological negation is to make possible concrete and practical affirmation. In fact the wager is both 'marvellous' and 'harrowing' because —ostensibly at least—it involves an affirmation composed only of those negations which preceded it. It is the peculiar virtue of this wager that it makes possible a transition from repudiation to predication simply by adding together a series of negatives in such a way as to obtain a positive result. This is the situation which gives to the second part of Camus' argument its special character. He is anxious to ensure that from the wager onwards his reasoning shall be dominated by awareness of the original negatives. As he explores the practical consequences of the wager and works out its ethical implications he is acutely conscious of the need to make only such positive assertions as will embody the earlier negations. Although he does not actually say so, it also follows that if he succeeds in his purpose the underlying arbitrariness of the wager will be made

65

much less obvious. The display of something approaching an organic relationship between the negative and positive halves of the argument will help to make the wager itself seem more logical and inevitable. This impression of logical coherence is also strengthened, of course, by the uniformly sober vocabulary used in both phases of the argument. Not only does the severe prose style of *Le Mythe de Sisyphe* seem particularly appropriate to the earlier analytical negations; by remaining the vehicle of later assertions it creates a strong impression in the reader that these negations are present just below the surface and that no affirmation which is made ignores them.

In deciding what kind of behaviour recognition of the absurd requires, Camus begins by looking at the main features of his position as expressed by the wager. He examines these features in order to be sure what qualities they contain, for these qualities must now provide the basis of a morality of the absurd. The two primary qualities that emerge from his scrutiny are lucidity and innocence. It is on this double foundation that he proceeds to build the absurdist ethic advocated in the later pages of the book. Lucidity is obviously a major preoccupation with Camus and dominates all his ideas. In the particular case of *Le Mythe de Sisyphe* it is a sustained effort of lucidity that has enabled him to disclose the reality and inevitability of the absurd. Now just as one can say that lucidity reveals the absurd, so it can be said with equal justification that the absurd, intellectually apprehended, necessitates lucidity. In other words, to assert the reality of the absurd and maintain awareness of it one must preserve lucidity as a constant attitude. The absurd is of such a nature that only an individual's lucidity enables it to be present to human consciousness. Clearly then, for the individual whom Camus a little unfortunately calls *l'homme absurde*, lucidity is a primary quality that must inevitably dictate the whole pattern of his behaviour.

Given this kind of lucidity which is an integral part of the absurd, it follows that innocence, at least as Camus uses the term, is an integral part of lucidity. He argues as follows: Lucidity is negative awareness in the sense that it denies the capacity of the mind to find meaning in experience, except in a very immediate and limited way. More particularly, it denies the capacity of the mind to demonstrate by itself the existence of abstract, universal truths. Lucidity about the absurd therefore reveals a world in which there is no transcendence for human beings, no set of absolute values by reference to which a man's behaviour can be absolutely sanctioned or absolutely reproved. This situation, in which *l'homme absurde* finds himself, is what Camus calls innocence. It follows necessarily from the revelation of the absurd by lucidity. To posit this kind of innocence, however, does not automatically lead to the conclusion that individuals have complete licence as to how they should act. It may well be, for example, that there are compelling human reasons, however individual or temporary in character, why a man should choose one particular course of action in preference to another when faced with a certain set of circumstances. This is not a point which Camus makes or appears to consider at this stage. Indeed he assumes in *Le Mythe de Sisyphe* that innocence and complete freedom of action go together. In writings published a few years later however, particularly in his *Lettres à un ami allemand*, he rejects his first interpretation of innocence and accepts the fact of limitations and responsibilities even within the context of the absurd. This is why it seems worthwhile to remind ourselves at this point that innocence and licence are not as logically inseparable as Camus first suggests. On the other hand, this interpretation of innocence does completely exclude the Christian interpretation of sin, and Camus is careful to make this clear. If *l'homme absurde* is asked to make the leap of faith he can find no evidence that would justify his doing so. If he is then told that he is guilty of the sin of intellectual pride this notion of sin is without meaning for him. He remains similarly unmoved and uncomprehending when told that hell and eternal damnation await him. Such ideas remain utterly alien to one who is aware of the absurd; they cannot survive the test of lucidity. At this point Camus continues, speaking of *l'homme absurde*: 'He is asked to admit his guilt. He feels himself to be innocent. Indeed his complete and utter innocence is all that he feels.' [1]

Camus does suggest, however, that the notion of sin can have meaning for *l'homme absurde* in one single situation. It is sin to reject lucidity and turn one's back on the evidence it provides. This seems to be the sense of a curiously compressed argument occurring a few pages before the passage just quoted. Camus refers to Kierkegaard's contention that lucidity must be renounced (by the leap of faith) if truth is to be found. He writes: 'In the Kierke-gaardian apocalypse this desire for lucidity must be renounced if it is to be satisfied.' He also refers to Kierkegaard's view that sin, in keeping with Christian teaching and contrary to the Socratic definition, lies in the will and not in the intellect. This I take, at any rate, to be the reference behind his next sentence which can only be intended as a paraphrase of Kierkegaard: 'Sin is not so much knowing (on this score everyone is innocent) as desiring to know.' Camus then re-interprets this statement in a very personal way in order to draw his own conclusion—a conclusion which is precisely the opposite of that intended by Kierkegaard. There are those, he says, whom the desire for fuller knowledge causes to ignore the limits already prescribed by lucidity. In fact they attempt to go beyond the boundaries of innocence which he posits. Now to reject innocence must be to accept sin. Therefore the leap of faith is sin for *l'homme absurde*. Camus says of this desire for complete knowledge:

This is precisely the one sin which makes *l'homme absurde* aware both of his guilt and his innocence. He is offered a solution which reduces previous contradictions to a mere game of polemics. But he did not experience them as a game. He must preserve their true character which is their inability to be satisfactorily answered.[2]

There are at least three objections to this piece of reasoning. Firstly, as in his earlier reference to Aristotle, Camus plays fast and loose with Kierkegaard's argument. There is something unsatisfactory in this method of making a point not with a straightforward argument of his own but by quoting or paraphrasing someone else's reasoning and then deriving from it a conclusion entirely contrary to that intended by the author concerned. Secondly, logic is outraged in the assertion that the absurd cannot be solved, therefore any solution offered must be rejected. The passage just quoted assumes in its premise the conclusion to which this premise allegedly gives rise. Thirdly, Camus can still only claim that evasion of lucidity is a sin by using some moral standard lying entirely outside the world of the absurd. It is impossible for him to produce from a world without transcendence, such as lucidity reveals, any standards by which he can assert that either acceptance or rejection of lucidity is sin. In fact, all these objections indicate again that an emotional determination to retain the absurd at all costs lies behind much of Camus' apparent logical detachment. It is worth mentioning here, incidentally, that even the pressure on *l'homme absurde* to choose lucidity and, later, to exercise freedom, makes of freedom and lucidity moral absolutes of the very kind that his fundamental innocence is held to deny. Camus claims to derive from the absurd values which the absurd, by definition, cannot recognize. The nature and weakness of Camus' whole position is expressed by Kierkegaard in his criticism of what he calls 'demoniac despair':

Revolting against the whole of existence, it [demoniac despair] thinks it has hold of a proof against it, against its goodness. This proof the despairer thinks he himself is, and that is what he wills to be, therefore he wills to be himself, himself with his torment, in order with this torment to protest against the whole of existence. Whereas the weak despairer will not hear about what comfort eternity has for him, so neither will such a despairer hear about it, but for a different reason, namely, because this comfort would be the destruction of him as an objection against the whole of existence. It is (to describe it figuratively) as if an author were to make a slip of the pen, and that this clerical error became conscious of being such—perhaps it was no error but in a far higher sense was an essential constituent in the whole exposition —it is then as if this clerical error would revolt against the author, out of hatred for him were to forbid him to correct it, and were to say, 'No, I will not be erased, I will stand as a witness against thee, that thou art a very poor writer'. *

In this passage Kierkegaard equates 'demoniac despair' with 'revolting against the whole of existence'. Camus, perhaps with Kierkegaard again in mind, claims that his twin foundations of lucidity and innocence (which strongly resemble the underlying aspects of demoniac despair) give rise to a morality of revolt. As he interprets them, lucidity and innocence are primarily negative in character. They form an integral part of his determination to say 'no' to any claim that existence can be made intellectually coherent or part of a system of absolute truths. Now such sceptical metaphysics, Camus argues, cannot permit of a renunciatory ethic: '. . . je ne puis concevoir qu'une métaphysique sceptique

* S. Kierkegaard, *The Sickness unto Death* (trans. Walter Lowrie), London, O.U.P., 1944, pp. 118–19.

Albert Camus

puisse s'allier à une morale de renoncement.' In fact, this negative metaphysical attitude necessitates a continuously defiant rejection of all suggested solutions and evasions since these cannot, in the nature of things, be successful or satisfactory. And so the first ethical consequence of the absurd is an attitude of perpetual revolt. At this stage revolt means for Camus a defiant rejection of the leap of faith and all other comforting doctrines, a rejection that is firmly rooted in the value of lucidity and the fact of innocence. He says of the individual who is aware of the absurd :

The absurd is maximum tension, and he continually preserves this tension by his own solitary effort, for he knows that through this awareness and this daily renewed revolt he bears witness to his only reality, which is defiance. This is the first consequence [of the wager].[3]

What Camus has done, then, is to make revolt the first practical result of the wager. We have seen already that lucidity and innocence were the main ingredients of this wager. But lucidity and innocence mean continual rejection of proposed solutions in order that awareness of the absurd may be preserved. Therefore to wager in favour of the absurd ultimately means an attitude of negative defiance which will provide the dynamic for a morality of revolt.

Camus now goes on to draw two further consequences from his position : freedom and intensity. The circumstances leading to defiant revolt also cause him to claim that a certain freedom of action, combined with the desire to live intensely, are two other characteristic features of *l'homme absurde*. In fact, as soon as he posits revolt he sees that it is closely bound up with freedom and intensity. It draws strength from them and offers them in return at least a limited objective.

In discussing freedom Camus is anxious to avoid abstraction. In the world of the absurd, which is without absolute values, there is no meaning in discussions as to whether freedom can be conceived of as a metaphysical entity, etc. Camus therefore emphasizes the practical nature of his approach :

. . though the absurd destroys all possibility of my knowing eternal freedom it does give me, in return, intensified freedom of action. This removal of hope and a future life means increased latitude for the individual.[4]

Both the certainty of death and the conviction that absolute values do not exist cause *l'homme absurde* to reject a full metaphysical notion of freedom. *L'homme absurde* is without hope of any eternal freedom, located perhaps in an after-life, that might nullify the effect of physical destruction. Yet Camus goes on to argue that an individual who has wagered in favour of the absurd is more free, in some ways, than one who has not become aware of the absurd at all. He begins with a criticism of the conventional notion of freedom. The majority of people, believing themselves to be free, 'choose' what course their life should take and attempt to give it a particular pattern. Thus one man concentrates on being an electrician, another a civil servant, and so on. Each sets himself a goal. But a very little thought shows that this idea of a goal also restricts a man. It involves conformity to a particular way of life, adherence to certain moral and social norms, subservience to a number of routines. Only a very limited freedom results. Now *l'homme absurde* is acutely aware of these restrictions. Indeed, part of his experience of the absurd depends precisely on their recognition. We saw in the last chapter that a sense of the absurd often arises from a feeling that the mechanical repetition which characterizes so many individual lives is without meaning or value. These routines, which Camus now calls 'le sommeil quotidien', turn out to be an inferior kind of freedom—perhaps even a negation of freedom. But the essence of the absurdist position, in this respect, lies in the fact that to wager for the absurd can liberate the individual from such restraints. The absurdist freedom that results from this situation is the only real freedom just because it is subject to mortal, human limitations.

There is surely something very unsatisfactory about the kind of freedom which Camus advocates here and about the way in which he argues on its behalf. This freedom is also severely limited. It is freedom to complain about the absence of absolutes but not freedom to fill this metaphysical void. It is freedom to act capriciously here and now (without fear of the consequences in an after-life, for instance), but not freedom that can outlast death. Camus describes it as a freedom that cannot draw cheques on eternity. He then goes on, in a sombre image, to compare it to the freedom experienced by the condemned man on the day of his execution. This really gives the case away. The condemned man's freedom of which

Camus speaks is, I imagine, something like the freedom defined by Spinoza as consciousness of necessity—what we may call freedom in sense A. Such freedom is clearly not lack of restraint—the meaning normally given to the term and what we may call freedom in sense B. Camus is unconvincing when he claims, in his enthusiasm for the absurd, that freedom in sense A is superior to freedom in sense B. Indeed, the reverse would seem to be true, since freedom in sense B is always free to become freedom in sense A, whereas freedom in sense A can never choose to become freedom in sense B. The whole treatment of freedom in *Le Mythe de Sisyphe* is unsatisfactory and fails to justify Camus' eventual assertion:

... death and the absurd are thus the principles underlying the only reasonable kind of freedom: that which a human heart can experience and put into practice. This is the second consequence [of the wager].'

The third consequence of the wager is intensity—what Camus calls *la passion*. The fact of death and the absence of absolutes combine with innocence and freedom to make intensity of living a coherent position for *l'homme absurde* to adopt. What matters is not that he should live as nobly as possible but as fully as possible. If one wagers in favour of the absurd one must accept the consequence of a quantitative rather than a qualitative ethic. As in the case of his two earlier consequences, Camus claims that he is considering not value judgments but what consistency demands. Therefore he says that should a quantitative ethic mean 'dishonourable' behaviour, consistent intellectual honesty may still require that he act 'dishonourably' in this sense of the word. Nevertheless, he also insists that the idea of quantity does not exclude the idea of ethical quality as automatically as some people assume. Indeed there is wide misunderstanding about the ethical significance of quantity and its relation to quality. We often find, for instance, that ethical values are related to experiences. The range and variety of a man's experience will contribute to the way in which he interprets a general moral code. Breadth of experience is what gives practical content to an abstract scheme for behaviour. This is one reason why ethical systems show such historical and geographical variation. It is obvious, in short, that a communal morality, if it is to become a reality and not remain an abstraction, has to be interpreted by each individual in the light of the amount of experience that he has had. Thus there is a direct connection between the idea of quantity and practical morality. In fact, quantity can create quality. This is not, of course, an original idea on Camus' part. He has presumably borrowed it from Hegel, or from Marx who took-it over from Hegel. What he himself does is to take an analogy from physics and point out that the scientist holds a million ions to differ from one ion in quality as well as quantity. One might also, I think, take an example from the sphere of ethics itself and say that tolerance almost always derives its quality as an ethical attitude from a quantity of experiences which must not fall below a certain minimum amount. Tolerance is often associated with richness and depth of experience. Now the quantity of an individual's experience, Camus continues, is arbitrarily given or withheld depending on whether his life is prolonged or prematurely ended by death. To this extent the individual may not be free to practise a fully quantitative ethic. But within this general framework the quantity of experience depends very much on the degree of intensity with which he accepts the various possibilities inherent in his life. Any period of life and experience, whatever the length that death finally gives it, thus becomes precious and irreplacable. Camus writes:

The present moment, together with a succession of such present moments experienced by constant awareness, is the ideal of *l'homme absurde*. Yet the word 'ideal' is out of place here. This is not even his vocation, but simply the third consequence of his reasoning.[6]

Camus here reaches a point at which he can give more definite form to the positive side of his argument. The fact of innocence, the necessity of lucidity, the possibility of freedom and the promise of intensity combine to form an ethic of revolt which is consistent with wagering in favour of the absurd. The argument that began as an invitation to commit suicide finally becomes an imperative to live life with passion. Courage and intelligence are necessary to practise this absurdist ethic. Courage is required if one is to live without the possibility of spiritual comfort. Intelligence is needed so that one has no illusions about the ultimately limited and hopeless life that such an ethic offers. We have seen that freedom is restricted and provisional for *l'homme absurde*. So also is intensity. Both are subject to the destruction of time and death. Thus the very affirmations of this revolt are sterile in the sense that they can hold out no promise of a golden age in the future. Self-respect may compel *l'homme absurde* to adopt an attitude of revolt, but this revolt as such cannot alter the basic character of the absurd. In other words this series of affirmations, made up of such terms as revolt, freedom and intensity, is still finally subject to those negations from which awareness of the absurd originated. Thus the ethic of revolt does not mean deliverance. It is revolt paradoxically based on acceptance—indignant acceptance of the immutability of the absurd.

Within the moral world of the absurd all actions become ethically equal in the sense that they are subject to no absolute standard of right and wrong. The ethic of revolt deliberately recommends neither crime nor virtue. But what commonly passes for virtue is not of necessity excluded. Camus points this out by saying, with something very like bitterness, that one can be virtuous merely through caprice. The important point is that the innocence implicit in the absurd negates the whole idea of moral guilt. The most that it preserves is a kind of responsibility. For example, the preservation of lucidity involves responsibility at least to oneself; but the consequences of this lucidity allow of no fundamental moral differentiation. It is this aspect, what one might call the moral equality of absurdist revolt, that causes Camus to stress quantity and not quality. His ethic of revolt is an ethic of quantity and concentrates on the immediate. It responds to the present moment, to a succession of present moments, and experiences their variety with the greatest possible degree of intensity. Experience itself, rather than the result of experience, becomes his goal. One is reminded of the *divertissement* described by Pascal, except that while Pascal sees it as escape Camus presents it as continued awareness. This ethic of revolt also recalls the ethic of quantity and intensity advocated in the final chapter of Pater's *The Renaissance*. Speaking of life as an interval between the void before birth and the void after death, Pater says: '. . . our one chance lies in expanding that interval, in getting as many pulsations as possible into the given time.' * What he calls 'multiplied consciousness' is in effect the ethical position adopted here by Camus as a way of living with the absurd.

* W. Pater, *The Renaissance*, London, Macmillan, 1922, p. 238.

The Emergence of Revolt

Any man can live in accordance with the absurdist ethic. All that is strictly required of him is lucid awareness. But lucidity combined with intensity produces some particularly striking examples of the kind of 'moralist' that Camus has particularly in mind. The quantitative ethic is seen in its clearest and fullest form in four human types: Don Juan, the actor, the conqueror and the creative artist. In each of these cases 'multiplied consciousness' is clearly an important characteristic. Camus now proceeds to examine each of these 'absurdist heroes' in turn having first said, with that sense of conventional morality which never quite deserts him, that an instance or illustration is not necessarily an example to be followed.

Camus' portrait of Don Juan shows familiarity with Kierkegaard's famous analysis of this legendary figure in *Either/Or*. Kierkegaard regards Don Juan as typifying what he calls the 'sensually demoniac'. By this he means, in effect, one who excels in the quantitative ethic. He points out, for example, that while chivalrous love is characterized by fidelity and singularity, sensual love (e.g. that of Don Juan) is marked by multiplicity and faithlessness. Faust, who typifies the 'intellectually demoniac', seduces only one woman, but Don Juan must seduce 1,003. In fact, Don Juan seeks the common, not the uncommon, and experiences unlimited sameness. In this way he is a striking representative of the quantitative ethic. His aim is to multiply experience, and Kierkegaard says of him in a memorable phrase that 'he hurries in a perpetual vanishing'.

Such characteristics of repetition and immediate response make Don Juan an obvious figure for Camus to choose as an example of one possible form that the quantitative ethic may take. Furthermore, his interpretation of the legend resembles Kierkegaard's in that it is deliberately unromantic. This can be seen in three separate ways. In the first place, he refuses to see Don Juan as a sad and desperate figure seeking perfect love and failing to find it. On the contrary, Don Juan emerges from Camus' account as one who has no illusions whatever about romantic love and who chooses to enjoy quantity rather than seek hopelessly for a quality of ideal love that does not exist. After all, Camus says, there is no compelling reason why love should be confined to one or two people in order to be experienced intensely: 'Pourquoi faudrait-il aimer rarement pour aimer beaucoup?' In any case romantic love, in its fullness, is always presented in literature as unrealizable or frus-trated in some way. It is repeatedly associated with death or suicide. At best it involves the attempt to annihilate oneself in the beloved, and this is another form of suicide. This means, in the last analysis, that ideal romantic love is impoverishment of others as well as of oneself. The complete identification of two people, which is the aim of such love, is impossible. Realizing this, Don Juan opts for multiplication rather than unification even though he may be pre-pared to admit that the quest for perfect and eternal love can be a moving and noble enterprise.

In the second place, Camus finds it ridiculous to make of Don Juan a man deeply versed in the Book of Ecclesiastes and over-whelmed by the vanity of existence. Don Juan would certainly regard hope in a future life as vanity, just as he holds romantic love to be an illusion. But the very absence of such hope and of abso-lute perfection makes enjoyment of this present life all the more desirable in his eyes. This interpretation is in keeping with the conclusion of Camus' wager and the quantitative ethic gives it practical expression. Camus says of Don Juan: 'This life gives him fulfilment, and to lose it is the worst thing of all. This mad-man is a great sage.'[7]

Lastly, Camus finds it necessary to insist that Don Juan is not immoral in any romantic way. He is certainly not a romantic figure courting damnation out of a desperate desire for eventual sanctity. He recognizes neither sanctity nor damnation as such, but is an ordinary seducer intent on a maximum of experience and pleasure. Within his own sphere he judges by results and not in accordance with a moral law. An ethic of quantity demands efficiency but has no place for the idea of immorality. In keeping with this view Camus interprets the Commander's statue ('cette pierre gigantesque et sans âme') as a symbol of all that Don Juan denies—eternal truth, absolute values, a universal moral code. Such conceptions are fittingly embodied in the cold lifelessness of stone. Thus two versions of Don Juan's end appeal particularly to Camus. He approves of the story which says that on the night Don Juan waited with Doña Anna for the Commander to appear the latter failed to turn up. Thus, once midnight had struck, Don Juan experienced to the full 'the terrible bitterness of those who are proved right' Camus accepts even more readily the versions in which Don Juan finished his days in a monastery. As one might imagine, it is not the edifying element that he regards as significant here. Instead he is impressed by the suggestion that such a final retreat from life into silent inaction is an inevitable outcome of the quantitative ethic.

Thus Don Juan is still interpreted by Camus as a tragic figure, but he has been deliberately shorn of the usual romantic associations. He embodies that cold, clear tragedy of the absurd which finds regrets and consolations equally vain.

The actor follows Don Juan as the second of the four figures chosen by Camus to interpret the absurdist ethic. Camus shows the actor to be an appropriate choice for his particular purpose here, but no doubt he was also influenced by his enthusiasm for the theatre. This enthusiasm has already been mentioned and it is apparent in the account which Camus now gives of the actor's profession. In the case of Don Juan he described the practice of quantitative morality by an individual; here he interprets acting as a symbol, not a practical application, of the same ethical attitude. There is therefore a clear difference between these two examples. Whereas Don Juan's career was a direct application of the quantitative ethic, the actor's life, with its repetition and multiplicity of rôles, offers instead a formal parallel to it. Don Juan displayed absurdist morality in practice whereas the actor illustrates the formal qualities from which such practice is derived.

The choice of the actor to symbolize a pessimistic view of life is, of course, a familiar one. In his remarks on the actor Camus refers to the rôle of the players in *Hamlet*, and one is also reminded of other familiar passages from Shakespeare that may have been in his mind: Jaques' view of the world as a stage, with men and women 'merely players'; Macbeth's reference to the 'poor player' strutting and fretting for an hour before his final exit. To this familiar image, however, Camus brings his own particular emphasis. He is presenting the actor as a symbol, not of any pessimistic view of life whatsoever, but specifically of the absurdist outlook, and this causes him to interpret the nature of acting along certain special lines. Before coming to this interpretation one odd feature in Camus' approach should be pointed out. He might have been expected, especially in view of his deliberately unromantic portrait of Don Juan, to adopt the same attitude to the actor. It would appear to be consistent with his reaction to the absurd that he should follow in general the still classic analysis of Diderot in *Paradoxe sur le comédien*. Diderot held the great actor to be a 'cold and calm spectator', and such a view would be in keeping with Camus' ubiquitous insistence on lucidity. Yet this is not his interpretation. On the contrary, he puts forward what should be called, in this context, a romantic view. Whereas Diderot preferred 'reflective' to 'soulful' acting, Camus reverses the order and says that the actor must feel intensely the emotions which he portrays: '. . . his art is . . . to simulate to the utmost degree, to enter as fully as possible into lives that are not his own.' [8]

Such a view of acting clearly rejects the paradox of detached identification proposed by Diderot. Presumably it is prompted by Camus' own experience and inclination as a one-time actor. One imagines that it is also stressed here, however, because it suits Camus' insistence on intensity as an integral part of the absurdist ethic. In the case of Don Juan, lucidity and intensity were satisfactorily reconciled, but by choosing the actor as his second example Camus is obliged to separate these two qualities. He stressed intensity, as the quotation above suggests, but lucidity is hardly considered. Lucidity and intensity can obviously represent two different general approaches to acting: acting mainly with the head or mainly with the heart. But Camus' choice of the second approach means that they are not reconciled here as the absurd requires them to be. Had he adopted Diderot's approach, or something very like it, this reconciliation between them would have been possible in the special case of the actor. Diderot says, for example, that the actor's tears should come from his brain, and this is just the sort of image that might have appealed to Camus. Certainly it is an interpretation of the actor's art that would have symbolized admirably that combination of lucidity and passion which he advocated earlier. By insisting on the need for the actor to identify himself as completely as possible with the dramatic character whom he portrays, Camus largely ignores the conception of lucidity and weakens the actor's symbolic rôle as an absurdist hero.

The actor is first contrasted with the spectator. The spectator of the play represents *l'homme inconscient*—the man who is either unaware of the absurd or who decides not to allow it to affect his way of life. The actor, on the other hand, who takes part in the play that the spectator only observes, represents *l'homme absurde* —the man who experiences and acts the immediate reality of the drama of the absurd.

From this contrast between spectator and actor Camus then turns to the differences between the actor and the writer. The actor's fame as an artist is much more perishable than that of the writer. His monument to his art—the actual performance he gives —cannot last in the same concrete and verifiable way as a poem or novel or play. It cannot be experienced repeatedly by succeeding generations. The actor, like *l'homme absurde*, has to stake his all on the present. He is conscious of the fact that his art cannot continue to exist as such. At best it becomes a memory and can only be judged and appreciated indirectly. After his last performance there is no further direct access to his art. This perishable immediacy makes the actor's achievement a suitable symbol of life as seen from the absurdist standpoint. But the conditions under which he performs his part also recall the world of the absurd. Each rôle that he creates is something complete and unique. It is perfected within strict limitations of time and space, and surrounded by a dark and alien element existing only on the other side of the footlights. In this way the theatre itself becomes a symbol of the conditions of life which the absurd reveals and under which *l'homme absurde* must exist. Its walls resemble those 'murs absurdes' of which Camus spoke in the early pages of the book. The stage itself represents that immediate, physical reality which is the element of *l'homme absurde*. The final curtain suggests the inevitability of death and oblivion. And yet the actor readily accepts all these limitations as a necessary part of his main activity—which is to lose himself in intensity and multiplicity. Within the limits of theatre and stage he can identify himself completely with the character whose experience he portrays. In fact, the intensification of these restrictions becomes a temporary liberation for him. He renounces his own personality in order to experience the emotional richness of other lives:

In the course of three hours he must experience and express a complete and unique individual life. This is what is called losing one's life in order to find it. During these three hours he goes to the end of a blind path, while the man in the stalls takes a lifetime to reach the same point.[9]

Albert Camus

The importance to the actor of his body also makes him a symbol of *l'homme absurde*. The body is his chosen means of self-expression, and on the stage, Camus says, the body is king. He adds that most of Shakespeare's plays are clear examples of this physical primacy. They are plays in which 'ce sont les fureurs du corps qui mènent la danse'. Thus Lear could never have 'kept his appointment with insanity' had he not made the brutal gesture that exiles Cordelia and condemns Edgar. For the actor then, as for *l'homme absurde*, the physical is his main means of expression. But there is a further similarity between these two types since the body is also the actor's most effective vehicle of knowledge. Here Camus repeats his view that acting requires identification with the dramatic rôle in question; he therefore claims that Iago can only be fully understood by an actor playing the part of Iago, *being* Iago. And this understanding of Iago comes to the actor through his body. Finally, this emphasis on the importance of the body causes Camus to see in acting the solution of a contradiction reflecting a similar solution offered to *l'homme absurde* by the quantitative ethic. The apparent contradiction in the actor is the contrast between the singleness of his body and the multiplicity of stage parts which this body encompasses in the course of a career. The actor, as an actor, unites in one activity both singleness and multiplicity. So it is with *l'homme absurde*. He too experiences a contrast between singleness and multiplicity—the singleness of his body and the multiplicity (e.g. the desire not to die but to extend each present moment indefinitely) which his mind craves for. In the world of the absurd the mind can never obtain satisfaction in mental terms; nevertheless, through the body, it can find an adequate though temporary substitute in the multiplied consciousness offered by the quantitative ethic. This ethic allows a similar union of singleness and multiplicity to that experienced by the actor. And so, quoting Hamlet's lines, Camus claims that *l'homme absurde*, when he practises the quantitative ethic, is among the blest:

> Whose blood and judgment are so well comeddled
> That they are not a pipe for Fortune's finger
> To sound what stop she please.

Camus concludes his observations on the actor with some brief comments on the historical relationship between the Church and the stage. The Church was bound to condemn the actor because he symbolized the opposite of everything the Church stood for. He represented physical intensity and multiplicity; his profession emphasized the present and the immediate by requiring him to live a succession of parts always completed and yet always renewed again; the essence of his art was to be as protean as possible, excelling in versatility. The Church stood for contrary values: for the spiritual rather than the physical, for the eternal rather than the temporal, for unalterable truth rather than change. The actor thus symbolizes a view of the world and a sense of values conflicting with those of Christianity. This is not the least of the several ways in which he represents the formal qualities of the quantitative ethic.

Some of the most bitter pages in *Le Mythe de Sisyphe* are devoted to an account of the conqueror—Camus' third absurdist hero. They take the form of an *apologia* spoken by the conqueror himself. It is certain that Camus does not mean by the conqueror a successful military leader, but the details of his conception of this human type are not very clear. Occasionally he uses the term 'adventurer' rather than 'conqueror' and this, I think, gives a better clue to his meaning. His conqueror, like the conquerors of Malraux, appears to be someone who is highly conscious of metaphysical solitude and who seeks a means of escape from himself. This he has in common with Don Juan and the actor, who both escape from themselves into other people or theatrical rôles. The conqueror is essentially a person who has adventured to the utmost limits of awareness about man's condition in the world and who lives in accordance with the results of this intellectual adventure. He may, like Garine in Malraux's *Les Conquérants*, seek to revolt against his condition by individual adventurous action. Or again, like Prometheus or Sisyphus, he may exemplify more passively the metaphysical revolt of humanism against man's situation in the world. In any event, he chooses history rather than eternity because history comes within his human experience while eternity represents a hypothesis which he cannot verify and which he distrusts: 'Between history and eternity I have chosen history because I like what is certain.' [10]

This is the way in which the conqueror reacts coherently to the absurd. From this point of view he represents the individual who, particularly since the coming of the machine age, has lost the serenity and the belief in eternal values that characterized most of his predecessors. Camus speaks of the Dutch painters whose calm and soothing work was done in the midst of bloodshed and strife. He also refers to the Silesian mystics whose prayers rose above the carnage of the Thirty Years War. Such art and prayer were possible, even in times of chaos and violence, because belief in a transcendent reality was still general. Such widespread confidence no longer exists, however, and having rejected the absolute and the eternal men have found themselves committed more and more to the temporal, the historical. The violence and brutality which still dominate individuals and nations are now faced with less confidence and a return to the old, eternal values becomes increasingly difficult. It is against this background that the conqueror assumes significance. He diagnoses his dilemma with lucidity and seeks release from it in intensity. Here again we have a reminder of the paradoxical nature of the quantitative ethic. It is derived from a lucidity that binds the individual, yet it is exercised with an intensity that frees him. He must die, but before death he can multiply and heighten his experiences.

The conqueror emphasizes in particular the element of revolt inherent in Camus' absurdist ethic. It is a revolt carried on in the name of man and of those desires and ideals that are thwarted by existence. But it also follows that for Camus' conqueror, as for Garine, revolt is not so much the attempt to solve a problem as the determination to maintain a protest. Camus calls it 'cet effort lucide et sans portée'. At best it leads to actions carried out *as if* things could be changed. And so the style of the revolt, the manner in which it is sustained, becomes more important than any goal to be reached. This is why the modern conqueror is not to be assessed in terms of territorial gains. For such a conqueror greatness lies in active protest and the ability to make sacrifices devoid of all promise or hope. Thus Prometheus, not Napoleon, is the model for the modern conqueror who says:

. . . I maintain my human contradiction in face of the underlying contradiction of existence. I set up my lucidity in the midst of that which denies it. I exalt man in the face of that which crushes him, and my freedom, my revolt, my passion are reunited in this tension, this lucidity, this boundless repetition.[11]

Expressed here in more consciously defiant terms we have the same
moral attitude as that applied by Don Juan and symbolized by the
actor. Lucidity and passion, combined in a series of repetitions
ultimately doomed by time, underlie the actions of all three types.
The conqueror differs from the other two mainly in degree. He
possesses heightened awareness of human potentialities. He is very
conscious of 'l'étonnante grandeur de l'esprit humain'. He stands
for the most militant kind of humanism which combines pride
with clarity, and by means of both recognizes the tragic ambivalence of all human creatures. The conqueror himself, like all
other men, is subject to this tragic ambivalence. He opts for man,
he refuses all 'compromise' with the eternal, and in the end he
dies. In the world of the absurd death is the final evil, 'le suprême
abus'. But it is the essence of the conqueror's freedom to know
that he is finally condemned to failure and death. The same intellect and consciousness that prompt him to choose the human and
the temporal also enable him to see the transience of their
splendour. It is in this consciousness of the human situation that
both his tragedy and his greatness lie.

Camus chooses the creator as his fourth exemplary figure. He
uses the term 'creator' to describe any artist, but more particularly
the writer. This kind of creator, he says, is the absurdist hero *par
excellence*. I referred earlier to the similarity between the quantitative ethic of Camus and that propounded by Pater. Another point
of resemblance between them is that each asserts the artist to be
a particularly suitable exponent of the kind of moral attitude being
discussed. Thus Camus describes the creator as '[le] plus absurde
des personnages', while Pater, in the last lines of *The Renaissance*,
claims that 'art comes to you proposing frankly to give nothing but
the highest quality to your moments as they pass, and simply for
those moments' sake'. It is not surprising, then, that Camus devotes
a long section to the creator—much longer in fact than those
dealing with the other three types. In the course of these remarks,
however, he strays several times from the immediate subject and
is led into making several important statements about the nature
of art. Because of this it seems better that comment on these pages
should be reserved for a later chapter on Camus' aesthetic ideas.

Before going on to discuss the creative artist Camus himself
returns to the three types of whom he has already spoken and

qualifies further his own personal attitude to them. He had begun by saying that they were chosen as illustrations, not necessarily as examples to be followed. He now makes this point more firmly, insisting that Don Juan, the actor and the conqueror do not imply any ethical judgment on his part but are simply pointers to a certain attitude to life. He does not commit himself on the moral consequences of this attitude; he uses these figures only to exemplify and explain the attitude as such. Thus Camus is now saying that he is more concerned with the intellectual starting-point of his models than with the practical content and consequences of their actions. And so he claims that the moral attitude required by the absurd is no monopoly of Don Juan, the actor and the conqueror; a model of chastity, a civil servant or a prime minister can equally well live lives consistent with awareness of the absurd. Lucidity and honesty about the human situation are what are required. Camus demands of the absurdist hero only that his actions should be consistent with his ideas and that he should not attempt to escape from the consequences of the truth as he sees it.

There must surely be some inconsistency in Camus' reasoning on this point. Indeed it looks as though he is taking back with one hand what he had given with the other. In his remarks leading up to the example of Don Juan, he was at pains to show that the seducer's quantitative ethic followed logically from wagering for the absurd. He specifically related the attitude to the consequences. Now he claims that he chose the most extreme examples only, that quite different kinds of behaviour can be deduced from the absurd, that the chaste man can live as closely in accordance with the absurd as the seducer. This view would be reasonable, of course, if Camus meant by the absurd simply the utter meaninglessness of everything. If he interpreted the absurd in the most radical terms, then all forms of behaviour would be equally valid. But this is not what he is saying here, nor does he interpret the absurd in this manner. By the absurd he means only the mind's inability to make contact with absolute truth, and this is not at all the same as saying that the world is utterly meaningless in itself. Furthermore, no one particular code of behaviour could be deduced in strict logic from radical absurdism. The only logical conclusion from such a position would be to say that *all* ethical systems were equally valid because ultimately pointless. Camus' second thoughts are therefore not concerned to say that any moral system will do, but rather that he is uneasy about the moral justification of his logical deduction from the absurd. He attempts to get round the problem by suggesting (*a*) that the moral behaviour of Don Juan or the conqueror was only one of several possible logical deductions from the absurdist position, and (*b*) that he is really only concerned at this point with the attitude behind the behaviour and not with the content of the behaviour itself.

These two positions are, I think, equally untenable. In the case of (*a*) one is struck by the fact that the only moral codes which he works out from the absurdist position—those of Don Juan and the conqueror—are precisely the moral codes that Camus now disowns. He asserts, in an apparently arbitrary way, that what normally pass for the opposite types of ethical behaviour could equally well be derived from the same absurdist position if this position were soundly held. But it is noticeable that he gives no actual illustration of this second assertion; indeed one finds it difficult to imagine how he could do so. He is saying in effect that although the only evidence he has produced points one way there is evidence (which he noticeably does not produce) that would point the other way. Such evidence would have to be considerable, and presented with great subtlety, before one could accept the contention that one and the same attitude to existence—particularly such an extreme attitude—can logically produce several quite different kinds of ethical practice.

As regards point (*b*) it appears as though Camus is really retreating from any practical judgment about the moral quality of behaviour. He is equating ethics with a view about man's position in the world but ignoring the sense in which ethics means practical conduct. Of course it is necessary that morality should have some kind of metaphysical derivation. This is as true of any so-called 'lay morality' or 'secular ethic' as it is of a code of behaviour based on religious convictions. But surely such morality becomes worthy of serious attention only when it has been discussed in terms of actual conduct, and when it has been applied at least to certain common human situations. Camus appeared to take this view when discussing Don Juan and the conqueror, but in the course of his second thoughts he withdraws into abstraction. It is difficult not to believe that he does so because of the practical moral consequences to which his abstract theory of the absurd has led.

The explanation of this hesitation and apparent confusion of thought is to be found, I think, in the chronology of Camus' views and writings about this time. To begin with, he himself has indicated that *Le Mythe de Sisyphe* does not quite accurately reflect the stage his own thought had reached at the period during which it was finally written. The writing of the book lagged behind the development of his ideas. He also claims that the book was not a personal statement of faith but an attempt to understand ideas which he found current among his contemporaries.* Thus *Le Mythe de Sisyphe* is more directly related to the earlier works— *L'Envers et l'endroit* and *Noces*—than to anything published afterwards. He was completing in it the fuller investigation of an earlier attitude, but his own ideas were nearer to those expressed shortly after that time in his *Lettres à un ami allemand* and, eventually, in *La Peste* and *L'Homme révolté*. It should also be pointed out that before *Le Mythe de Sisyphe* was published Camus had not only witnessed the German invasion of France but had returned there and joined the Resistance. It seems probable that he found it impossible to retain the absurdist ethic in the face of a particular, concrete situation. A quantitative morality might have led as easily to the black market as to the Resistance—indeed it did so in many cases. Consequently I am inclined to interpret Camus' hesitations about the ethical implications of the absurd as the result of this experience. The quantitative ethic could not satisfy him in the circumstances of the Occupation, yet by the time *Le Mythe de Sisyphe* was completed he had still not worked out fully how a more morally acceptable code of behaviour was to be made the equally logical result of absurdist premises.

It is difficult, nevertheless, to be completely satisfied by Camus' disclaimers on the subject of the absurdist ethic. He speaks of having simply analysed an idea (the absurd) current among his contemporaries, and suggests that *Le Mythe de Sisyphe* represents an extreme by which he was tempted, not a deeply held conviction of his own. And yet, in the first half of the book particularly, it is difficult not to feel that he is personally involved to a considerable extent. There is, at best, an ambiguity of attitude at various points.

* See his essay, 'L'Énigme', printed in *L'Été*, pp. 123–38.

Perhaps the best explanation is to be found in a statement made by Camus in 1939: 'To establish the absurdity of life cannot be an end but only a beginning.' *

I think this remark justifies the suggestion that *Le Mythe de Sisyphe* is really Camus' essay in methodological doubt. We have seen already how he uses a negative method and yet derives certain positive affirmations from it. *Le Mythe de Sisyphe* now emerges more clearly as that negative beginning, that destruction of facile assumptions, in which many thinkers have indulged whose ultimate purpose was to establish values. It is the method of Descartes and Pascal. The analysis of the absurd, often made with more conviction and personal involvement than Camus is now perhaps prepared to admit, was a way of showing that positive conclusions, alien to both physical and philosophical suicide, could be arrived at even on such an apparently negative basis. He was still not clear, I think, about the detailed nature of these conclusions, but the general impression at the end of *Le Mythe de Sisyphe* is one of qualified optimism.

This last feature is seen most clearly in Camus' comments on the myth that gives the book its title. Sisyphus is an absurdist hero both by his life on earth and by the nature of his subsequent punishment in the afterworld. He disclosed the misdemeanours of the gods to certain mortals, he temporarily conquered and chained Death, he greatly enjoyed physical existence—indeed so much so that when he returned, for what was to be a brief period, from the Shades to the earth, Mercury had to force him back to the under-world where his stone awaited him. Thus Sisyphus, like *l'homme absurde*, scorned the gods, hated death and was passionately attached to life. His 'absurdist' punishment, however, makes him a less hopeless figure, according to Camus, than one might at first think. Each time he tries again to push the rock to the top of the slope he is conscious of his torment and of the hopelessness of his task. Nevertheless, despite this knowledge, he continues his task. He realizes the nature of his destiny, and Camus claims that this consciousness makes him superior to it. The lucidity necessary to his torment is part of his victory over it. One is reminded of Pascal's claim, in one of his most famous *pensées*, that although man is so

---

* Article in *Alger-Républicain* for 12 March 1939. ('Constater l'absurdité de la vie ne peut être une fin mais seulement un commencement').

fragile a creature in the physical world his consciousness of what can destroy him—a consciousness that the illness or the avalanche themselves can never have—also constitutes his superiority over a potentially malevolent universe. The myth of Sisyphus means for Camus that the most appalling truths can lose their power over us once we have resolutely recognized and accepted them. He points out that the 'all is well' of Sophocles' Œdipus is prompted by final knowledge of his true condition. Therefore in the end Sisyphus is interpreted not as a symbol of despair but of obstinate happiness. Camus' last word on the subject is: 'Il faut imaginer Sisyphe heureux'. In other words, the assertion of a particular kind of happiness that was the final outcome of *Noces* is reiterated in *Le Mythe de Sisyphe* on similar grounds of lucid revolt. In this second case, however, the idea of happiness is further strengthened by a much fuller analysis of all the apparent reasons against it. What is still uncertain is the precise form that behaviour resulting from this attitude should take. At this point Camus has further clarified the idea of revolt. He has still not made clear the kind of moral conduct to which he thinks such revolt should give rise.

Apart from the hesitancy displayed by Camus here, one is also likely to be struck by the very self-centred nature of his ethical views at this stage. The absurd, as he interprets it, seems to produce a solipsistic moral world. Real consciousness of other people such as a sound ethical attitude surely requires is noticeably lacking. This is a weakness in Camus' moral position to which he turned his attention shortly afterwards, but as far as *Le Mythe de Sisyphe* alone is concerned it is one more element in that generally unsatisfactory impression which the book makes on the reader.

Part Two

REVOLT AND POLITICS

5 THE THEORY OF REVOLT

Malheureusement, l'expérience s'est refusée à offrir
l'exemple de la Révolution, conforme à la prophétie
marxiste et aux espoirs humanitaires.

RAYMOND ARON

On its publication in France in 1951 Camus' *L'Homme révolté*
made a deep and widespread impression. Except for the near-
silence of the French Communist Party it was vigorously discussed
in print and speech by people of all political shades. Some regarded
it as a quite outstanding contribution to anti-Marxist theory; others
held it to be the potential source of a purified and rejuvenated left-
wing militancy. It was also important enough to call down thunder
from *Les Temps modernes* and was the immediate cause of the
celebrated quarrel and rupture between Camus and Sartre. An
English translation, *The Rebel*, made no comparable stir in this
country. Indeed several reviewers found it abstract, unrealistic
and inclined to make a good deal of fuss over rather remote issues.
The English translation of Simone de Beauvoir's novel, *Les
Mandarins*, which deals with similar topics from another angle
and contains an almost literal account of the Sartre/Camus controversy, was also treated by some reviewers as a curious specimen
injudiciously transplanted from the hothouses of Saint-Germain-
des-Prés. The reasons for this kind of attitude are fairly clear. On
the one hand they have to do with the persistence in France since
1789 of a lively revolutionary tradition, with French abstract thinking and with the presence in post-war France of a large and influential Communist Party. On the other hand they are connected
with English empiricism, the absence of doctrinaire socialism in
England, the British monarchy and geographical and ideological
separation from continental Europe. My own view would be that
the issues discussed by Camus in *L'Homme révolté* are important
in themselves and also essential for an understanding of the post-

war climate of opinion in France. Apart from this they involve an interesting development beyond the somewhat sterile conclusions reached in *Le Mythe de Sisyphe*. This latter point makes it necessary to discuss them here, and a fuller understanding of their significance for Camus should help, at least indirectly, to explain his own importance for his French contemporaries.

The development of Camus' thought along more historical and political lines was foreshadowed in his *Lettres à un ami allemand*. The first of these four letters, written in 1943 after the publication of *Le Mythe de Sisyphe*, indicates something of his dissatisfaction with the possible practical consequences of the absurdist position. He attributes the rise of Nazism, or at least of the 'philosophy behind it, to the putting of machiavellian nationalism into the moral void created by an acute sense of the absurdity of existence. Nazism is thus interpreted as a form of revolt against the absurd, but a revolt which did not distinguish between self-sacrifice and mystification, energy and violence, strength and cruelty. In the fourth letter, written in 1945, the problem is discussed more fully. Here Camus admits that he agreed with the diagnosis of the absurd made in the 'thirties by many Germans. He shared their disillusionment concerning moral absolutes. But many who felt this way in Germany proceeded to accept the law of the jungle, of force, violence and deceit. Man was held to be of little account; human life was cheap. The escape from the apparent senselessness of existence took the form of *Realpolitik* and the adventure of power. Writing these letters in the 'forties Camus now found himself in the Resistance fighting against the Germans. Starting from the same absurdist basis as the Nazis he was now in the opposite camp. The only explanation he can offer is his passionate desire for justice and his conviction that the absurdity of the world can only be affirmed by reference to some prior conception of coherence and sense. Man himself possesses meaning and value precisely because he is the one creature whose desire for these things is constantly frustrated. What ultimately allows a man to condemn the absence of divine morality in the universe is his deeply-felt need of an ethic that will satisfy him as a human being. Camus says that he and the Nazis derived such different forms of revolt from the principle of absurdity because the Nazis had already accepted despair too easily whereas he had not.

This apparent change in Camus' thought calls for two comments. In the first place we must be clear that the assertion of absurdity was always regarded by him as provisional only. He considered it to be a negative attitude which could eventually lead to positive recommendations. As early as 12 March 1939, in the newspaper *Alger-Républicain*, he wrote that to ascertain the fact of absurdity can only be a beginning, not an end. It must be a stepping-stone to eventual affirmation. Again, in the interview given to G. d'Aubarède in 1951, and already referred to in Chapter 2, he is reported as saying:

When I analysed the feeling of the absurd in *Le Mythe de Sisyphe* I was in search of a method, not a doctrine. I was exercising methodical doubt. I was seeking to make that 'clean sweep' which precedes constructive effort.[1]

In theory, then, the somewhat attenuated nihilism of *Le Mythe de Sisyphe* had always been too negative for Camus. In practice—and this is the second point—historical events soon dictated the main lines of those positive recommendations which had always been part of his intention. The circumstances of the Occupation emphasized the fact that an absurdist or quantitative ethic could not satisfy the demands of his humanity. Moral choices and responsibilities arose which could mean life or death for others, depending on how they were interpreted. An instinctive moralist like Camus was unable to put the quisling or the informer on a level with the Resistance fighter. And so I imagine that this concrete situation did much to give both urgency and form to positive revolt against the absurd rather than negative connivance at it. The *Lettres à un ami allemand* contain a first tentative expression of the long and searching 'examen de conscience' which he then undertook.

These letters, prompted by the pressure of political circumstances, thus form a link between the different positions of the two major essays, *Le Mythe de Sisyphe* and *L'Homme révolté*. This last work is a more profound result of the 'examen de conscience' first indicated by the letters. It is the outcome of careful and patient self-interrogation in the course of which Camus has the courage to re-examine a number of his earlier conclusions. It is an honest effort to face apparent contradictions and scrutinize them more thoroughly. Not least, it contains a revised analysis of the moral implications of the absurd. Such an enterprise quickly leads Camus from self-interrogation to wider issues. Starting with his own conception of the absurd he goes on to consider the two most positive reactions—metaphysical revolt and political revolution—to which the absurd in one form or another has historically given rise. Having traced the history of metaphysical revolt, as we find it expressed in literature, he then turns to the question of political revolution, which has sometimes been associated with it. The fact that revolution, however idealistic in its origins, seems ultimately to involve murder and terror, is attributed mainly to an obsession with the 'philosophy of history' prompted by German metaphysics. A deformation of history and of moral values follows—rational in the case of Marxism, irrational in the case of fascism, pernicious in both instances. The essay ends by advocating revolt, not revolution. But the revolt now prescribed is not that of the nineteenth- and twentieth-century poets and novelists. It resembles most closely the revolt of certain Greek thinkers with its emphasis on man and with its sense of limitation. It amounts to a resolute humanism seeking a middle course between the deism latent in romantic metaphysical revolt and the deification of history apparent in doctrinaire political revolution.

The general purpose of *L'Homme révolté* is stated in its opening pages. It is an attempt to understand those forms of contemporary violence and inhumanity which have an ideological basis and which proclaim, in apparent contradiction of their deeds, that human well-being is their goal. We are no doubt aware, even without Camus' reminder, that we live in a world where mass murder has become a common technique of government. Although it is sometimes argued that individuals have gained or retained power by this means since the earliest times, it would still seem that 'rational murder', as Camus calls it, has reached an unequalled pitch of technical perfection. In addition, it is now justified by unparalleled moral claims and supported by detailed philosophical theories. Governments asserting that they serve the cause of ordinary men massacre ordinary men by the thousand. Slave camps and mass deportations are defended in the name of freedom or said to represent the will of the people. This situation is, I suppose, absurd in a macabre way. And the violence which dominates it at least suggests links with the absurd as Camus defined it in *Le Mythe de Sisyphe*. If nothing has meaning, if there are no values, then murder and violence are neither right nor wrong. One will do 'good' or one will do 'evil' merely by caprice. Camus himself says that it will apparently be a matter of moral indifference whether one adds more victims to the gas-chambers or devotes one's life to curing lepers. The logic of the absurd seems to say that murder and medicine are equally legitimate. This is a conclusion which Camus cannot accept. He therefore embarks on a re-examination of 'the logic of the absurd'. Before coming to the historical and political discussions forming the main subject of *L'Homme révolté* he prepares for them by some closely argued abstract reasoning in the course of which he derives new consequences from the concept of absurdism.

The reader is referred first of all to *Le Mythe de Sisyphe*. In this earlier essay the argument which centred round the problem of suicide began, on the lines of the logic above, by pointing to self-destruction as the consistent outcome of the absurd. But, as we have already seen, when this conclusion was investigated more fully it had to be replaced by the absurdist wager. This required determined confrontation of an absurd universe by the individual who judged it to be absurd. To commit suicide would have been to connive at the absurd—an action morally, if not logically, inconsistent with the 'scandalized resistance' which revealed it in the first place. Now if a coherent attitude to the absurd really demands the preservation of one's existence, it follows that it actually emphasizes, if only by contrast, the value of human life. Far from making life something of little or no account it gives it an almost dramatic importance. Once this argument is accepted Camus claims that the problem of murder raised above is also resolved. The reasoning leading to the rejection of suicide must also lead to the rejection of murder. The final logic of this attitude to the absurd condemns calculated self-destruction and rational killing alike.*

Camus' reasoning, as he himself frames it, is perhaps more convincing than this bare summary would suggest. Yet even if this

---

* This position gives added interest to Camus' resolute opposition to capital punishment (e.g. in his *Réflexions sur la peine capitale*, written in collaboration with Koestler).

is so it still seems a poor argument. To have read *Le Mythe de Sisyphe* is to realize that his case rests on an unsatisfactory analogy. We have already seen that the argument against suicide depended on using the term 'logic' in several different senses thereby concealing an arbitrary choice under the appearance of rational inevitability. In addition, Camus draws an entirely unsupported conclusion from this unsatisfactory analogy. What he is really saying is that if suicide (i.e. killing oneself) is illogical, then murder (i.e. killing someone else) must necessarily be illogical also. It seems as though he is again confusing moral choice with logical necessity.

That Camus himself may have been conscious of the unsatisfactoriness of his argument is suggested by the fact that at this point he looks at the implications of the absurd/suicide relationship yet again. He sees a new contradiction in accepting the fact of the absurd and still continuing to preserve one's life. As soon as the absurd is interpreted as requiring one to continue living, the very act of living is seen to necessitate choice and judgement. But choice and judgement could not be exercised in a world that was irremediably absurd. They presuppose some meaning if they are to exist at all. Either the world is irremediably absurd and renders life impossible, or else the absurd is not as radical as first appeared and life can be lived. Radical absurdism could never be given practical, living expression. Now if the absurd is incompatible with the act of living it is also incompatible, on the same grounds, with discussions about its own nature. A 'philosophy of the absurd' runs into contradictions as soon as it is expressed in words since such expression assumes at least a minimum of coherence at the very centre of that incoherence which it sets out to analyse. A logically satisfactory analysis of the absurd would have to be silent and unexpressed.

It is the realization of these difficulties—one might call them Camus' antinomies—which now prompts him to compare his earlier absurdist attitude to the systematic doubt of Descartes. This is why he now says that *Le Mythe de Sisyphe* offers a method of argument but does not contain a body of doctrine. In fact, 'l'absurde en lui-même est contradiction'. Camus thus has the honesty, at this point, to admit a fundamental inconsistency in *Le Mythe de Sisyphe*. According to the argument used above, the book is even self-contradictory by the very fact of having been written at all. On his own showing the argument in his essay on the absurd has little significant content. But he still claims that it does represent a negative methodology enabling him to reach certain positive conclusions. This he now considers to be its main value and justification.

The manner in which Camus now obtains positive values by a negative method again calls Descartes to mind. We have seen that awareness of the absurd means doubt concerning the value of existence. We have also seen that this doubt must eventually be extended so as to include the very possibility of thinking or living in accordance with any interpretation of the absurd. Nevertheless, however radical such doubt may become it is always accompanied by the sharp awareness of the absurd which ultimately causes it. Whatever the correct logical deductions to be made from the absurd there is no doubting the experience behind it. Now this experience of the absurd is, in essence, a sense of scandal and revolt. The absurd scandalizes the reason and, in time, the moral sense. It arises from something which is at least a negative kind of revolt. If the analysis of such revolt is taken further, however, it becomes apparent that revolt is not the wholly negative attitude it might first appear to be. In accordance with the argument used earlier, to recognize the absurd is to do so in the name of some value by which it is judged to be absurd. To become aware of the absurd is to have rebelled to the extent of saying 'no', in some form, to a certain state of affairs. But to do this is also to say 'yes' to something which is not that state of affairs. The absurd is recognized by a movement of revolt that is affirmation as well as negation. The act of revolt thus reveals within an individual the presence of something against which the absurd is an offence. One cannot say that all values necessitate revolt, but it does seem to be the case that all revolt invokes values. To say 'no' is to impose limits, and this is to imply that within these limits values of some kind are being safeguarded.

At this stage in the argument the full nature of these values may be obscure, but it is at least certain that three related values are revealed by an attitude of metaphysical rebellion. In the first place, to revolt against the absurd is to rediscover oneself. Rebellion reveals to a man the existence of a part of himself which he holds to be important, by means of which he identifies his essence as a human being, and in the name of which he confronts the absurdity of existence. The first value indicated is that of individual human worth, of potentialities that can only be expressed and fulfilled by such an attitude. But the individual has already seen that this worth is what identifies him as a human being, as a member of the human race. It thus transcends his personal destiny and has to do with the nature of man in general. And so something resembling a universal human nature is the second value revealed by revolt. This leads directly, according to Camus, to a third value —human solidarity. He replaces the famous Cartesian formula by one of his own: 'Je me révolte, donc nous sommes', and sums up the matter by saying: 'Although apparently negative because it creates nothing, revolt is positive in a profound way since it reveals those elements in man which must always be defended.' [2] *

The underlying moral intention of revolt emerges from this quotation. The revolt which Camus has in mind will certainly include attacks on traditional morality, but it will do so in the name of what it considers to be a higher and purer ethic emptied of direct self-interest. The impulse behind metaphysical revolt is essentially spiritual, even if Camus attempts to describe it only in logical terms. It is spiritual in the sense that Greek teaching was spiritual when it claimed the human spirit to be the measure of all things. It is not, of course, spiritual in a strictly religious sense since it refuses to recognize a divine purpose permeating human existence. Realizing the spiritual possibilities—in the humanist sense—of revolt, Camus makes two interesting observations on its relationship to religion.

Firstly he explains his belief that revolt and atheism do not begin by being synonymous or even compatible, although in time they tend to merge into one another. Revolt, he says, is more a question

of defiance than negation. It must be directed against a state of affairs, and then, ultimately, against someone responsible for this state of affairs. Metaphysical revolt in basically theistic. (This is presumably the logic behind certain writings of that contemporary *homme révolté,* Marcel Jouhandeau, in which he attacks God's being while resolutely affirming his existence.) In time, however, revolt really becomes atheistic. It subjects God to human judgement, it begins to treat him as an equal, it refuses to grant him omnipotence. Once God's transcendence is taken away his death is soon proclaimed:

The uprising against the human condition takes the form of an unbridled foray against the heavens. The king of the heavens is brought back a prisoner, his downfall is declared and he is then condemned to death.[3]

The historical development of this process from revolt to mortal condemnation could be traced successively through the writings of Sade, Baudelaire and Nietzsche. Camus does something of the kind shortly afterwards in his essay.

Having described the connection between revolt and atheism, Camus goes on, in the second place, to relate revolt to Christianity. The theoretical foundation of such a relationship has already been referred to—the fact that metaphysical protest can only have meaning if one posits a God who is the creator of all things and responsible for them. Historically, however, revolt and religion have been related in a less direct way. In western Europe they have alternated with one another and succeeded one another in time. In very general terms Camus sees the history of civilization as successive phases of metaphysical reconciliation and metaphysical revolt. There are religious phases in which most men feel adjusted to their human condition and accept the official answers given to gradually replaced by reconciliation with the divine will, particularly through the mediatory person and doctrine of Christ. The Christian form of the *sacré* lasted for many centuries. By the nineteenth century reconciliation, in its turn, had again begun to be replaced by revolt. France, in fact, had a notable eighteenth-century precursor, in the person of the Marquis de Sade, of a new, extreme and entirely blasphemous revolt against God. With the romantic movement in Europe some of the metaphysical rebels—Vigny, for example—even annexed the reconciliatory figure of Christ to their own cause. They emphasized his suffering, his cry of despair on the cross, his death (suffering, despair and death were precisely the grounds of human revolt against the deity), and by treating him as a victim of Jehovah they cleared the way for renewed attacks against God. Later nineteenth-century poets also rebelled and looked in some cases for alternative answers to the Christian account of ultimate reality. More recently, in the present century, surrealism has accentuated revolt by renewed emphasis on the absurdity of existence.

We ourselves may thus be said to live in a phase of revolt that already has two centuries of history behind it. Such is the tradition of revolt that Camus now proceeds to describe. At this point, therefore, he moves from a theoretical discussion to an historical narrative of revolt. After a few pages of comment on the pre-Christian revolt of Epicurus and Lucretius he jumps across the intervening Christian *sacré* to the revolt of Sade.

It would be tedious to paraphrase in detail Camus' comments on revolt from Sade onwards. A few points, however, should be made briefly. Camus has the honesty and good sense, despite the current fashion, to say that Sade's achievement as a writer is greatly exaggerated at the present time. He holds Sade to be important mainly as an example and a warning concerning a possible and dangerous misunderstanding of the true nature of revolt. Sade did not rebel in the name of principles. He did so on behalf of the instincts and was thus led to his well-known advocacy of 'le crime universel, l'aristocratie du cynisme et la volonté d'apocalypse'. The freedom which he demanded was unbridled licence. As a result the moral values which should be an integral part of revolt were swamped by the violence of his rebellion. Determined self-interest and a growing advocacy of evil similarly weaken the value of revolt from the Romantics to Baudelaire. Their revolt, like that of Sade, was quite different from the revolt of the ancient world and Camus' excellent analysis of the literary dandy in the nineteenth century shows this difference to have been a deterioration also:

Dostoievsky, on the other hand, advocated a type of rebellion which Camus admires as he admired the revolt of Epicurus and Lucretius. It is a rebellion which recognizes values in seeking the reign of justice for man rather than the arbitrariness of divine grace. This, for Camus, is the primary function of authentic revolt. It is his high-minded conception of revolt which leads Dostoievsky's hero, Ivan Karamazov, into a terrible conflict between the nihilistic logic of the absurd ('everything is permitted') and the moral aspirations of his original rebellion. Once Karamazov scrutinizes the full consequences of the absurd he finds to his horror that murder is logically acceptable and virtue cannot be positively justified. Eventually he accepts logical rather than moral revolt, allows his father to be killed and ends in madness. Camus claims that this logical revolt, and the rational killing associated with it, reached its apotheosis in Stalinism.

The same logical revolt was a major preoccupation with Nietzsche. He discussed it in terms of the question whether it is possible to continue to live while believing in nothing. Nietzsche answers his own question in the affirmative. He does so in his later works by preaching systematic negation rather than systematic doubt. This leads him eventually to his doctrines of the superman, the will to power and fidelity to the earth. Man can at least become a momentary god. Camus' general conclusion is that Nietzsche's nihilism was pure in intention but lethal in its effects. Nazism drew inspiration from it, although Camus claims that it did so by misunderstanding Nietzsche. The tone of Camus' comments on Dostoievsky and Nietzsche shows how much his own thought has been influenced by them both.

The longest comment on the increasing deviation of revolt towards nihilism is reserved for the section in which Camus discusses Lautréamont, Rimbaud and the surrealists. There is an acute analysis of the contradictions between nihilism and banal conformism which he finds in Lautréamont and Rimbaud. Yet although there is contradiction in one sense, he claims that this particular kind of nihilism was ultimately bound to end in conformity. The contradictions of nihilism are considered in most detail in the surrealists, particularly since they claimed, at one period, to combine metaphysical revolt with political revolution. Revolt in the previous century, from the Romantics to Nietzsche, had been primarily individualistic. But for some time surrealists like Éluard and Aragon claimed to reconcile their subjective anarchy with the objective principles of Marxism. Camus traces this combination of revolt and revolution to the extreme nihilism of surrealism. Not only did it seek to violate language and the rational processes of thought; the famous statement was also made that a proper surrealist action would be to go into the street with a revolver and fire casually at the passers-by. The violence thus announced, in theory at least, against conforming members of society became focused for a time on society as an institution. Marxism, as the surrealists imperfectly understood it, came to be regarded as a means of liberating and furthering their desires. Incidentally, communist 'double talk' eventually set them an example in the violation of words ('freedom', 'democracy', 'will of the people', etc.) which far outdid their own earlier experiments with language. Camus sees nihilism as the common factor in surrealist revolt and the surrealist conception of revolution: '. . . these madmen wanted "any sort of revolution", something or other to release them from the world of tradesmen, and of compromise in which they were obliged to live.[4] The revolution of their dreams was not something to be brought about by technical skill and detailed, patient organization. It was a myth that gave them consolation, and it was not necessarily less dangerous on that account. Indeed, Breton really looked upon political revolution as the handmaiden of surrealist nihilism. The revolution, if it removed social injustice, would thus ensure that the latter did not obscure the metaphysical injustice of the universe. The rationalism of a Marxist society would primarily serve to throw into unmistakable relief the absurdism of the human condition. There was therefore a deep conflict between the politico-economic aims of Marxism and the frustrated metaphysical aspirations of surrealism. Breton, along with others, realized this after some time. Today he is anti-Marxist and his nihilism has led him to propose a provisional return to traditional morality which recalls the later conformism of Lautréamont and Rimbaud. His continuing cry, 'nous voulons, nous aurons l'au-delà de nos jours', suggests that surrealism cannot be a political movement. To Camus, whose sympathy with some of Breton's theses is clear, surrealism appears rather as 'une impossible sagesse'.

This survey of revolt during two centuries leads Camus to the conclusion that it has become lethal to life and liberty by failing to maintain the tension inherent in all metaphysical protest. While the tension remained, moral values could exist, but once the tension was dropped death, violence and moral nihilism were inevitable. What Camus calls the intemperance of absolutism has repeatedly led either to advocacy of suicide (absolute refusal of the absurd) or advocacy of murder (absolute acceptance of the absurd). It is the latter form of extremism which has become dominant and has betrayed the nature of metaphysical revolt. Camus now turns to an examination of its growth in the form of political revolution or, as he calls it, 'la révolte historique'.

The term 'révolte historique' is used by Camus because it indicates the nature of the link between metaphysical revolt and political revolution. The 'death' of God was followed by the deification of man. The temporal creature was raised to a status previously attributed to a deity who, by definition, existed outside the bounds of time. The *révolté* thus replaced vertical and extra-temporal transcendence, or grace, by horizontal and temporal transcendence, or history. Failing to find eternal salvation he began to look for salvation through time. Political revolution was the result, representing a deformation of original metaphysical revolt by the deification of history.

Revolution is a betrayal of revolt because it ignores the fact that there are no absolutes for *l'homme révolté* any more than for his elder brother *l'homme absurde*. Political revolution deliberately takes an imperative absolute which the 'death' of God denied and transfers it to history. This betrayal of revolt brings dangerous consequences. For example, historical thinking and horizontal absolutes encourage men to sacrifice the present to a hypothetical future. The temptation to adopt any temporary means of hastening historical ends is a powerful one. Furthermore, a strictly historical perspective also introduces, inevitably, the idea that efficacity is a sufficient justification of action. This is why revolution in the name of freedom has led so quickly to the guillotine and the purge. The desire for freedom may initiate revolution, but at a certain stage freedom is indefinitely suspended in the interests of efficacity, and the reign of terror begins. This is why Camus says that revolt, as an expression of human consciousness, is innocent, whereas revolution, as an historical enterprise, is guilty.* It is this story of guilt, from the French to the Russian revolutions, that he now takes up. He is not concerned with the political and economic causes of revolution but with the reliance of its theory on some of the major themes of metaphysical revolt.

Camus begins with the French regicides, the origin of whose theories he traces to Rousseau. These origins have to do with belief in human innocence and in the supremacy of the general will of the people. The tradition deriving from Rousseau, being deistic, could not attribute the blame for human despair and frustration to a rational supreme being. Instead it placed the source of evil in the current organization of society. This is Rousseau's well-known claim that society has corrupted man's primal innocence. With Saint-Just the ideas of Rousseau, particularly those expressed in *Le Contrat social*, were further extended and also given practical application. Reason itself, rather than a rational deity, became the new absolute, along with Virtue. Thus even during the French Revolution the sky was not entirely empty although the death of God had left a large gap. Saint-Just aimed at establishing what he called 'a universal tendency towards the Good', and the worship of Reason was also instituted. Now just as God had been replaced by Reason and Virtue so also the king—God's appointee to society—was executed and the general will of the people made sovereign. Thus Camus regards the execution of Louis XVI as a turning-point in the enterprise of revolution because it marks the de-spiritualiza-

---

* Another fundamental difference between Camus and Sartre is apparent here. Sartre, in his essay on Baudelaire, takes the opposite view to Camus on the question of the relative merits of revolt and revolution. The aim of the metaphysical rebel, he says, is to keep intact the abuses from which he suffers so as to be able to continue his rebellion against them. The revolutionary, on the other hand, is actively concerned to change the world of which he disapproves. He seeks future values by inventing them and fighting for them here and now. From Sartre's point of view Camus' preference for revolt over revolution is sentimentality, ineffectualness and 'bad faith' in the existentialist meaning of the term.

tion of history and the secularization of God. All that remained of God was the presence of some abstract principles in an otherwise empty sky.

These principles, by the very fact of their abstract character, were insufficient to ensure the reign of universal virtue and reason. Being abstractions they lacked the concrete, human, moral content of authentic revolt. Also, because they were abstractions, they ignored the fallibility of human nature. The word 'sin' is not acceptable to Camus, but he does say: 'A day comes when ideology conflicts with psychology.' Thus even a revolution like that of 1789, laying as it did such genuine emphasis on reason and virtue, accepted within a short time tyranny and terror.

If abstract moral principles were unable to halt this movement, the removal of even these principles could only make matters worse. So long as the general will of the people was accepted as an ideal, thought and action could still be humane in intention, if not always so in practice. But a further dehumanization of the idea of revolution was brought about by Hegel's philosophy of history. Camus admits that Hegel has often been misinterpreted, particularly by the left. He also agrees that some of Hegel's most dangerous doctrines are offset by statements in other parts of his work: 'il y a dans Hegel, comme dans toute grande pensée, de quoi corriger Hegel'. But for his purpose here the important fact is that an interpretation of Hegel's system, whether accurate or not, led to the final and utter degradation of the revolutionary ideal. After Hegel the view was taken that man did not direct his own destiny but was carried along by the historical process. What he thought to be a free action on his own part was in reality part of the inevitable course of events. And this deification of history, for this is what it turned out to be, meant that the conqueror was necessarily right and the conquered were necessarily wrong. History had passed judgment on them. The one moved forward with history; the others were outstripped by history. The Russian anarchists of 1905 were to form what Camus calls an 'aristocracy of sacrifice'; those who led other revolutions formed what might be called an 'aristocracy of success'.

The aristocracy of success was bound to place the values it respected in the historical process:

Truth, reason and justice were suddenly embodied in the becoming of existence. But, by giving them perpetual motion, German ideology mistook their motion for their real nature and placed the fulfilment of this nature at the end, if there was such a thing, of the historical process.[5]

Consequently, Camus adds, these values ceased to be signposts and became destinations. Once they had been placed in some hypothetical future the means of judging the methods used to bring about their realization were removed. Here, then, we see the real source of evil in historical revolt. Means, as such, were removed from the sphere of moral judgment. Only the unrealized values they were meant to serve, the ends, could be used to justify or condemn them. As a result actions were judged on the basis of their success, not in accordance with moral values. Morality was rendered provisional and constantly shifted in accordance with the requirements of the historical situation (e.g. the posthumous condemnation of Stalin's 'crimes' by his comrades and henchmen). To place moral values in the future and suspend their immediate operation was also to open the way for the assumption of general human guilt. This is a major point of difference between Saint-Just who accepted Rousseau's doctrine of innocence and later revolutionaries who accepted Hegel's ideas of guilt. And naturally, once the general guilt of human beings was assumed, they could be treated accordingly. In fact, however, political revolution led to murder and destruction in both cases. One must kill in order to destroy those individual exceptions who sully human innocence, or one must kill in an age of guilt in order to usher in the age of innocence. Camus puts the point neatly when he says: 'Il faut détruire ceux qui détruisent l'idylle ou détruire pour créer l'idylle'.

A problem arises here to which Camus gives no clear answer. He produces many examples to show that when revolt is treated in terms of historical becoming it is altered and debased. But he seems to waver between attributing this historical debasement to metaphysical flaws and to practical misapplications. At times he seems to say that thinkers like Hegel and Nietzsche misunderstood the limits of authentic revolt and succumbed to the temptation of nihilism. At other times he inclines more to the view that these thinkers were misinterpreted by practical men or even that no system of government could give them satisfactory expression (cf. Proudhon's contention that government, by the very fact of being government, cannot be revolutionary). I shall have more to say on this point later. For the present it should simply be pointed out that the second kind of interpretation would explain Camus' apparent leanings towards anarchism and his later approval, during the positive conclusions of *L'Homme révolté*, of anarcho-syndicalism.

This tendency may be observed also in the account which Camus now goes on to give of the Russian anarchists. It might at least be argued that all of them exceeded the limits of authentic revolt, yet they are treated with considerable indulgence. This is particularly the case with the group of youthful terrorists, Kaliaev, Dora Brilliant and others, who assassinated the Grand-Duke Serge in 1905. They are called 'les meurtriers délicats' in *L'Homme révolté* and 'les justes' in Camus' play of the same name. He even claims that they provide the supreme and also the last example of the genuine spirit of revolt. First, however, he reviews briefly the ideas of those successive generations of Russian anarchists who preceded the 'meurtriers délicats'. He comments on the Decembrists, Bielinski, Pisarev, Bakunin and Nechaev. He criticizes with some severity the *Catechism of a Revolutionist* written by Bakunin and Nechaev. Where Kaliaev and his comrades hated murder and only accepted the necessity for killing others by sacrificing their own lives, men like Nechaev used murder as an avenue to power. And so it is only of the 'meurtriers délicats' that Camus says:

The victory they won at the cost of exhaustion was finally betrayed. But by their sacrifice, and even by their out-and-out negations, they gave tangible form to a value, or a new virtue, which even today continues to oppose tyranny and helps authentic liberation.[6]

The 1905 terrorists were the culmination of nearly thirty years of assassination or attempted assassination of heads of government in Europe and the U.S.A. From the very depths of nihilism, Camus says, many hundreds of dedicated and courageous young men and women tried to create the values they ardently desired by means of guns, bombs and the ready sacrifice of their own lives. They deliberately accepted guilt and death in an effort to guarantee the victory of their ideals. In describing their attitude Camus makes a statement of implied approval which seems to be in conflict with his earlier analysis. He says: 'The future is the only world of transcendence for men without God.' [7] This 'historicism' was held earlier to be a major factor leading to degradation of the idea of revolt in the practice of revolution. Camus justifies the statement here by saying that although these young nihilists thought they were serving values to be realized in the future they in fact gave birth at once to the true values of revolt by the nature of their action. They set great store by fraternity, they experienced and practised a strong sense of solidarity, and they enhanced these values by a remarkable capacity for self-sacrifice. Furthermore, although they chose political assassination as the means to realize their ends, they spared women and children—unlike the later Marxist revolutionaries.

The element of special pleading seems clear in these various arguments, though Camus is not speaking less than the truth when he describes the continual moral scruples which made Kaliaev and the others almost unique figures: 'Although they lived a life of terrorism . . . they never ceased to be harrowed by it.' [8] Once again this is not, in itself, a justification of terrorism, but Camus interprets it as living the tension and paradox of authentic revolt. Their unconcern for their own lives existed side by side with concern for the lives of others; they found violence to be inevitable and yet they were unable to justify it. But they accepted all the consequences of such paradoxes. They kept both terms of each paradox alive. In this they were unlike later revolutionaries who suppressed one of the elements in the tension of revolt and regarded violence and death with cold equanimity. Kaliaev, Dora Brilliant and their comrades demonstrated the fact that revolt must avoid dogmatic satisfaction if it is to preserve its true character. By the willing sacrifice of their own lives they also found some sort of final solution to the paradox which their lives had to preserve. They accepted their own death as the price that must be paid for the element of guilt in the paradox. Here again Camus seems to me to be over-indulgent when he treats the sacrifice as though it removed the guilt. After all, the acceptance of their own death by the terrorists was, in its inevitability, an elaborate form of suicide. On these grounds alone it is open to Camus' earlier objections since it means that the paradox is 'resolved' only when it is no longer being lived. If the absurd is not to be 'elided' in this way, neither is the contradiction of revolt. In any case, it can hardly be seriously maintained that one death cancels another. Camus' own insistence on individual human worth would make this impossible. The assassin, by accepting his own execution, cannot thereby nullify the assassination he has committed. Camus makes no allowance for such objections, however. He ends his account of the 1905 terrorists with a final reference to their rôle as exemplars of true revolt: 'Kaliaev doubted to the very end, but doubt did not prevent him from taking action; this is why he offers the clearest image of revolt.' [9]

Camus' analysis of individual terrorism makes it appear to have more value as an attitude or gesture than as a practical policy. One may even suspect that it has more to do with solving the emotional problems of the terrorists themselves than with changing the existing political and economic structure. This latter task was soon taken up again, however, by the followers of Marx. The transition was made, at the same time, from individual terrorism to state terrorism. With state terrorism the paradoxes of revolt were suppressed. Murder was accepted as legitimate, the historical situation became the arbiter of morals, techniques were perfected for the seizure of power and the state was made an object of worship. It is this 'betrayal of revolt' that Camus studies in the next main section of *L'Homme révolté*, beginning with some brief observations on the fascist and nazi revolutions of the present century. These were not revolutions in the same sense as the French and Russian revolutions. They did not depend on the same deification of history. Indeed, they looked on history as the chance interplay of brute force and in this way deified irrationality rather than reason. Nevertheless, they are part of the history of revolt, since Mussolini and Hitler claimed to derive many of their ideas from Hegel and Nietzsche respectively. The two dictators exemplify clearly that increasing deification of the state to which revolutions have always led. They instituted an irrational state-terrorism devoid of all values except the criterion of success.

The rational form of state terrorism, ultimately derived from Hegel and Marx, found expression in the Russian revolution and the communist state. The ideological development is traced by Camus during a series of comments on the teaching of Marx. This section of *L'Homme révolté* obviously had a good deal to do with the book's success in French right-wing circles, but it should be pointed out that Camus' criticism of Marx is not of the kind often applauded today. For one thing, he gives a refreshingly novel impression of actually having read Marx. His criticisms are the outcome of serious consideration, not of out-of-hand rejection. Furthermore, he admires aspects of Marx's thought. He praises the denunciation by Marx of the social hypocrisy of the nineteenth-century bourgeoisie. Marx, he says, showed convincingly that the middle-class family virtues praised by the conservative press relied on an economy that sent less fortunate men and women half naked down the coal-mines. The reigning moral principles of the period, if not consciously hypocritical, were thoroughly misleading, and Marx performed a real service in uncovering the immoral economic situation that lay behind them. In fact, Camus generally praises the moral impulses activating Marx. He recalls that it was Marx who said that 'an end requiring unjust means is not a just end'. Of course Camus is quick to admit—indeed this is his main point—that the practice of Marxism from the Russian revolution onwards calls for severe criticism. The moral principle just quoted was flagrantly ignored by those who were concerned to make of Marxist theory an effective reality. This is particularly so because Marxist practice allowed justice to be swallowed up in the historical process and thus deprived of a solid and immediate ethical justification. Nevertheless, as in the case of Nietzsche, Camus sees that many of the causes of later decay were already present in the system elaborated by Marx. It was bound to prove unworkable because of the inconsistencies it contained. Once these faults had been exposed by historical events immoral methods were more and more frequently adopted in an attempt to salvage Marx's ultimate ideals. The majority of his more immediate historical predictions having proved inaccurate the emphasis was placed on ensuring, by the most effectual means, the fulfilment of his long-term prophecies. In his comments on Marx Camus first points out contradictions in his thought and then goes on to give an explanation of the way in which various theories failed in practice.

Although Marx claimed that his theories were scientific, the opposite is the case. His method was a contradictory mixture of determinism and prophecy, practical analysis and utopian dreaming. His criticism of an existing society had scientific foundations, but his account of the future development of society was little more than supposition. Again, a contradiction existed between his theories concerning materialism and those to do with the dialectic. Camus shows the failure of the dialectic to support Marx's claim that thought is determined by a prior, material reality (*L'Homme révolté*, pp. 245–6). The dialectic itself gives rise to another kind of conflict which proved most dangerous in practice by making the full development of capitalism (i.e. increased injustice and suffering for the proletariat) a prerequisite of ultimate proletarian happiness and justice. The determinism of the dialectical process also produces a dilemma because of the active and passive conclusions which Marx seems to draw from it at different times. Furthermore, there is no real reason for supposing that the dialectic of history, if it is a fact, has a foreseeable end in time. In other words, its very nature would seem to refute the claims of Marx himself that the class struggle must come to an end and be replaced by a classless society. Finally, the form to be taken by the proletariat's seizure of power was described in conflicting terms in several different works and Marx allowed these inconsistencies to remain unsolved.

If the theoretical reasoning of Marx had its inconsistencies, its practical application showed up even more striking errors. For example, society did not develop along the lines foreseen by Marx and this made the application of his system, in its complete and original form, impossible. Methods which he might well have disavowed came to be used in order to deal with this immediate failure, while seeking to ensure that his long-term prophecies would still come true. In his analysis of society Marx seriously underestimated the economic rôle of the peasantry. As a result the Russian kulaks turned out to be five million historical exceptions and the Marxists of the 1917 revolution used death or deportation as the only methods of reconciling them with Marxist theory. Again, Marx was proved utterly wrong in thinking that universal proletarian solidarity would be a stronger force than nationalism. The failure of the Second International alone showed the reverse to be true. Finally, the sudden and striking acceleration of technical progress brought into being a new form of oppression of the working-classes which Marx did not foresee. He recognized money and the military as means of oppressing the proletariat but he made no provision for the tyranny of technocracy to which the workers were submitted, not least by his later disciples.

Inconsistencies and miscalculations of this kind seriously hampered the implementation of Marx's political philosophy. New methods had to be found in order to make it work. Perhaps the most damning criticism of Marx lies in the fact that these new methods were justified by the re-interpretation of other elements in his system. The communist theory and practice which emerged as a result led to those features of contemporary Marxism which Camus most deplores and which he regards as an utter betrayal of the original nature of revolt. These observations on Marxism end with a restatement of the differences between metaphysical revolt and political revolution:

Revolt demands unity, historical revolution demands totality. The first starts from a 'no' based on a 'yes', the second starts from absolute negation and condemns itself to every kind of slavery in order to create an affirmation transferred to the end of time. The one is creative, the other nihilistic.[10]

Before coming to his final comments on the nature of revolt and how it is to be safeguarded from political excesses, Camus describes the relationship between revolt and artistic creation. This is a topic which will be discussed in Chapter 7 in connection with the aesthetic theories behind Camus' novels. I shall therefore ignore it for the moment and conclude the present chapter with an account of the particular kind of revolt commended in the closing pages of *L'Homme révolté*. To advocate any kind of revolt at all after this historical account of its failure must strike one as a difficult undertaking. The whole burden of Camus' lengthy exposition has been the abortiveness of all attempts to give revolt accurate and effective political expression. What he does in these closing pages is to re-examine some of the political failures already described. This re-examination emphasizes again the faults of post-Christian revolt, faults of extremism which Camus criticized from Sade onwards. But by the same token these political shortcomings make it evident, at least to Camus, that pre-Christian revolt, the revolt expressed by the ancient world, preserves those features of limitation and moderation necessary to a solution of the political problems he discusses.

Albert Camus

In the end therefore, with characteristic fidelity to his mediterranean origins and the world of *L'Envers et l'endroit* and *Noces*, he advocates what he calls 'la pensée de midi' as the source of a new spiritual and political renaissance.

The question arises whether one should even contemplate revolt any longer because of its degradation in practice. Once political measures are taken to make it a practical reality the values which gave it its moral character are indefinitely postponed or lost in a hypothetical future. The formula, 'je me révolte, donc nous sommes', is replaced by 'je me révolte, donc nous serons', and violence and slavery are the outcome. Violence had already proved a problem in relation to the absurd. At that stage, however, it remained a theoretical difficulty and could be refuted on logical grounds (or at least Camus thought so). But once revolt took the form of political revolution violence became a pressing moral problem and seemed to defy all practical solutions. It looks, then, as if *l'homme révolté* is faced by an insuperable dilemma. He has a clear conception of justice but finds himself perpetrating injustice in its name; he aspires to goodness but fatally employs evil methods which make its realization impossible; his desire for freedom leads him to institute slavery; theory and practice contradict each other despite his attempts to reconcile them.

These contradictions are followed by two sets of political antinomies between violence and non-violence and between justice and freedom. In principle, revolt demands the renunciation of violence out of respect for human life; but revolution, which gives political expression to the idea of revolt, takes its origin and nature from the principle of violence.* Thus, short of complete withdrawal, one must either renounce revolt and connive at evil or choose revolt and commit evil. Again, justice and freedom are the goals of both revolt and revolution. But revolution, in order to obtain justice for its adherents, must at least suppress the freedom of the ruling class. Later, in order to retain freedom for its adherents, it must deny justice to counter-revolutionaries. There is an apparently irreducible contradiction between the moral demands of revolt and the practical requirements of revolution.

---

* The fact that revolution must mean the sudden replacement, *using violent means*, of one political system by another is convincingly argued by Raymond Aron in *L'Opium des intellectuels*, Paris, Calmann-Lévy, 1956, pp. 47 ff.

These dilemmas and antinomies seem to face us with an unenviable choice between the moral ineffectiveness of the yogi and the moral cynicism of the commissar. It is at this point that Camus returns to his concept of revolt. Such problems arise, he claims, because the assertion of limitation, and therefore of moderation, inherent in authentic revolt, has been ignored. For instance the freedom demanded by revolt is by no means total. On the contrary the rebel reacts precisely against the unlimited freedom being exercised against him by a superior power. His very revolt sets limits to freedom. Camus writes:

No doubt the rebel demands a certain freedom for himself; but in no circumstances does he demand, if he is consistent, the right to destroy the person and freedom of someone else. He degrades no one. The freedom which he demands he claims for everybody; that which he rejects he forbids all others to exercise. He is not simply a slave opposing his master but a man opposing the world of master and slave.[11]

To the values already derived from revolt the value of moderation is now added. This is precisely the value that political revolution has continually ignored. Extremism has been its hallmark and this extremism has given rise to unnecessary but inevitable dilemmas. The deification of history is a striking example of one such extreme position. Not only is it a betrayal of genuine revolt but Camus now sees it as being, in itself, a logical impossibility. He argues, following Jaspers, that it is impossible for men to conceive of history in its totality because they are themselves a part of history. They cannot stand outside it to judge and interpret it in an infallible way. Indeed, from this point of view, 'il n'y a pas d'histoire, à la limite, que pour Dieu'. Thus it is equally impossible for men to carry out plans embracing the totality of history. All action in time, whatever the intentions or theories that guide it, must contain a large element of uncertainty and this inevitable margin of error makes all dogmatism and doctrinaire rigidity unjustifiable.

Revolt founded on a 'philosophie des limites' now emerges as a means of resolving the two political antinomies mentioned above. First of all there is the question of violence and non-violence. The violence that betrays revolt does so because it is systematic and reduces men to mere objects in the service of some distant historical goal. For *l'homme révolté* violence must be assumed as an indi-

Albert Camus

vidual responsibility and can never serve an abstract doctrine. Revolt will therefore take up arms only on behalf of efforts to eradicate violence, not to codify it. Camus says, for example, that a revolution is not worth dying for, is not justified in taking human life, unless it immediately abolishes capital punishment. Within the context of authentic revolt violence is only justified by the subsequent establishment of non-violence and will only be employed to this end.

A rather similar argument is used in the case of justice and freedom. Genuine revolt, with its awareness of limits, emphasizes relativity in the sphere of justice and freedom. With this sense of relativity goes the realization that the ends it sets out to achieve must begin by being approximate. In order that this approximation may become more and more accurately defined revolt will allow free expression of opinion. In this way it will give force to that human solidarity which justifies it in the first place. In particular it will ensure the permanent expression of justice as a legal concept. Justice will become an increasing reality because of the freedom of protest and genuine human communication. Absolute justice and absolute freedom are incompatible, but the interplay of relative justice and relative freedom, if both are dedicated to preserving the values of revolt, will eventually lead to harmony between them and a satisfactory measure of each.

Genuine revolt will therefore open a path that leads one safely between the extreme positions of the yogi and the commissar. It will preserve the moral aspirations of political revolution in its daily practice. To do so it will be focused on a 'philosophy of limitation' whose origin is to be found, not in the dominant metaphysical revolt of the last two centuries but in ancient Greek thought. For this reason Camus commends what he calls 'la pensée solaire' or 'l'esprit méditerranéen'. This mediterranean tradition, inherited primarily by progressive Italian, Spanish and French thinkers of the nineteenth century, was overshadowed and finally overcome by German ideology and historicism (Hegel, Nietzsche, Marx, Engels etc.). Consequently, Camus regards the decisive struggle of our own century as being not so much between Marxism and Christianity as between:

... nordic dreams and the mediterranean tradition, eternally adolescent violence and mature strength, nostalgia, aggravated by learning and books, and courage tempered and enlightened by experience of life; in short, history and nature.[12]

Revolt that draws its inspiration from the mediterranean tradition can be effective as a political ideal precisely because the values which it discovers are not mere abstractions. The dignity and fraternity which it reveals and the moderation it enjoins are values that owe their whole existence to the actions of men and their personal experience of revolt. Genuine revolt does not claim that these values have existed from all eternity or that they will inevitably exist at some future date. It sees them as a present reality which can only be preserved by that unflagging awareness of tension and exercise of moderation which are the essential features of revolt. As an example of revolutionary practice which keeps intact the values of revolt Camus cites revolutionary syndicalism—a movement which still has adherents in France and possesses its own periodical. In reply to the charge that it is politically ineffectual Camus credits this movement with improving conditions for the workers and being instrumental in the advance from a sixteen-hour day to a forty-hour week. It is founded, he says, on human and economic realities ignored by the doctrinaire extremism of Marxism. Its down-to-earth gradualism has done more for human happiness than dialectical materialism. It works in the opposite direction from Marxism, progressing from the particular to the general, from real men to abstract ideas, from practice to theory. In this way even anarcho-syndicalism, if not always avoiding violence, must always avoid terror, slavery and that degradation of man which has characterized revolution for more than 150 years. Camus emphasizes that he is not putting syndicalism forward as a complete solution; it is no more than an example of the kind of political thinking and action required today. It reflects the essence of mediterranean wisdom (its most lasting appeal has been to several mediterranean countries and parts of South America) because it takes its stand on concrete realities including a proper conception both of human dignity and human limitation. By so doing it reminds us that political wisdom must be inspired by love of man as he is; it must be characterized by an attachment to his present well-being; it must reject ideologies which sacrifice present happiness to doctrinaire promises of its future fulfilment.

6 THE PRACTICE OF REVOLT

Si vraiment toute action est symbolique, alors, les livres sont à leur façon des actions.

MAURICE MERLEAU-PONTY

Many people would probably wish to disagree with Camus over points of detail in his historical account of the course taken by revolt and revolution since the end of the eighteenth century. It is hardly possible, however, not to be deeply impressed by the broad general lines of his narrative. His criticism of metaphysical revolt and political revolution since Sade and Saint-Just is at once profound, disturbing and, I think, essential to a proper understanding of present world problems. The most dangerous features of Marxism are lucidly and intelligently exposed, and yet the reasons for its success in Europe also emerge clearly. *L'Homme révolté* reveals a most sensitive moral consciousness and a striking nobility of mind on Camus' part. When one has said this, however, one has to admit that the book remains unsatisfactory. The last part in particular, with its constructive and positive intentions, seems to have been rendered unconvincing in advance by the very analysis leading up to it. Near the end, the book begins to fall apart. Despite Camus' eloquence and ingenuity it is difficult to find a genuine link between the criticisms he has made and the conclusions he draws. The final pages strike one as an unsuccessful attempt to turn a fundamentally negative argument into a positive one. In this connection there is a notable change in style towards the end of the book. After 350 pages of admirably clear and direct prose Camus allows himself a series of lyrical flights and makes increasingly hermetic statements based on his dominant image of 'sunlit thought'. The following are three examples of statements whose meaning, even when agreed upon, is difficult to relate to any precise reality: '. . . des paroles de courage et d'intelligence qui, près de la mer, sont même vertu' (p. 374); 'Et déjà, en effet, la révolte, sans prétendre à tout résoudre, peut au moins faire face. Dès cet instant, midi ruisselle sur le mouvement même de l'histoire' (p. 376); 'Nous choisirons Ithaque, la terre fidèle, la pensée audacieuse et frugale, l'action lucide, la générosité de l'homme qui sait' (p. 377). Phrases such as these incline one to think that the moderate revolt finally commended is a highly private vision on Camus' part and not a practical policy of general application. The very effectiveness of his earlier criticism seems to leave him without a solution that can be widely understood and put into practice. I suspect that his eloquent pleading in these final pages is an attempt to conceal the fact that he is advocating a point of view held independently of the earlier analysis. Lacking a close logical argument and convincing practical examples he tries, probably quite unconsciously, to conceal these flaws behind an increasingly poetic vocabulary.

One further comment should be made on this same point. The advocacy of 'la pensée solaire' or 'la pensée de midi' is, as these expressions themselves suggest, a mystical hymn of praise to the virtues of sunshine and light. The vocabulary of the closing pages is dominated by references to light. For example: 'le courage durci et *éclairé*'; 'l'intelligence est sœur de la dure *lumière*'; 'cette lutte entre *midi* et minuit'; 'attend son *aurore*'; 'des volcans de *lumière*'; 'une *lumière* pourtant est inévitable'; 'une limite, dans le *soleil*, les arrête tous', etc. This obsession with light is a major feature of Camus' whole sensibility. Sunshine and the open sea are symbols, in his novels and plays as well as in his essays, of the values which he cherishes. A complementary preoccupation with darkness and confined space can also be traced in the same works —the 'absurd walls' of *Le Mythe de Sisyphe*, the dominant image of *L'État de siège,* the picture of Oran cut off by an epidemic in *La Peste*, Czechoslovakia denied direct access to the sea in *Le Malentendu*—and these dark, imprisoning images symbolize the forces that enslave man. Here, in *L'Homme révolté*, the 'midnight' reigning in political affairs is to be counteracted by the 'midday' of Camus' dreams. Nordic obscurity is opposed by mediterranean light. A continual contrast of this kind is surely an oversimplification. The images of sunshine and darkness are all too often a source of misleading generalization in Camus' more philosophical works.

His preoccupation with light and shadow ends by falsifying his arguments. One also notices that it leads him to underestimate the 'luminous' tradition in German thought from Goethe to Nietzsche, while he sees no contradiction in emphasizing the Judaic (and therefore presumably mediterranean) concern with historical fulfilment. In general this emotional attitude to light gives to *L'Homme révolté* an element of private myth-making which detracts in an unfortunate way from the outstanding merit of much of the argument.

There are some other faults in the book which should be mentioned briefly. First of all I would make a general objection, ultimately connected with the previous points, that the book begins by emphasizing the virtues of revolt and ends with what is really a plea for moderation and gradual political reform. This strikes one as an obvious inconsistency, and the reason for it is to be found, I think, in Camus' lack of clarity concerning the nature of revolt itself. He begins by considering revolt as the proper way of reacting to one's discovery of the absurd. This means that revolt begins as a metaphysical concept and a philosophical attitude. In the closing pages of the book, however, revolt has come to mean refusal to accept political extremism and the Marxist interpretation of history. Revolt in this sense is something quite different and has become a brand of political philosophy. It is no longer a response to the human condition in the broad sense of this term. It now has to do with a particular historical situation. I am not here criticizing this use of the term as such; I am simply making the point that 'revolt' means two quite different things in two different parts of the book and an organic relationship between them is not shown. Camus not only fails to draw attention to these two interpretations of revolt. He also fails to explain the nature of the transition from one to the other and complicates matters further by using the master/slave analogy several times to explain the nature of both kinds of revolt. In fact, we have in *L'Homme révolté* a multiple use of the term 'revolt' which causes confusion as did a similar use of the term 'absurd' in *Le Mythe de Sisyphe*.

In addition to these objections one may also take exception to the fact that Camus traces all political revolution to that particular form of revolt which arises from experience of the absurd. Such an explanation holds good in some cases but it is certainly not true of all of them. He is right to argue from this viewpoint in so far as his own experience of both revolt and revolution has been of this kind (the element of self-examination in *L'Homme révolté* is again apparent in this way). But this limitation of the meaning of revolt, with its restricted explanation of revolution, gives rise to another weakness in the argument. It means that Camus' description of the transition from revolt to revolution is a very summary one. He ignores the many social, political, economic and other factors which cannot be dismissed in an adequate account of revolution both as a political doctrine and as a historical occurrence. Revolutions have their material as well as their spiritual and intellectual causes. Marxism may err in concentrating almost exclusively on these material explanations, but Camus surely conveys an equally misleading picture by taking no account of them at all. By limiting revolt to revolt against the absurd, Camus also pays no attention to what might be called Christian revolt. I think it would be expecting too much of him, and perhaps it would be tantamount to asking for an entirely different book, if this point were heavily insisted upon. Nevertheless one wonders where Péguy or Léon Bloy, for example, fit into his scheme of things. The fact remains, too, that Camus greatly admires the social ideas of a Christian *révolté* like Simone Weil. This in itself might have prompted him to consider the kind of revolt, within Christianity, of which she was such an outstanding example.

The emphasis on revolt as rejection of the absurd also explains, I think, the uneasy relationship between the subject-matter of *L'Homme révolté* and Camus' handling of it. The central subject has to do with society and history, but an approach from the absurd gives rise primarily to considerations of the individual and nature. Although the standpoint of the individual and nature (the mediterranean outlook) enables Camus to criticize society and history (the nordic outlook) with such force, it fails, at the same time, to produce a convincing and positive solution. One feels that the right weapons of attack cannot also be adequate instruments of reconstruction. This explains, I think, the sharp contrast that emerges in the final pages of the book between an awareness of moral nobility and a feeling of political inadequacy. One admires the moral tone of the whole discussion but one cannot see how the final advocacy of moderate revolt, admirable though it may be in the abstract, could prove an effective answer, in the middle of the twentieth century, to the problems previously analysed with such insight. At best Camus properly reminds us of what, both individually and socially, we ought to be. He does not really tell us how this ideal is to be effectively realized.

Charges of political ineptitude and sterile moral aloofness were soon levelled against Camus by Sartre and by his disciple Francis Jeanson. In the previous chapter I indicated one or two general differences between the ideas of Camus and Sartre, and something further should now be said about the public quarrel that arose between them after the publication of *L'Homme révolté*. This quarrel is of interest, and perhaps of importance, for several reasons. In the first place it is a controversy that could hardly be conceived of as occurring anywhere else than in Paris. A communist state would certainly not have tolerated it, and the social and intellectual conditions in our own country or the U.S.A. would have made it appear unreal and irrelevant. By the same token, however, it throws light not only on a certain type of high-powered intellectual life in France but on the whole complex of historical and political factors which led to its being followed with such attention and interest. In the second place it gave to the public further clarification of the political views held by Camus and Sartre. It also showed that their disagreement was not simply a question of different political policies but had to do with subtle moral and philosophical issues. Thirdly one may say that this quarrel summed up the main points of what both Camus and Sartre regard as the fundamental debate of our time—the argument between Marxism and the non-Marxist left. Its importance in this respect is suggested, I think, by Raymond Aron's only partly facetious reference to it as having taken place in the year VII of the cold war. Briefly what happened was that Jeanson reviewed *L'Homme révolté* in a long and highly critical article published in *Les Temps modernes* in May 1952. Three months later the same periodical published a sixteen-page letter of self-defence addressed by Camus to Sartre, and this letter was accompanied by lengthy and detailed replies from Sartre and Jeanson.

For some years after World War II Camus was widely referred to as an existentialist. It became clear in time that the label had been misapplied, but one can see why it was used. There was, in fact, a good deal of similarity between the broad philosophical tendencies of Camus and Sartre. Both maintained an atheistic and humanist position, rejecting moral and metaphysical absolutes. They found their values in experience, not in *a priori* reasoning, and they had confidence in man's ability to fulfil himself without supernatural aid. Both also emerged from the war with a common concern for political questions. They denounced the same things—bourgeois hypocrisy, economic exploitation, colonialism, the colour bar, Franco Spain, etc. They collaborated in Sartre's Rassemblement Démocratique Révolutionnaire during its brief existence. It is not surprising that Sartre should write, in his reply to Camus of August 1952:

For us you were—and can be again tomorrow—the admirable meeting-point of a personality, a life of action and a literary achievement. That was in '45: we discovered the Camus of the Resistance as we had discovered the Camus who wrote *L'Étranger* . . . you summed up in your own person the struggles of the period and you transcended them by the ardour with which you lived through them. You were a *person* of the most rich and complex kind . . .[1]

It is useful to remind ourselves in this way of the amount of common ground between Sartre and Camus. We are then better able to see that the quarrel between them had more to do with differences of interpretation than with principles and that these differences sometimes depended on very fine shades of meaning. In general they have tended to give different interpretations to a common anti-absolutist position. Sartre has opted for the efficacy of collective endeavour—always at the risk of mistakes and failures —and the creation of values through action in time. Camus finds his values in the individual consciousness, independent of action and history. They are still human values, not absolutes, but we have seen that he finds them to have been degraded by collective historical experiment whereas Sartre holds that they can exist in any useful sense only by being fashioned in political activity. As a result Sartre insists on the necessity of accepting moral short-comings and possible guilt in the service of the revolution. Camus, on the other hand, gives the impression of preaching an impracticable moral austerity. Both Jeanson and Sartre accused him of priggishness and Sartre added wryly that he appears to carry with him 'a portable pedestal'. He accounts for Camus' position as follows. He says that Camus' conception of revolt was metaphysical, not social, from the very beginning. It had to do with the individual and nature, with man's search for inner happiness in the face of an incomprehensible or malignant universe. In other words, this confrontation between man and his human condition pointed to an eternal injustice which could never be changed but only resisted. It is unaltering and unalterable tragedy. Sartre adds:

You chose and created yourself such as you now are by meditating on misfortunes and misgivings which were your personal lot; the solution you have found for them is a bitter wisdom which seeks to deny time.[2]

For a period, during the Occupation, Camus took part in direct historical action. He describes himself in the *Lettres à un ami allemand* as having 'entered history' at this time. But Sartre asserts that Camus, for these reasons, identified history with war, regarded it as 'la folie des autres', and thus he entered history only for the purpose of fighting against it. The final proof is that after the war Camus returned to his metaphysical preoccupations and directed the spirit of revolt away from the world, where it could have been effective, towards the sky, where it quickly dissipates its strength.

This is not, I think, a fair or an accurate account of Camus' position. He does not say that history should be ignored nor does he advocate withdrawal from all political action. It is true that he commends a certain kind of political action which Sartre despises. One may argue that his policy has little chance of success given the present social and political conditions in France. But this is not a withdrawal from history and indeed we shall shortly see that he has readily taken up a position on all the main political controversies since the war. What Camus rejects is not history as such—it would be impossible for him to do so—but historical absolutism of the kind described in *L'Homme révolté*. He makes his position clear by saying that, in the world as it is today, complete anti-historicism is as misplaced as complete historicism.

Sartre makes the charges he does only because he refuses to give up his faith in Marxist revolutionary doctrine. This makes him regard any other approach as automatically ineffectual. Consequently, although this quarrel is between two non-communists, Sartre resolutely defends the Marxist ideal and this is why I referred earlier to an argument between Marxism and the non-Marxist left. If Camus sometimes comes closer to the position of the yogi than he himself realizes or admits, Sartre is clearly very near to the other extreme of the commissar. In fact, throughout this argument, Jeanson and Sartre both rely very much on the Marxist doctrine of efficacity. Since they identify the interests of the proletariat with those of the Communist Party as an article of faith, they regard revolution, with the Communist Party as its instrument, as the quickest and most efficient means of giving the workers the conditions and the authority which should be theirs. This is why, as Camus complains, they refuse to distinguish between reactionary political ideas and any criticism of Marxist dogma. Anyone not on their side, for whatever reasons, is held to be serving reaction *objectively*, in the special communist sense of this word.

The question behind this part of the discussion really is—can a non-Marxist left be effective in present-day political conditions? This kind of question may not seem to be of any vital importance in Britain, for instance, or the U.S.A., but it has pressing relevance in countries like France and Italy. In time, too, it will almost certainly become an increasingly important question to answer in newly emerging African and Asian communities. Sartre's view is, of course, that there can be no effective non-Marxist left. He pours scorn on Camus' criticism and rejection of both the extreme right and the extreme left and says:

You blame the European proletariat for not having publicly denounced the Soviets, but you also blame the governments of Europe for admitting Spain to UNESCO; in these circumstances I see only one solution for you: the Galapagos Islands.[3]

There is a real difficulty here, and Sartre puts his finger on the contradictions of a dilemma experienced by an increasing number of European intellectuals who wish to take a clearly left-wing stand while rejecting communism. There seems to be no simple and satisfactory answer to this problem, or at least I myself find it impossible to produce one. But some general points can be made. Camus' attitude of attacking both left and right may seem like self-righteousness on occasions, but it is infinitely preferable to a retreat into a political cynicism because of the difficulties of the problem. The fact also remains that racialism and colonialism, for example, still exist in both right-wing and left-wing forms. It seems right that Camus should attack evils in whatever camp they may be found just because honesty of this kind is an essential attitude for any intellectual. Sartre is no more a practical politician than Camus. He is primarily a writer and as such he must have a duty to speak the whole truth and not justify half-truths on one side in the name of efficacity. There is cogency and some subtlety in Sartre's reasons for not publicly denouncing slave camps in the Soviet Union, yet his attitude is surely wrong. Camus has shown clearly enough that once one begins to suppress facts in the interests of political expediency this suppression, which began as a political manoeuvre, becomes a lasting feature of the system built up in this way. It remains true, of course, that the moral position is often ineffective. But one may easily forget that even today sufficiently strong and widespread protest may still influence government policy. Some political observers have claimed, for instance, that the Soviet Government yielded to this kind of pressure when the affair of the doctors pointed to a new wave of anti-semitism behind the Iron Curtain. It would be evading the main issue, however, and no doubt ignoring events in Hungary in October 1956, to claim a great deal on behalf of such protests in general. Nevertheless, even if the issue is mostly an unavoidable choice between integrity and political expediency, the intellectual must, I think, choose integrity. Sartre's slighting reference to Camus as public prosecutor of the 'République des Belles Ames' does not alter the necessity of choosing in this way.*

It is this question of intellectual honesty which prompts Camus to ask whether or not Sartre and Jeanson regard the Soviet régime as a satisfactory fulfilment of revolutionary Marxism. Jeanson's uneasy reply is that the Soviet régime is not authentically revolutionary but that it has the merit of being the only system of government which even attempts to be so. Therefore one may disapprove of certain methods used but one must applaud the purpose of the enterprise. Even its imperfection is infinitely preferable to its destruction. The Soviet Union is treated with this elaborate care by Jeanson and Sartre because it comes closest to fulfilling Marxist historical theory. Camus now goes on to assert that such an

---

* There is an interesting discussion of this whole problem of the non-Marxist left, from the French angle, in Jules Moch's *Confrontations*, Paris, Gallimard, 1952.

argument involves existentialists in a contradiction. Existentialism is incompatible with Marxism precisely because of their different ways of interpreting history. The theoretical contradiction between them makes nonsense of political co-operation and explains the unwillingness of Sartre to affirm complete and open identification with the practical programme of the Communist Party. This kind of argument does not, of course, make Camus' choice of integrity rather than expediency intrinsically more sound. But it does at least show that Sartre's particular choice is less inevitable and intellectually sound than he might like to claim. It is true, after all, that existentialism regards the passage of history as a succession of free choices, whereas Marxism interprets it as the necessary and inevitable unfolding of the dialectic. In the first case history is 'open', but in the second case it is 'closed'. Thus *l'homme révolté*, not *l'homme communiste*, comes nearest to the existentialist interpretation of reality. Given present communist theory and practice it is no answer for Sartre to say that Marx only ascribed a foreseeable end to 'prehistory' (i.e. history up to the establishment of the Marxist state) and not to history in the broadest sense. Nor is it an adequate reply, for the same reasons, to quote Marx as saying that history is simply man's pursuit of his own ends and to argue that to reject the Marxist interpretation of history is to turn one's back on oppressed and struggling humanity.

As one reads the various arguments put forward by both sides it becomes clear that the basis of the whole quarrel between Camus and Sartre is ultimately a philosophical one. This is true despite the repeated discussion of political efficacity. Sartre, refusing any prior human nature, sees man as the sum of his acts. Camus, although agreeing that man exists physically in history, believes him to be a creature of such a kind that he also transcends history by virtue of his participation in what might be called 'the human spirit'. This is why Sartre accuses Camus of vague and empty transcendentalism. Jeanson even goes so far as to say that Camus is much more preoccupied with God than with man. This last statement is patently untrue, but the fact remains that the close connection between revolt and the absurd, together with frequent use of the master/slave analogy, suggests that Camus' thought is continually tending in a transcendental rather than a historical direction. It would not be impossible for him to develop some kind of theism out of a re-examination of the absurd. His thought has a lot in common with that of Gabriel Marcel, for instance, despite the obvious political and religious differences. To pursue this point, however, would be to embark on vague speculation. For the present one can only say that Camus refuses to diagnose the human situation, and therefore to try to solve it, in purely political terms. He holds certain values to exist in the mind prior to their embodiment in temporal action. These values are logically prior as well as prior in time; otherwise, how could we judge historical acts to be good or bad? What Camus seems to have in mind is the fact that the actions of Hitler, for instance, can be judged only in a way that satisfies the human conscience by reference to criteria which are unaffected by considerations of time. He presents Sartre with another dilemma when he says:

If man has no purpose that can be treated as a mark of value, how can history have a meaning that is discernible here and now? If history has such a meaning, why does man not make that his purpose? And if he does so, why does he experience the terrible and unremitting freedom of which you speak? [4]

To these questions Sartre replies:

Man participates in history in order to pursue the eternal. He uncovers universal values in the concrete action which he performs with a specific purpose in view. [5]

This last statement seems a very reasonable one, but it also shows that Sartre has not escaped from the dilemma. In fact, his surprising use of the concepts 'the eternal' and 'universal values' suggests that he is unconsciously assuming something remarkably close to Camus' own position while rejecting the political inferences that Camus draws from it.

One's final impressions of this celebrated quarrel are bound, I think, to be confused. No clear line of action emerges from the arguments of either Camus or Sartre. Both speak, to a considerable extent, from inside a peculiarly French kind of intellectual vacuum. Camus lays bare inconsistencies between Sartre's philosophy and his political views, but Sartre in turn shows how real are the temptations of abstraction and political abstentionism in Camus' outlook. Many will think that Camus is profoundly right in feeling, however vaguely, that the most acute human problems are not political and cannot be solved by political action. (This, incidentally, is very much the view of Malraux also.) At the same time, however, one admires the restless desire of Sartre to improve the lot of men and women by direct action here and now. He gives an impression of political realism and practical common-sense that sometimes contrasts strongly with Camus' quixotism (for example, the latter's support in *Combat*, during 1948 and 1949, of Garry Davis and the 'world citizenship' movement). In the end, perhaps, Sartre is telling us what we could do, but we feel we ought not to do it in view of the form that Marxism has taken. Camus, for his part, is telling us what we ought to do, but we feel that our chances of being able to do it to any purpose hardly exist at present.

I have just said, for the second time in this chapter, that Camus' political ideas, though morally admirable, do not seem likely to be realized in our present world. In all fairness I have to add, however, that he himself has considered the charges of political unreality levelled against him and rejects them most strongly. He has also stated his increasing political optimism on several occasions and asserted that the hopes of progress, on the lines he advocates, have increased rather than diminished. The exposition and defence of these ideas may be found in various editorials, letters, speeches and articles collected in *Actuelles, chroniques 1944–1948* (published in 1950)* and *Actuelles II, chroniques 1948–1953* (published in 1953). The main positions adopted in these writings should therefore be examined before taking leave of Camus' political views.

A word should first be said about Camus' conception of his responsibilities as a writer. He recognizes a very general similarity of intention in both art and politics since each is, in its own way, an attempt to give coherence and form to the disorder of experience. But an important difference exists between them since political extremists, both left-wing and right-wing, want to impose an ideological totality of their own on the world whereas the writer of revolt seeks his unity by harmonizing elements already present in the world. The political conqueror works by force and hatred in the service of totality; the artist by comprehension and example in the service of unity. The artist remains a rebel against

---

* Not, in fact, called *Actuelles* I. Presumably Camus did not foresee *Actuelles II* in 1950.

the existing order of things. The politician becomes a tyrant on behalf of much more dogmatic pretensions. This political ambition of totality, aided by police and propaganda, means that the writer in his turn may become an object of pressure. Indeed he does so twice over—as a man and as an artist—and his very existence means some degree of involvement in politics. Seen against this background Camus' conception of 'commitment' is not that of existentialism. He makes the following distinction: '. . . it is not the [political] battle which makes artists of us, but art which forces us to enter the battle.' [6] The writer's main rôle is that of a witness to freedom. He is concerned above all with defending that human reality and individual uniqueness which are his normal preoccupations as an artist. The politician, on the contrary, is more taken up with abstract ideas and with large groups of people. In contrast to the politician, too, the writer is 'condemned', as Camus puts it, to try to understand those who differ from him or are his enemies. Above all, in a world where systematic killing is part of the established order the writer must bear witness to those qualities in the human spirit which cannot be killed. Yet his loyalty remains a divided one. He must serve suffering and humiliated humanity (i.e. write on social and political topics), but he must also serve beauty (i.e. not sacrifice art to political preaching and dogma). His attitude has thus not led Camus to complete and direct identification of literature and political activity. He regards them as being connected but also holds that they remain separate. It is this point of view, I think, which has given a high standard of literary excellence to Camus' political journalism and also resulted in many of his imaginative works having important social implications. His artistic sense does not allow him to be a practitioner of 'socialist realism', but he has never hesitated to express clear views on political issues. He has written on most of the controversies that have arisen in France since 1945: the post-Liberation 'purge'; Madagascar and the Raseta affair; the campaign against the E.L.A.S. in Greece; the communist 'coup' in Czechoslovakia; the case of the Rosenbergs; colonial wars in Indo-China and North Africa; the Henri Martin affair; the East Berlin rising etc. I do not propose to discuss Camus' detailed views on these and other questions, but it does seem worthwhile to look at the general attitude behind them. His articles have a recurring emphasis on such concepts as peace, freedom, truth, justice, and he defines these values by reference to specific events and situations such as those mentioned above.

Camus is very much concerned to avoid political dogmatism. He is conscious of living in an age of confusion—a confusion felt particularly strongly in France following the collapse of the Third Republic and the morals and politics which it represented. In the preface to *Actuelles II* he says that the articles contained in it offer neither a dogmatic message nor a formal moral system. They simply claim that it is possible, though exceedingly difficult, to introduce certain basic moral standards into political activity. What Camus chiefly offers, then, is a kind of pre-politics. He is attempting to reconstruct and test some political principles which will remain faithful to the left and to the revolutionary outlook while rejecting the excesses of the revolutionary ideal as perverted by contemporary communism. He claims not to minimize the difficulty of such an undertaking but insists that its absolute necessity should be obvious to us all since we live in the atomic age and under the shadow of possible self-destruction by the human race. The alternatives are a world of values or a world in ruins. We must now refashion our civilization, or perish. We live, according to Camus, in 'le siècle de la peur'. This fear is not only caused by the contemplation of atomic warfare. It arises also from the more general fact that the world seems to be controlled by blind forces which ignore the individual's will and are deaf to his supplication and his protests. We can no longer even be sure that we shall obtain humanitarian reactions from another human being if we speak the language of humanity to him. In the years since the first World War we have seen a frightening amount of duplicity, propaganda, violence, deportations, torture. Almost always these things have been carried out by people who would not listen to argument or be persuaded by appeals to their humanity because they were certain they were right. They were no longer real human beings at all but the dogmatic and dehumanized vehicles of an ideology. The dialogue, which Camus regards as the sign of political health and the essence of democracy, is being replaced more and more, even in the democracies, by silence until one is spoken to, and by the receiving or giving of orders and directives. We are told, he says, that we must not mention the purge of Russian intellectuals because this will assist the forces of reaction. But we are also told not to object to American aid to Franco because to do so would be to play into the hands of the communists. Thus the dialogue is suppressed from more than one direction, a conspiracy of silence is enjoined, and fear is the main instrument used. We live in a century of fear not only because atomic warfare is a possibility but because coercion has replaced persuasion, political expediency has ousted values, technical and ideological abstractions ignore the individual's instinct for freedom, happiness and justice.

Camus is therefore pleading for the application of morality to politics. As early as 1944 he admitted that such an enterprise might prove utopian—as it would seem to have done in the past even in the hands of such eloquent advocates as Tolstoy and Romain Rolland—but he claims that the only proper way to answer this question is to give morality a genuine trial. Political 'realism' has had its innings and the results are plain for all to see. It may turn out that there is no temporal salvation for humanity, but such a conclusion is not justified until the attempt has really been made to apply scrupulous moral principles in all political action. At the same time Camus is aware of the tendency of such a moral position to degenerate into moralism—the systematic attitude of the judge or the professor of morals. It is a short step from one attitude to the other. This danger is a temptation to which many moralists have succumbed but it must be avoided in an age already confused by an excess of dogma. It can be guarded against by the continual exercise of self-criticism and by a sense of relativity. Such relativity involves a tension not unlike the kind described earlier by Camus in connection with the absurd and with revolt. It must be built up on a combination of negation and affirmation which will hold a middle course between the rôles both of executioner and victim. Above all, the danger of a rigid and abstract moralism can be avoided by the unfailing embodiment of values in concrete realities. For example, the general basis of the moral approach to politics, as Camus defines it, is freedom for each and justice for all. This principle, however, is of little use in itself. Realizing this he says that the principle has to be defined with increasing precision by being put into practical effect. It begins as a very rough guide to behaviour only and a useful meaning gradually emerges as it is applied to political affairs. This is why he says of justice:

Justice is both a concept and a warmth of the soul. Let us ensure that we adopt it in its human aspect without transforming it into that terrible abstract passion which has mutilated so many men.[7]

The idea of freedom must similarly be given positive human meaning. Freedom has to do first and foremost with *free individuals*. An effective working relationship between justice and freedom will gradually be achieved by such practical application if it is guided by common sense and the realization that real values are defined in human terms and not against an absolute and abstract standard.

In the end Camus is simply asking for sensible and practical moderation in politics. This means that in some ways his attitude is much closer to the English political tradition than to the doctrinaire approach so widespread in France. Like many other counsels of moderation, however, it fails to please a great number of people of different shades of opinion. In France some of Camus' political opponents hold his attitude to be too lukewarm towards the enduring political myths which they still worship. He has been accused of betraying the political faith of the left, of making unacceptable concessions to the right and the left, of commending a spineless gradualism. This kind of criticism has led even his sympathizers to wonder whether his ideas have the remotest chance of genuine acceptance, given the doctrinaire and fragmentated nature of the French political parties. In some ways his views would make better sense in Britain but the emphases would still be rather peculiar because he is all the time assuming a bitter, doctrinaire atmosphere which scarcely exists, even potentially, on this side of the Channel.

Although he preaches moderation, Camus means moderation of a particular kind. He holds intellectual moderation and the avoidance of dogmatic extremism to be necessary for sound social theory and human happiness. But the mediterranean in Camus regards emotional moderation as a despicable attitude. He sees it as often resulting in a lukewarm approach towards suffering and injustice, and says: 'Our world has no need of lukewarm spirits. It needs ardent hearts that can place moderation in its proper perspective.'[8] At the same time, of course, intellectual moderation does not mean intellectual mediocrity. On the contrary, it is an attitude which only genuine intelligence can fully maintain. And so one finds Camus stressing more than once the need for high intellectual qualities in political life. He points out, for instance, that dictatorships instinctively attack intelligence and the genuine intellectual. He remembers that Vichy attributed the responsibility for defeat mainly to 'intellectualism'—'les paysans avaient trop lu Proust'. Intelligence must be defended and exercised in politics because it produces coherent thinking, a scale of values, balance and moderation in practical affairs. Indeed it is the main bulwark against dangerous instincts, insidious forms of propaganda and irrational excesses such as racialism and chauvinism. He realizes, of course, that a certain kind of intellectual subtlety, common enough in France and elsewhere, has its own peculiar dangers. He admits there is a type of intellectual who can be 'a potentially dangerous and treacherous animal'. But he is commending intelligence which recognizes duties as well as rights; an intelligence based on moral awareness and solid human experience. This has little or nothing to do with purely logical subtleties.

As the enemy of dogmatic extremism intelligence is also necessary as a force against the more childish and bigoted aspects of party strife. Like many reflective Frenchmen, Camus would possibly like a reduction in the number of political parties though he does not say so in either volume of *Actuelles*. What he certainly does want is an intelligent attitude that will distinguish between essential and inessential differences; an objectivity that will recognize those occasions when party intransigence should take second place to the well-being of the nation. Party government is an essential feature of democracy but democracy is betrayed by the worst kind of party government. The latter thrives too often on obstinate wrangling and underhand dealing with the result that the same problems repeatedly reach the same dead ends. In such circumstances independent voices, if they are raised at all, are drowned by the furious barking of the watchdogs of sectional interests. Genuine democracy presents a very different appearance: 'After all, the democrat is a person who admits that his opponent may be right. He therefore allows him to express his views and agrees to think about them.' [9] Camus also describes another quite different way in which intelligence may be fruitfully applied. He takes it as axiomatic that France can no longer be a great power in a politico-economic sense. In these circumstances intelligence, if it replaces emotional bombast, can save the country from costly and therefore weakening delusions of grandeur. In addition, intelligent democracy within her own national boundaries could make France an important moral influence in the world—and therefore a great power in another sense—by setting an example for international democracy to follow.

The general framework of Camus' political doctrine thus consists of intelligent moderation and an insistence on moral standards. Now such ideals would be considerably strengthened if they could be supported by honest and responsible political journalism. And so we find in *Actuelles* examples of this kind of journalism, as Camus conceives it, and also an account of the press it would serve. During his editorship of *Combat* Camus produced a daily paper that came commendably close to his ideal standards. In particular, the editorials which he himself wrote maintained a remarkably high level of intelligence, balance and positive moral commentary on the affairs of the day. It is worth pointing out, incidentally, that his 'ideal press' was not such a quixotic venture in 1944 when he first outlined its main features. The Liberation had given birth to a new press statute which made possible, at least for some years, the appearance of newspapers and periodicals that made their political comments quite independently of business and financial pressures. *Combat* itself ran into financial and political difficulties later, but even today it retains clear traces of its high beginnings. No doubt the most remarkable post-Liberation paper is the evening *Le Monde* which has preserved an admirable independence and perhaps is now the nearest approach to the ideals of serious, objective and independent comment envisaged by Camus.

Having briefly though trenchantly criticized the pre-war press which, he says, increased the power of some but lowered the morale of all, Camus insists on the need to free the French press from business and financial interests so that it may speak truthfully and independently. Having obtained such a press—and France seemed to have done so immediately after the Liberation—the important point is to conserve its character and use it properly. It can only be used properly if it is guided by a profound sense of responsibility. This sense of responsibility was an integral part of clandestine journalism during the Occupation when an article could mean prison or death for its author. Such concern with what is said and the way it is said must be an active force in peacetime journalism also. Words should be carefully weighed and responsibly used. The old tricks and clichés of pre-war journalism can no longer be accepted. The watchwords of the new press should be vigour, objectivity, humanity, not rhetoric, hatred and mediocrity. Only in this way can the press, as the nation's voice, speak worthily on the nation's behalf. Camus also makes the familiar distinction between news and comment in journalism. Both aspects have an important part to play and both can be improved. As regards news items he would like to see journalists not only indicate the agency from which they have come but add informed comments on the likely reliability of the agency in question. In certain cases too it might be useful and salutary, for the public, to print conflicting pieces of allegedly factual news in adjoining columns. He wants, in fact, what he calls 'un journalisme critique'. Where comment on the news is concerned this should be most carefully and clearly written avoiding in particular the facile use of empty abstractions and catch-phrases designed simply to arouse unthinking emotional responses in the readers. In this way the press will have some chance of preserving that scrupulousness which should be a dominant feature of all journalism.

I have spoken of Camus' moral approach to politics and of the reformed press in which he hoped to give this approach regular expression. I now want to end the present chapter by describing three particularly characteristic attitudes he was led to adopt in consequence. These may briefly be described as internationalism; the rejection of all forms of racialism; continuing opposition to the Franco régime in Spain. Without making a completely unreal distinction between national and international politics Camus puts repeated emphasis on the need for parliamentary and economic internationalism as the only alternative to the most dangerous kind of power politics. In addition, the changed conditions of our modern world make it a necessity. From the point of view of travel and technological development we live in one world and this world is constantly growing smaller:

Today we know that there are no more islands and that frontiers are useless. We know that in a world of increasing speed in which the Atlantic is crossed in less than a day, in which Moscow speaks to Washington within a few hours, we are forced to adopt solidarity or collusion, depending on the circumstances.[10]

A similar situation exists in the sphere of economics:

> . . . no economic problem, however secondary it may appear to be, can be solved today outside the framework of international co-operation. Europe's bread is in Buenos-Ayres and Siberia's machine-tools are manufactured in Detroit. Today tragedy is collective.[11]

The speed of communications, the consequent 'shrinking' of the world, the economic interrelation of the most distant countries and, one might add, the rapid increase in the power and range of weapons of destruction, mean that the problems of peace and of political thought as a whole can no longer be purely national, continental, even western or eastern. They must be universal. Material circumstances alone make world unity in some sense inevitable sooner or later, and this unification can only come about in one of two ways. The first way is complete world domination either by the U.S.A. or the U.S.S.R. Camus says that such a prospect naturally dismays him both as a Frenchman and as a mediterranean though he is prepared to dismiss this objection, with a touch of irony, as being a sentimental one. The real objection is that this kind of unification, by either great power, could only be brought about by another war, or at best the extreme risk of war. Even if world hegemony were not obtained by atomic warfare—Camus believes that this is precisely the way it would be achieved—another war of any kind would leave the human race so mutilated and impoverished that the idea of a subsequent world 'order' makes no sense. And the speed at which new and more powerful weapons of destruction are perfected means that a war in which they were used would destroy the possibility of the 'victors', from whichever side they came, enjoying the so-called fruits of war. With such a prospect before us the second method of world unification is the only one that can be contemplated without dismay and despair. This is of course the peaceful method of agreement on basic issues between all different groups. It is what Camus calls 'la démocratie internationale'. His plea for parliamentary internationalism reaches its culminating point when he writes:

> What is national or international democracy? It is a form of society in which those that govern are subject to law, a law that expresses the will of all and is represented by a legislative body. Is the attempt being

made today to bring about this state of affairs? It is true that an international law is in process of elaboration. But this law is made and unmade by governments, that is to say, by the executive body. We therefore experience the rule of international dictatorship. The only way of escaping from this situation is to place the international law above all governments. This means making the law, having a parliament, creating this parliament by means of world-wide elections in which all peoples will take part. And since we do not possess such a parliament the only course open to us is to resist international dictatorship on an international level using means that will not conflict with the end which we pursue.[12]

What we must realize at once, according to Camus, is the fact that political thinking is being more and more quickly outdistanced and made obsolete by events. Practically speaking, he says, international political practice today is an attempt to legislate for the world of the future by using outdated eighteenth- and nineteenth-century concepts connected with the beginnings of modern industrialism and scientific evolutionary optimism. Other sciences are rapidly growing and developing but the science of international relations is practically static. There is a lack of any real correspondence between our international political behaviour and present historical realities. In politics at least we forget that in the last fifty years things have changed more radically than in the 200 years preceding this period. Statesmen shortsightedly continue to argue over lines of political demarcation. They disagree about frontiers in a world where frontiers have become an unreality. For many Europeans the German problem looms large, yet Camus asserts that it has already become secondary. Even the U.S.A./U.S.S.R. argument and the problem of peaceful co-existence are in process of becoming secondary. Within the next fifty years erstwhile colonial countries in Africa and Asia will grow so powerful that the whole of Western civilization, capitalist and communist, will be called in question. The immediate need is to prepare for this situation now by creating a world parliament which will not simply be a remote collection of ministers but a collection of genuine representatives of all peoples and their peaceful wishes. And international democracy of this kind will have to be economic as well as parliamentary. The major means of production, oil, uranium, coal, must be internationalized so that they belong to no individual country or group while being indispensable to all countries.

In these various schemes for internationalism Camus is aware that the charge of utopianism will be made against him. Indeed, much as one may agree ideally with his solutions it is extremely difficult to see how they could be given practical effect under present conditions. At the very least the difficulties are enormous. Camus' answer to this reaction is twofold. True liberals throughout the world must give these ideas a real chance, he says, by combining together to defend and further them. Those who are still sceptical must be made to realize that the alternatives before them are 'utopianism' or war. The world's statesmen have to choose between anachronistic thought and relatively utopian thought. The former, which is what they have chosen so far, bids fair to destroy us. Only the latter offers any real hope of salvation and has yet to be given a serious trial. Thus Camus goes on to argue also that the true 'realists' are those who are prepared in this way to defend forthwith the ideals of international toleration and persuasion against the present methods of violence and domination. They are genuine realists if they work actively for the international idea in education, in the press and in public opinion. Above all they are genuine realists because they take into account the future as well as the present and seek the maximum benefit from the minimum sacrifice.

It seems logical that as well as being a passionate internationalist Camus should also be a determined opponent of all forms of racial discrimination. This is the second of his political attitudes to which I referred and it can be dealt with quite briefly. In a *Combat* editorial of May 1947 he drew attention to various instances of renewed racial prejudice in France itself. He mentioned particularly the assumption by certain sections in France of innate superiority over coloured colonials and also criticized signs of anti-semitism. Shortly afterwards he wrote eloquently about the plight of Jewish refugees from Europe attempting to emigrate to Palestine. His preface to Jacques Méry's *Laissez passer mon peuple* is a bitter indictment of the general indifference or hypocrisy shown by France, the U.S.A. and the U.S.S.R. towards this problem. He claims that those who suffer or have suffered persecution in the world are so embarrassingly large in numbers that the big nations either salve their consciences by pretending to be ignorant of the facts or exploit the sufferings of the Jews and use them as another stick with which to beat their political opponents. Mention should also be made of a letter written by Camus to *Le Monde* in July 1953 in which he severely stigmatized the racialism behind the shooting down of North Africans by the police in Paris. In all these cases he shows a fine humanity and a capacity for writing in angry and stinging terms. Racialism is something to which he reacts very strongly and he insists that his reaction is not a sentimental one:

. . . there is no question here of pleading on behalf of a ridiculous sentimentalism which seeks to mix up all races in one tender-hearted confusion. It is true that all men are not alike; I am well aware of the deep differences in tradition between myself and an African or a Mohammedan. But I am also well aware of what binds me to them— something in each of them which I cannot despise without degrading myself.[13]

Mention must finally be made, briefly again, of Camus' articles and speeches attacking the Franco dictatorship in Spain. He feels very strongly on this subject and regards the increasing friendship shown by the West to Franco as a denial of the conception of morality in politics. One of his plays, *L'État de siège*, is set in Spain and as we shall see later it contains, among other things, a severe attack on political dictatorship. In a review of the play in 1948 Gabriel Marcel objected to the choice of Spain and received a reply from Camus which makes three main points. Having recalled that he has already spoken as clearly as possible against Russian slave camps and Stalinist dictatorship he insists that the particular circumstances described in *L'État de siège* have a much more general application. He is attacking dictatorship as such, whether it is to be found in Spain, the U.S.S.R., Germany or elsewhere. In reply to Marcel's objection to his choosing Spain rather than any other country he speaks of his concern that the iniquities of the Spanish dictatorship should not be conveniently forgotten in the interests of anti-communism. He considers it immoral and inexcusable to condone or minimize tyranny in the West because it exists on a much larger scale in the East: '. . . you are prepared to keep silent about one case of terror in order to fight another more effectively. There are some of us who are not prepared to pass anything over in silence.' [14] He had one further reason for placing the action of *L'État de siège* in Spain. He did so as an act of dissociation from the behaviour of Vichy, which handed over various republican exiles to Franco on Hitler's orders and thereby sent them to their death.

Camus' most detailed attack against the Franco régime is contained in a speech which he delivered at the Salle Wagram in November 1952. The occasion was the admission of Spain to UNESCO and the speech contains scathing attacks both on the Spanish dictatorship and the attitude of the Pinay administration towards it. More particularly he examines three different arguments commonly used to justify 'acceptance' of Franco. It is widely claimed, for example, that the principle of non-intervention in the internal affairs of other countries means that what happens in Spain is the sole business of the Spaniards themselves and obliges us to recognize and accept their government. Much could be said, of course, about the illogical way in which this principle is operated so that it is applied to some countries and ignored in the case of others. Camus is content to remind his audience that Spain is ruled by a dictator using the familiar instruments of a state police, the execution or imprisonment without trial of political opponents, etc. Therefore, he argues, to accept the dictator as an educator and to strengthen his international standing is not non-intervention but very definite intervention *against* his victims.

A second argument used to justify Franco's admission to UNESCO is the fact that he is uncompromisingly anti-communist. Apart from contradicting the first principle of non-intervention this kind of reasoning is dangerous since to accept such an ally weakens the democratic pretensions of the non-communist world and strengthens communist propaganda. It could well increase the number of communist sympathizers in countries like France and Italy where the party is influential. Connected with this argument there is a third which emphasizes the strategic importance of Spain. Although confessing himself 'un éternel débutant' in matters of military strategy, Camus returns to the previous argument that co-operation with Franco, whether military, economic or cultural, could easily lead to an increase of communist strength elsewhere. In such circumstances the strategic gain of Spanish bases would be offset by democratic set-backs in other parts of Europe and the possibility of war might even be increased. He sums up by describing the admission of Spain to UNESCO as the cultural façade behind which a sordid military and political deal has been carried out. He adds:

But even as a deal it cannot be justified. It may finally bring more wealth to some market-gardeners, but far from serving any country or any cause it merely does a disservice to those few reasons which the people of Europe still have for continuing the struggle.[15]

There is no need, I think, to sum up comprehensively Camus' political ideas, but two or three points can briefly be made. His comments on political affairs show a mixture of what is perhaps extreme pessimism and extreme optimism. This extremism, if such it be, arises from the two lone alternatives with which he faces us. He is a pessimist because of the apocalyptic vision of mass suicide which he sees at the end of the political road on which we are at present travelling. He is an optimist because of his belief that another road is open to us. But if these are the only alternatives, and if this second road is as he describes it, I think many will feel that the nature of his optimism ultimately serves only to intensify the pessimistic analysis accompanying it. On the other hand, his untiring defence of certain moral principles in politics makes Camus the conscience of his times. In so far as democracy must keep its conscience alert and active if it is to retain its true character Camus has performed an essential if thankless task. Above all he is an exemplary figure in the sense that his political journalism has given expression to the aspirations and fears of thousands of ordinary men and women. He has proved to be their spokesman and their champion and has lived his own life in strict conformity with the high ideals he defends.

Conclusion

Part Three

REVOLT AND LITERATURE

7 THE ART OF THE NOVEL (I)

> *Le roman moderne est, à mes yeux, un moyen d'expression privilégié du tragique de l'homme, non une élucidation de l'individu.*
>
> ANDRÉ MALRAUX

I have been careful so far not to use the content of Camus' novels and plays for the purpose of illustrating his philosophical and political views. Several considerations oblige one to disregard his imaginative writings in this way when dealing directly with his ideas. There is the simple and obvious fact, for instance, that a novelist often attributes to one or other of his characters statements about life with which he himself is not in agreement but which can be expected from the lips of a particular character which he has created. It may even be that the novelist does not identify himself with any single character at all, or share the viewpoint of the book as a whole. In such circumstances the task of deciding which views expressed in an imaginative work are those of its author will often be an impossible undertaking and always a hazardous one. No doubt complete and utter objectivity is impossible for a novelist, but it is equally true that much critical comment on novels assumes too readily a transparent subjectivity on the writer's part. As far as Camus is concerned he makes it clear that his own ideal is objectivity in imaginative writing. In the course of some complaints about his public status as a pessimistic prophet of the absurd he describes as a puerile legacy of Romanticism the belief that a writer must portray himself and embody his private convictions in a work of art. He *may* do so, but Camus contends that he may equally well be primarily interested in other people, in his own age or in certain familiar myths.*

A further reason for disregarding Camus' imaginative writings

---

* See *L'Été*, pp. 131-3. In an ironical passage Camus says that, as far as he knows, Sophocles did not murder his father or dishonour his mother although he wrote about such crimes.

when dealing primarily with his ideas lies in the fact that he has written separate books and essays in which he specifically sets out his views on various philosophical and political questions. At the same time it must be admitted that his imaginative and discursive works often show a good deal of surface similarity, and this is presumably why he has been treated as a subjective novelist. His first novel, *L'Étranger*, and his essay on the absurd, *Le Mythe de Sisyphe*, appeared within a few months of one another, and it was soon clear that the novel could be interpreted as the application to an imaginary individual of the ideas expounded in the essay. Most critics said, in effect, that the novel embodied the *experience* of the absurd while the essay provided its *rationale*. One can easily see the reason for this kind of statement, yet as a critical approach to *L'Étranger* it remains an incomplete account both of the novel and of the relationship between it and the essay. In fact, the point of critical interest lies not in the similarities between these two books but in their differences. For example, *Le Mythe de Sisyphe* attempts to be a rational and systematic exposition of the absurd whereas Meursault, the main character in *L'Étranger*, lacks any real system in his ideas and actions. If his experience is too closely related to the arguments of the essay he is consequently endowed with a self-awareness, or at least a coherence, which are completely alien to the whole essence of the novel. *Le Mythe de Sisyphe* can too easily deprive Meursault of that uncomplicated spontaneity which Camus is anxious to create and preserve in the novel. There is also another, and more important, difference between the two books. *L'Étranger* is primarily a novel, a work of art. It is not simply the statement of a philosophical viewpoint in the way that *Le Mythe de Sisyphe* is. Thus too-frequent reference to *Le Mythe de Sisyphe* will put too much emphasis on the content of *L'Étranger*, just as using *L'Étranger* as an appendix to *Le Mythe de Sisyphe* will be to interpret the novel as a philosophical statement of equal reliability. In either case the literary quality of the novel, its prime existence as a work of art, will tend to be forgotten. Now this existence of the novel as a work of art is of great importance to Camus himself. It is quite clear that a discussion of the ideas in his novels, or an examination of his characters as though they were new neighbours, is an inadequate response to his conception of fiction. This kind of approach must have some value, of course, but Camus insists on a basic concern with the way in which a novel organizes and shapes experience. The novel, in his view, poses certain aesthetic questions first of all.*

Before coming more directly to Camus' theory and practice of fiction it is necessary to pay some attention to his interpretation of art in general. An early exposition of his aesthetic ideas is contained in *Le Mythe de Sisyphe* where art is placed in the context of the absurd and the artist is described as '[le] plus absurde des personnages'. We have already seen that one of the chief features of the absurdist outlook is its realization that intellectual explanations of the world are vain. *L'homme absurde* is sealed off from transcendence and rooted in the world of immediate appearances. Now this, according to Camus, is the world of particularity in which the artist also must work. This is the source from which he takes the materials of his art. Thus the outlook and activity of the artist, in their basic forms, direct attention to the fact of the absurd. The artist joins Don Juan as an exemplar of absurdism. It is clear, at the same time, that Camus does not romanticize art as an escape from the absurd. He sees it rather as being, in its own way, a conscious or unconscious acceptance of the evidence by which *l'homme absurde* is faced. The work of art is situated at a point where the desire for transcendence and the impossibility of transcendence conflict—'elle marque le point d'où les passions absurdes s'élancent, et où le raisonnement s'arrête' (*Le Mythe de Sisyphe*, p. 132). Art, for Camus, is imaginative confirmation of the absurd.

Confirmation of the absurd, when experienced in this way, eventually leads to a measure of renunciation. It is when the mind recognizes its inability to find a logical pattern in the world that it renounces this approach to reality and explores the possibilities of imaginative transformation. The work of art arises from an act of renunciation dictated by confirmation of the absurd. Camus says that it arises from the inability of the intellect to make adequate sense of the world it finds. The work of art, as we shall see shortly, embodies the ambition to achieve an imaginative re-creation of experience and attempts to go beyond a mere intellectual duplication of it.

According to Camus, therefore, artistic creation is an activity

---

* See particularly Camus' article, 'L'Intelligence et l'échafaud', collected in *Problèmes du roman* (ed. J. Prévost), Lyon, Éditions Confluences, 1943, p. 218.

which confirms the fact of absurdism and thereby renounces the attempt to find order and coherence in the world as directly experienced by *l'homme absurde*. The view of art set out in this way in *Le Mythe de Sisyphe* shows several similarities to Malraux's aesthetics. This influence of Malraux, which Camus himself has admitted in general terms, is even more noticeable when he goes on (mainly in *L'Homme révolté*) to analyse the impulses governing artistic creation. If the nature of artistic creation involves confirmation of the absurd and renunciation of the logical interpretation of reality, the human impulses behind it are the need to revolt against the given world and the desire to replace it by some better alternative. Confirmation and renunciation ultimately lead to revolt and replacement.

Confirmation of the absurd relates the artist's activity to the world of physical appearances. Yet, although such a world is the artist's particular sphere, renunciation of a logical interpretation of reality shows that he is related to it in a negative way. In one sense the artist must accept the world of appearances as the only certain reality, yet in another sense he rejects it as unsatisfactory and inadequate to his desires and ideals. This appears to be Camus' meaning when he says that art extols and denies at one and the same time.* Thus art must have its roots in the world of sense, but it expresses itself actively as a rejection of its own natural element. This recalls Malraux's description of art as a 'permanent accusation' of the world—a rebellion against the limitations of physical existence and the fact of death. Such rebellion cannot destroy the world it is seeking to reject, but it can at least create a world of forms and ideas that corresponds more closely to its own aspirations. One of the mysteries and triumphs of art is its rôle in enabling the eternal human prisoner to create, from the conditions of his imprisonment, the image of a free life that he has never known. Camus therefore regards art not only as an aspect of revolt but as the creation of a universe of replacement. It gives positive substance to revolt against the absurd. Camus goes on to assert that art transforms the world, but this is little more than a romantic, and loose, use of words. All he can really claim is that the work of art, without altering the world itself, offers an imaginative

---

* See *L'Homme révolté*, p. 313: 'L'art aussi est ce mouvement qui exalte et nie en même temps'.

alternative to it. This alternative is conceived, of course, as an improvement. Camus quotes Van Gogh's remark that God should not be judged by this world which is one of his unsuccessful sketches. Every artist, Camus adds, seeks to improve the sketch and give it a style which it lacks. Thus the greatest artists do not merely transcribe the world in their works; they indulge in what Stanislas Fumet called 'culpable rivalry' with God. This doctrine of replacement and rivalry also reminds one of Malraux. In particular, it recalls his remark that the acanthus possesses the shape that man would have given to the artichoke if God had asked his advice.

When Camus turns from art in general to the novel in particular we find him making the same main points. He regards the ideal novel as one which confirms the fact of the absurd while also embodying revolt against it. The relation of the novel to the doctrine of revolt is stressed several times, as when he writes: 'The novel is born at the same time as the spirit of revolt and reflects, on the artistic level, the same aim.' [1] Here Camus means not only that the novel represents, intellectually, a form of revolt, but that the growth of the novel corresponds, historically, to the beginnings of modern metaphysical revolt described in *L'Homme révolté*. A few pages after the quotation above he returns to the idea of replacement by speaking of the novel as an attempt to 'correct' the world so that it may conform more closely to man's deepest desires. The 'universe of replacement' represented by fiction must still be composed of materials found in the world itself, but the novelist is free to decide which materials he will choose. In fact all art, however realistic or naturalistic, involves choice; the novelist is at one with other artists in being able to accept some materials, to reject others, and to rearrange them so that they compose a new imaginative pattern. In this way form and style assume fundamental importance in the novel—hence Camus' statement that the novel poses aesthetic questions first of all.

In view of Camus' reasoning it now becomes clear that this remark of his does not imply an artificial distinction between form and content. In fact he deliberately relates form to content. He insists several times on the obvious point that the writing of a novel always necessitates selection. Complete realism is impossible because it would entail infinite enumeration. To write at all is to choose, and from this act of choice form and style first arise. The style of a novel, as Camus understands the term, is thus not simply formal excellence; it is an artistic ordering of the disorder of experience requiring intelligence and depth of character as well as technical dexterity. The type of novel that Camus most admires—the classical novel of Mme de Lafayette, Constant, Stendhal and Proust—is not, despite Stendhal's own phrase, a mirror held up to life. It is instead a *redistribution* of certain elements found in experience. Novels in the dominant French tradition are what Camus calls 'schools of life' precisely because they were first conceived as 'schools of art'. The attempt to 'correct' the world by words and by a redistribution of elements taken from reality is, for Camus, style in a novel. It emerges from the encounter between the mind and experience. Its main effect is to create a new and reorganized unity. Style in this sense thus becomes another sign of authentic revolt. Camus writes:

> If the stylization is exaggerated and obvious the work is pure nostalgia: the unity which it seeks to achieve has no basis in physical existence. On the other hand, if reality is transmitted in its raw state and stylization is almost nil, physical existence is presented without unity. Great art, style, the authentic features of revolt, lie somewhere between these two heresies.[2]

This conception of style casts some more light on a matter mentioned earlier—the difference between Camus' novels and his discursive essays. These essays analyse human experience of the world and try to show its true nature; the novels select more rigorously from human experience of the world and try to give it an ideal nature. The stylization resulting in the latter case means that the novels differ profoundly from the essays and must be discussed in quite different terms.

This theory of fiction, with its emphasis on style, means that Camus differs from many of his French contemporaries because he writes novels which attempt to embody revolt while continuing to employ the traditional resources of art. Unlike Camus, most novelists of metaphysical and moral revolt have tended increasingly in recent years to reject accepted aesthetic standards in fiction. In France, indeed, a so-called 'anti-literature' has gradually come to the forefront both in poetry (the 'a-poème') and in the work of such novelists as Blanchot, Robbe-Grillet and Nathalie Sarraute. These writers would be worthy contestants for that *prix de l'anti-littérature* which, significantly enough, was established in Paris a couple of years ago. There is no doubt that Camus' own concern with the fact of the absurd and the need for revolt has caused him to write at least one novel—*L'Étranger*—which resembles the fiction of the anti-literature type. Indeed we shall shortly see that *L'Étranger* is virtually an 'anti-novel'. Nevertheless, the chief impression given by Camus, particularly in his incidental comments on the art of fiction, is that he is trying to escape from this situation and to bring about some kind of reconciliation between the non-artistic implications of absurdism and the artistic aspirations of revolt. Behind his novels there remains a general conflict between the nihilistic statement in *Le Mythe de Sisyphe:* 'It makes no difference whether one creates (artistically) or not',[3] and the positive claim made in *L'Homme révolté:* 'Destiny is made to measure by the novel. Thus the novel competes with the creation and gains a temporary victory over death'.[4] The three novels Camus has so far written might be interpreted as progressive stages in the attempt to give the novel the effective status suggested in the second of these two quotations. His novels also show, I think, an increasingly successful effort to avoid the impasse of anti-literature. I am not necessarily claiming that *L'Étranger, La Peste* and *La Chute* are on a rising scale of literary excellence. It does seem true, however, that each represents a further step forward in Camus' attempt to overcome the aesthetic intransigence of his philosophical ideas and to produce a novel coming close to the artistic ideals of the best French novelists of the eighteenth and nineteenth centuries.

One of the features which Camus disapproves of most in contemporary fiction, and which he tries to combat in his own novels, is the lack of fully dimensional characters. He finds among many of his contemporaries in France the attempt to portray man in such general, philosophical terms that the characters in their books lose all individuality and human particularity. In his introductory essay to the Pléiade edition of Roger Martin du Gard's works he complains that the secret of portraiture in depth has practically been lost. He holds the combined influence of Kafka and the American 'behaviourist' novel to be responsible for this situation in France. He adds that the difference between the characters of the older and newer fiction is rather like the difference between characters on the stage and cinematographic figures. There may be more general animation in some contemporary novels, but there is less human substance and flesh.

The increasingly direct metaphysical aspirations of modern French novelists are no doubt mainly responsible for this situation. Their concern to express truths about 'the human condition' has often produced mere ciphers and encouraged a turning away from the creation of convincing individuals. Many people would argue that this is inevitable and that metaphysics and fiction do not mix. An automatic distinction is often made between the abstraction of philosophy and the concreteness of art. Camus, however, refuses to accept this view. He sees quite clearly, of course, that philosophy and art have not been satisfactorily combined by many fellow novelists, yet he believes himself that they can and should be harmonized.

According to Camus the traditional opposition between art and philosophy is an arbitrary one. It is true, he says, that each activity possesses its own particular climate, but this type of statement merely emphasizes the obvious fact that art is not philosophy and philosophy is not art. Clearly they do not coincide, but there can exist an interpenetration between them and both embody, at the present time, a common disquiet and similar anxieties. One may point out here that since the early novels of Malraux there has been a noticeable *rapprochement* in France between metaphysics and fiction. The most influential writing during the last twenty years or so has produced a predominantly philosophical literature, and the reason appears to be twofold. In the first place the existentialists, and also certain individual writers like Camus, emphasize the concrete and individual nature of what they consider to be sound philosophical thinking. They avoid timeless generalities and look for truth in immediate human experience. Most of them have in common a desire to divert philosophy from abstract intellection towards concrete and particular description. As a result literature, particularly the novel, becomes a natural and appropriate vehicle for the expression of such philosophical bias. Art moves most readily in the sphere of immediate particularity, and immediate particularity is the chosen field of much contemporary philosophical reflection.

Albert Camus

There is a second reason for the close identification of philosophy and literature in recent French writing. The ideas of writers such as Malraux and Camus, with their insistence on the absurd and the need to revolt, have produced philosophies of drama and tension. Similar results have followed from the existentialist emphasis on freedom and choice. Now the individual conflict which these philosophies exhibit can only be adequately conveyed by demonstration, not intellectual discourse. Once more, therefore, literature in general and the theatre in particular serve this purpose admirably. One finds, in fact, that all these writers frequently put their philosophy on the stage or in novels. They are philosopher-dramatists and philosopher-novelists who set in motion situations which are available to direct personal experience but which, by the same token, cannot be adequately conveyed or discussed in the language of 'pure' philosophy. Such abstract and analytical discussion would entail a confidence in logical generalities which the nature of the absurd, as variously interpreted by Malraux, Camus or Sartre, denies. It is from this point of view that Camus comes very close to self-contradiction by writing his essay on the absurd. His novels and plays on aspects of the absurd are more consistent with his metaphysics. It might even be argued, as Simone de Beauvoir has done briefly in the case of Kafka,* that in view of Camus' ideas the novel and the drama are his only really satisfactory means of expression.

These last points concerning the relationship between literature and philosophy in Camus' novels severely inhibit a certain kind of literary criticism. Given the sense in which I have claimed his fiction to be a specially apt vehicle for his ideas, a critical discussion of these ideas will tend to undo the work of the novels while adding nothing new to them. Except where some elucidation of the ideas seems essential, I therefore propose to examine primarily the technical achievement of the three novels. The attempt to see how Camus has created imaginative literature out of the ideas already discussed in connection with his essays will be in keeping with his own dictum that a novel should mainly give rise to artistic considerations on the critic's part.

* See Simone de Beauvoir, *L'Existentialisme et la sagesse des nations,* Paris, Nagel, 1948, p. 118.

Apart from this peculiarly inviolate status of the ideas in Camus' novels it may even be argued, in the particular case of *L'Étranger*, that to summarize its story would be to do violence to its nature. A summary that is regarded as satisfactory is likely to give an air of coherence to the events with which it deals. In *L'Étranger*, however, Camus is at pains to show the incoherence of experience. He uses various devices to emphasize the discontinuity forming part of the absurd. Too neat a summary would therefore destroy one of the main purposes of the book. Perhaps the most one should say about the subject-matter of this novel is that it purports to be narrated by an Algerian clerk, Meursault, who fails to be grief-stricken by his mother's death, who shoots an Arab without really understanding why, and who is condemned to death by a court of law. During these events Meursault never says more than he really feels. This honesty about his own feelings makes him an *étranger*, an outsider, where society is concerned; the nature of the feelings themselves shows him to be a metaphysical outsider also.

L'Étranger contains, of course, many ideas and attitudes referred to in *Le Mythe de Sisyphe*. What makes it a work of art, however, and sharply differentiates it from the essay, is the remarkable congruity between the view of life that it implies and the embodi-ment of this view of life in literary terms. In order to achieve this congruity Camus uses several technical devices which raise his subject-matter from the straightforward content of the essay to the artistically wrought content of the novel. These devices are used in connection with the narrative viewpoint, the vocabulary, the treatment of time and the tense employed. An examination of each of these matters in turn, in the light of Camus' ideas, will enable us to demonstrate more clearly the striking unity of content and form in this novel.

L'Étranger is written in the first person: the narrative view-point is an individual and subjective one. Traditionally, the first-person narrator in fiction has possessed a high degree of self-knowledge and has enjoyed a privileged insight into the thoughts and motives of his fellow-characters. His task has normally been to enlighten the reader and guide him towards a full understanding of those events and experiences which make up the story. In fact the first-person narrator has possessed virtual omniscience, being the mouthpiece of a novelist who accepted as axiomatic his own ability to understand and interpret aright the data of experience. The omniscient narrator argued, in short, a coherent and comprehensible universe. Immediately one begins to read *L'Étranger*, however, one is struck by the fact that the narrator, who is also the main character, appears peculiarly ill-equipped, by traditional standards, for his task. His intellectual powers are unimpressive, his psychological insight is almost non-existent, and in general he appears bemused by experience. He also lacks an accepted ethical sense and generally displays moral indifference. In other words, Meursault is the direct opposite of his counterpart in nineteenth-century fiction. Whereas the latter was confident of his ability to understand what he saw and attempted to describe, Meursault makes frequent reference to his own inadequacy, his failure to understand, his apparently genuine ethical indifference. The novel begins, for instance, on a note of moral unconcern and emotional deficiency:

Mother died today. Or perhaps it was yesterday; I'm not sure. I received a wire from the home: 'Mother dead. Funeral tomorrow. Sincere good wishes'. That doesn't mean anything. Perhaps it was yesterday.[5]

In a similar way there are frequent references to Meursault's inattention towards events around him and his inability to grasp their significance. He describes himself on different occasions as being confused, and unable to concentrate or think or understand. Thus it is that in *L'Étranger* the meaningful world of the first-person narrator, which was at one time accepted without question, is replaced by a world of incoherence, a world where rational analysis has little scope and where moral purposes and responses are conspicuously absent. In this way Camus gives force and in-dividuality to his novel by the unusual method of adopting Meursault's uncomprehending and disjointed narrative viewpoint. By the same means he conveys a direct impression of how the absurd may be experienced. Meursault, by telling his own story in his own way, exemplifies the relationship which gives rise to the absurd and which Camus calls, in *Le Mythe de Sisyphe*, 'the disunity between man and his life, between the actor and his backcloth . . .'[6]

There are some other ways in which the narrative viewpoint here is particularly appropriate to the subject-matter. I think it is clear, for instance, that Meursault's attitude would be much less acceptable if we saw it from the outside only. Society, with which he himself cannot make adequate intellectual or emotional contact, condemns him through lack of understanding. If the reader were also to see him primarily through society's eyes the point and impact of the novel would be largely lost. By seeing experience as it presents itself to Meursault we are helped to understand better what would otherwise be a much more disconcerting and perplexing attitude to life. The fact that Meursault remains outside society makes it necessary for Camus to take his readers right inside his hero. By using the first-person narrative Camus thus ensures that the absurdist attitude will at least be more understandable, if not finally acceptable, to the greatest possible number of readers. We are more likely to be convinced by direct contact with Meursault's reactions than by the author's second-hand account of them.

A second and related point arises here. In *L'Étranger*, in contrast to *Le Mythe de Sisyphe*, Camus is concerned to convey the experience of absurdism rather than to expound it rationally. He is writing a work of art, not a treatise. No doubt a treatise would necessitate some explanation of the fact, for example, that life can only appear absurd by reference to an implied rational standard, and attributing an origin to such a standard could lead one into many difficulties. In a novel, however, this point need not, and perhaps should not, arise. The first-person narrative is the ideal vehicle for conveying an experience like this which hinges on the failure to explain. Meursault's experience, by its nature and by his nature, precludes explanation. Now it is important that this impossibility of explanation should not appear to reside in an omniscient third-person narrator, much less in the novelist himself. It must be the distinguishing feature of a character within the novel's own world, and this character must speak directly, in his own person, to the reader. Camus manages to do this by using as his narrator a person who is also the central character of the novel and whose own telling of his story shows that, although his senses are finely receptive to experience, his mind gives it no meaning.

One more point connected with the narrative viewpoint seems worth making. By using Meursault to tell his own story Camus exploits fully the psychological unconventionality of *L'Étranger*. In his way he gives it a particular kind of exoticism. The exotic element in this novel, despite its North African setting, consists much less in its geographical location than in its psychological singularity. The first-person narrative naturally increases the impact of this exoticism on the reader. More important, however, is the fact that it conveys a necessary sense of authentic, personal human experience existing at the very centre of psychological singularity. In this way the first-person narrative ensures both the fact of psychological exoticism and its acceptance by the reader. It enhances the whole novel by making its theme less abstract, and more convincing in purely human terms.

Turning from the narrative viewpoint of *L'Étranger* to its vocabulary we find that this latter is severely restricted and remarkably concrete. All the critics have pointed this out and vary only in the words they use to describe it: 'style sobre', 'style dépouillé', 'grisaille étonnante', 'écriture blanche', etc. Before commenting further on the vocabulary a preliminary point should be made which links it to the preceding discussion of the narrative viewpoint. The impact of the novel is partly due, in fact, to the combined effect of choosing the first-person narrative and using a non-analytical vocabulary. The first-person narrative, particularly within the tradition of the French *roman personnel*, is associated with subtle and searching introspection. In *L'Étranger*, however, Camus uses a vocabulary that is continually and uncompromisingly objective. An unusual discordance results between language and narrative method, and Camus uses this discordance in order to sharpen our sense of the incoherence lying at the heart of Meursault's experience. This is one more example of the way in which the novelist uses a technical device in order to emphasize the point of his novel without resorting to direct comment. The first-person narrative gives an impression of authentic directness. The severely restricted vocabulary prevents analytical complication. And by bringing authentic directness and lack of analytical power together in the same character Camus conveys a strong impression of the void felt by someone who experiences the absurd.

This first point is one of many indications that Camus is greatly interested by the whole question of language. His imaginative writings in particular show a cautious use of words which goes beyond artistic fastidiousness. He appears to be suspicious of his inevitable medium as a writer. This suspicion of words, particularly of abstract words, was referred to in the first chapter and is widespread among contemporary writers. It represents a revolt against what Sartre has called (in *Situations II*) 'a vocabulary that has been dislocated, vulgarized, softened and stuffed with "bourgeois-isms" by a hundred and fifty years of middle-class domination'. This view of language is suggested by some of Meursault's remarks to Marie and to the prison chaplain. One may go farther and say that the criticism of society explicit in the trial scenes, and in the novel generally, is implicit in Camus' rejection of the vocabulary and literary style of that same society. A formal device again reinforces the content of *L'Étranger*. Meursault's status as a social outsider is emphasized by his refusal to accept society's interpretation of certain words and by his general verbal restraint.

But Meursault is also a metaphysical outsider, and Camus uses the particular vocabulary of his novel to convey a metaphysic as well as social criticism. The use of words to express a metaphysical attitude emerges most clearly from his continual rejection of the language of causality. Events are not only described with economy; the whole vocabulary of interpretation, motivation and attribution is avoided. Conjunctions involving cause or effect, purpose or consequence, are rare, and the syntax is correspondingly abrupt. In place of the coherence indicated by *ainsi* or *parce que* we find the simple succession of *et* and *puis*. In other words, the discontinuity of experience which is a major element in Camus' conception of the absurd is reflected in his deliberately discontinuous style. He does not keep on reporting to the reader that the human condition is absurd; he conveys, through vocabulary and syntax, a direct impression of fragmentariness and abruptness. The following passage, when kept in the original French, is a typical example:

Il s'est alors levé après avoir bu un verre de vin. Il a repoussé les assiettes et le peu de boudin froid que nous avions laissé. Il a soigneusement essuyé la toile cirée de la table. Il a sorti d'un tiroir de sa table de nuit une feuille de papier quadrillé, une enveloppe jaune, un petit porte-plume de bois rouge et un encrier carré d'encre violette. Quand il m'a dit le nom de la femme, j'ai vu que c'était une Mauresque. J'ai fait la lettre. (p. 49).

One is reminded of Hemingway's similar use of abrupt phrasing in *Fiesta:*

Albert Camus

We drank three bottles of the champagne and the count left the basket in my kitchen. We dined at a restaurant in the Bois. It was a good dinner. Food had an excellent place in the count's values. So did wine. The count was in fine form during the meal. So was Brett. It was a good party.*

These two passages help to emphasize another quality of Camus' style in *L'Étranger*, apart from its fragmentariness. By presenting events as a *succession*, not a *sequence*, his account of experience also takes on a certain ingenuous air. This appearance of innocence arises particularly from the fact that he often makes statements, especially statements of liking or disliking, which are unaccompanied by any explanation or justification. We are reminded of a certain stage of candour in a child's limited vocabulary and self-expression when we read, for example: 'I remembered that it was Sunday and this fact annoyed me: I don't like Sunday.' [7] This sentence, and many others like it, suggests that the elliptical style of *L'Étranger* represents not only a *hantise du silence*, as Sartre termed it, but also what might be called a *nostalgie de l'innocence*. Once again the style faithfully reflects and reinforces the thought, since both these attitudes are important elements in Camus' reaction to the absurd. He is not using fiction to explain or justify his ideas; instead, by a simple formal device, he conveys such a strong sense of what the absurd is like that any attempt at intellectual justification would only weaken the whole impression.

The very restrained character of Camus' vocabulary in *L'Étranger* leads to another interesting feature of his prose which was first pointed out by W. M. Frohock.† There is one particular situation—Meursault's experience just before he shoots the Arab—which is described, not in severe and sober prose, but in a passage packed with metaphorical expressions. One might of course be tempted to regard this passage as a lapse on Camus' part, but I think it is clear that it would be a mistake to do so. Indeed we shall see that he is using colourful prose here very deliberately, and in a way that is fully consistent with his disapproval of rhetoric. By isolating these metaphors in an otherwise virtually non-metaphorical narrative Camus attracts attention to them and gives

* This is also a feature of much modern French poetry. One thinks in particular of Michaux and Prévert.
† See *Yale French Studies*, II, 2, pp. 91–9.

them special significance. Immediately prior to the passage in question (which occurs on pages 83–7 of the French edition) it is the passivity of things, a sense of inertia, which is conveyed. Stillness and silence reign between the sea, the sand and the sun. Then the mood and language change abruptly. The sea, the sand, the sun, etc. are personified and take a noticeably kinetic quality in contrast to the preceding inertia. Motion and personification become the basis of various metaphors. The heat 'leans' against Meursault; the sand 'vibrates'; light 'squirts' from the blade of the knife. Although he does not refer to the kinetic aspect of these metaphors Frohock points out that there are twenty-five of them in the space of six paragraphs, compared with only fifteen in the previous eighty-three pages of the novel.

The reason for Camus' use of metaphorical language at this point begins to emerge once one realizes that he is making his vocabulary serve a double purpose in the passage. He uses the same set of words both to carry forward the narrative and to convey the psychological reasons for it. The accumulation of metaphors ultimately turns out to be a clever economy by which he dispenses with the necessity of treating narration and motivation as two separate operations. He narrates in such a way that the motivation is implied without being explicitly formulated. In short, although an explanation of the killing of the Arab by Meursault is, as it were, embedded in the narrative of this event, explanatory statements are absent. This device is not only consistent with Camus' verbal reticence elsewhere in the novel. It also enables him to present the crucial action of *L'Étranger* in such a way that Meursault's deed, though explicable to the attentive reader, remains inexplicable—and therefore inexcusable—in the eyes of the law. What really happens is this. Camus uses a series of metaphors whose characteristics of personification and motion combine to create a noticeable impression of hallucination. As the metaphors accumulate, so Meursault's hallucination increases. The 'cymbals of the sun' ultimately cause him to commit murder. During this mounting tension the Arab in the distance fingers his knife. The blade glints in the sun and the light, reflected from it, strikes Meursault's eyes. It is at this moment that Meursault suffers the final hallucination, and his mental confusion becomes complete. The reader is encouraged to assume that he mistook the flash of light on the blade for the blade itself. Thus it seems as if Meursault really shot the Arab through an instinct for self-defence, an automatic reflex, and because he was momentarily deluded into believing that he was actually being attacked. Camus removes even more responsibility from Meursault by describing the trigger of his gun as 'giving way' rather than being pressed.

It now becomes clear that Camus' temporary use of rhetorical prose, far from suggesting failure to sustain the sobriety that otherwise marks his use of words in *L'Étranger*, is in strict accordance with his attitude to language elsewhere in the novel. This attitude is dictated by a distrust of rhetoric and the belief that it obscures the real nature of experience. He is therefore being entirely consistent when he uses rhetorical phrases to convey a confused state of mind—Meursault's momentary and fatal failure to distinguish between reality and phantasy. The point at which Meursault's language becomes fanciful and metaphorical is also the point at which he wrongly interprets experience—as distinct from simply failing to understand it—and becomes a murderer.

There is one main point to be made regarding Camus' treatment of time in *L'Étranger*. The narrator, Meursault, undergoes an important change which he fails to understand yet whose nature is conveyed to the reader by the way in which Camus handles the time element. He achieves the difficult but necessary feat of retaining Meursault's imperceptiveness and yet enabling him to explain himself clearly by implication. This appears to be done in the following manner. The novel is divided into two parts of equal length, but whereas the first part covers eighteen days the second deals with a period of close on twelve months. The first half shows acute and continued awareness of time. This is the period during which Meursault finds his existence ultimately meaningless, but in which he responds actively to physical pleasure. Once the murder has been committed, however, and the second half begins, time almost ceases to have any significance at all. The first six chapters contain a large number of references to time, but the last five virtually ignore it. They contain instead allusions to such symbols of eternal recurrence or permanence as day and night or the sky and the stars. There are also explicit references to the fact that time appears to have stopped for Meursault. He says, for instance: 'Pour moi c'était sans cesse le même jour qui déferlait dans ma cellule ...'

(pp. 114–15) This transition from a sharp consciousness of time to apparent unawareness of its passing is a technique effectively used for other purposes by Malraux in *La Condition humaine*. Here, in *L'Étranger*, it reflects and reinforces Meursault's progress from a purely sensual appreciation of experience to an attitude in which he gradually grows indifferent to physical existence as he contemplates his approaching execution and death. Time is manipulated in such a way that we are helped to realize more fully Meursault's withdrawal from temporal existence in the world of sense into more speculative and timeless self-awareness. In this way the consistency of the main character is preserved. Camus does not present him as suddenly articulate and aware of his own mental processes, for this would be to split his character into two irreconcilable parts. What he does do, by presenting this transition in mainly temporal terms, is to preserve the impression of Meursault's lack of understanding since he himself is only dimly aware of the change that events have wrought in him. Meursault is unable to analyse this change, yet its character is clearly conveyed, in spite of this, by the gradually altered nature of his allusions to time. Camus' treatment of time in *L'Étranger* enables him to get round the difficulty that arises from having chosen as his narrator a person of low intelligence whose experiences must nevertheless be understood by the reader.

A consideration of the tense used in *L'Étranger* brings us to the last main way in which the novel displays a striking fusion of idea and form. One of the most noticeable features of this novel is the fact that the story is recorded almost exclusively in the perfect tense. This use of what is called in French *le passé composé*—what used to be called *le passé indéfini*—is unusual in a straightforward literary narration of past events. It may be argued, of course, that Camus uses this tense simply because it is the most natural form of spoken narrative in French. This is to say that Camus chose it in order to give authentic directness to Meursault's story and to avoid a too-literary narrative. No doubt this is true as far as it goes, but to stop at this point is, I think, to oversimplify the matter. I believe it can be shown that the perfect tense corresponds to Camus' subject-matter—the experience of the absurd—in several more subtle ways.

The peculiar quality of the perfect tense lies in the fact that although it describes a past action it also retains, to a considerable degree, a feeling of presentness. It preserves something of that latin form from which it derives, which consisted of present tense plus adjective rather than auxiliary plus past participle. The action formulated in the perfect tense, though occurring at a point in time past, is presented as somehow holding good up to the present moment. Thus one is always aware of latent possibility in the perfect tense. There is something provisional about it. Whereas the preterite seals off an action in time the perfect tense confers a less precise temporal limit upon it. This, I take it, is the difference in French between the definiteness of 'il rentra chez lui' and the indefiniteness of 'il est rentré chez lui'. The second phrase holds out more promise than the first that we shall also be told what happened next. It is more forward-looking. One might perhaps say that the preterite is the tense of *lived* experience whereas the perfect is the tense of *living* experience. In fact this quality of presentness added to the past, of temporal indetermination, is suggested by the earlier description of the perfect tense in French as *le passé indéfini*. Thus the point made above is confirmed. The use of the perfect tense in *L'Étranger* helps to impart directness, to bridge the gap between the novel as author-narration and as reader-experience. It gives to events an actuality which virtually makes a composite present out of the author's presentation of time and time as experienced by the reader.

If the distinction I have made between the two tenses is correct, there are three closely associated ways in which the use of the perfect tense corresponds to the attitude to experience conveyed by other means in *L'Étranger*. Firstly, the indeterminate nature of the *passé indéfini*, its air of continuing possibility, enables Camus to carry his narrative forward while avoiding a set pattern and air of finality about the events described. The tense used renders very strong the impression that one is experiencing these events directly, before they have been analysed, classified—and misrepresented— by rational scrutiny. In this way the tense achieves the same effect as the narrative method and Camus' use of syntax. Secondly, the indefiniteness of the perfect tense also emphasizes that gratuitous and arbitrary quality of experience which is associated with the absurd. This tense, with its ultimate inconclusiveness, strengthens the impression that nothing is irrevocably settled and that events might still assume a different character. It contributes to that *a priori* arbitrariness of things which is an important element in experience of the absurd. Thirdly, the prolongation of the past into the present, which characterizes the perfect tense, gives to the events of *L'Étranger* a quality of continuation from their occurrence up to the moment of their narration by Meursault. This means that each event, because of the way in which it is recounted, possesses a distinct and separate presentness marking it off from every other event. The result is a 'succession of present moments' which we saw Camus describe, in *Le Mythe de Sisyphe*, as the ideal of *l'homme absurde*. In this way too the discontinuity conveyed by the syntax is reinforced. The following passage, when kept in the original French, shows how tense and syntax combine to convey an impression of fragmentation:

Raymond a eu l'air très content. Il m'a demandé si je voulais sortir avec lui. Je me suis levé et j'ai commencé à me peigner. Il m'a a dit alors qu'il fallait que je lui serve de témoin .... J'ai accepté de lui servir de témoin. (p. 57)

There are those who would no doubt wish to argue at this stage that too great a degree of self-consciousness in his use of language is being attributed to Camus. I think Camus' own observations on language—not least of all in his essay of 1943 on Brice Parain—could be used to refute this argument. It also seems to me that a careful reading of *L'Étranger* itself weakens such objections considerably. In fact, it is clear that a high degree of self-consciousness in the use of words must inevitably affect a novelist who is presenting the absurdist view of experience. The prose of *L'Étranger* is singularly lacking in adjectival colour precisely because a profusion of adjectives would suggest a confidence in appearances, a leisurely attitude to time, a certain lack of tragic urgency—all attitudes that are directly contrary to the absurdist outlook. It is very much focused on verb and tense since these aspects of the vocabulary emphasize the distrust of abstraction and the sharp awareness of man as a victim of time which characterize absurdism. To read *L'Étranger* in this way is to see its verb-centred prose as particularly effective in presenting experience with a minimum of cerebration and in contributing to the general atmosphere of tragic action. In fact we have in this novel an example of the way in which Camus, like many of his contemporaries, uses a highly intellectualized artistic medium in order to convey a direct and unintellectualized impression of human experience.

At the end of this discussion of *L'Étranger* we come back once more to Camus' statement that the novel poses aesthetic questions first of all. In his own first novel at least, with its complicated attempt to appear uncomplicated, the truth of this remark is clear. And in particular one is struck, I think, by the way in which the various artistic devices associated with narrative viewpoint, vocabulary, time and tense combine together and reinforce one another. These different formal contrivances do not simply give additional support and emphasis to the subject-matter; they combine together in such a way that in themselves they form an organic unity in which each part contains something of the other parts and assists them to function properly. And yet, much as one may admire the appropriateness and co-ordination of these techniques their success has its dangerously negative aspects. Before leaving this novel, therefore, a final word remains to be said concerning the undesirable consequences which seem to follow from its formal devices.

Camus makes no secret of the fact that much of his technical procedure in *L'Étranger* is of American origin. In 1945 he gave an interview to Jeanine Delpech, and part of their conversation was printed in *Les Nouvelles littéraires* for 15 November. In reply to Jeanine Delpech's remark that *L'Étranger* recalled certain novels of Faulkner and Steinbeck, Camus replied that the similarity was not an accidental one. He added that he used a certain American novel technique because it exactly suited his purpose in *L'Étranger*. I myself should have been inclined to suggest Hemingway and James M. Cain, rather than Faulkner and Steinbeck, as Camus' models for his first novel, but the important point is that he recognizes a debt to the technical example of certain American writers. Having acknowledged this indebtedness, he goes on to regret the widespread influence of the 'tough' school of American novelists on his French contemporaries, suggesting that the French novel is being diverted from its traditional path and severely impoverished in consequence. He is reported as saying in the same interview:

The Art of the Novel (1)

A widespread application of these methods would lead to a world of automata and instincts. This would mean considerable impoverishment. That is why, although giving the American novel its due, I would exchange a hundred Hemingways for a Stendhal or a Benjamin Constant. And I regret the influence of this literature on so many young writers.[8]

It is clear, then, that Camus realizes that there are dangers involved in a general application of the methods which he used in *L'Étranger*. The more one thinks about it the more one realizes that some of the most effective technical devices in *L'Étranger* would do more harm than good to most novels in which they appeared. In fact, *L'Étranger* suggests at least three observations on this kind of novel. In the first place, characterization is alien to the absurdist novel. From the absurdist standpoint the motivation and analysis of human behaviour are more likely to mislead than enlighten. In the end they prove useless, and this means that one of the chief preoccupations of the great novelists of the past tends to be denied to their absurdist successors. Secondly, events do not conform to any coherent pattern in the eyes of the absurdist onlooker. All experiences are equivalent to *l'homme absurde*, events are no longer evaluated and fused into an artistic whole, and the absurdist novel may suffer from a measure of structural disintegration as a result. Thirdly, the absurdist novel not only turns away from character-analysis and plot-construction; it holds in deep suspicion the very medium that the novelist is bound to use. The absurdist caution about language has much to justify it, and Camus' application of it in *L'Étranger* is very ingenious, but a certain impoverishment of the prose medium follows. If, therefore, characterization and coherence of plot are removed, and if at the same time words and syntax are deliberately reduced to bare simplicity, there seems little point in writing more than one novel on this basis. One might claim, indeed, that further novels of this kind would merely be replicas of the first one. My own view is that *L'Étranger* must be regarded as a remarkable technical achievement, but that it also hints at a limit, a point of non-renewal, in the art of fiction. I imagine it is no accident that Camus' second novel, *La Peste*, explored adjacent territory by using quite different methods.

8 THE ART OF THE NOVEL (II)

L'effort de fabulation de l'homme tend toujours à fixer, par un symbolisme concret, certaines situations essentielles, et à hâter leur dénouement.

PIERRE EMMANUEL

In recent years the word *mythe* has become almost indispensable to the vocabulary of French intellectuals. Like other fashionable words it has taken on a prestige value and is often used as much to impress the hearer as to bring him genuine elucidation. In most cases, as used by contemporary French critics, it represents a considerable departure from the original sense of the word.* It has come to mean a widely shared attitude or an idea shaping the outlook of a large mass of people; it is no longer confined to the dictionary definition of an ancient story embodying significant actions performed by legendary or supernatural beings. This earlier and more precise meaning of the word still persists, however, and myths of this kind characterize much recent writing, particularly in France. In the French theatre, for example, classical myths are frequently recreated and freshly interpreted. One thinks of well-known plays by Giraudoux, Gide, Sartre, Anouilh and others. In its turn, such refurbishing of classical legends has not been the only mythologizing activity to be found lately among French writers. There has also existed, to some extent in the theatre but more strikingly in the novel, an attempt to create 'contemporary myths'. A great imaginative effort has been made to put into fiction situations and plots which do not simply deal with some universal human trait but are meant to express universal truth about man's situation in the world. The search for a myth is closely linked with

---

* That lively and original French critic, Roland Barthes, is a case in point. Between 1954 and 1956 he contributed a regular monthly article to *Les Lettres Nouvelles* in which he investigated the 'mythologies' attaching to many widely differing subjects including detergents, Greta Garbo, the Tour de France and strip-tease.

the increasingly metaphysical aspirations of the French novel. The myth has proved a means whereby men of letters have taken over the rôle of commentators on human destiny—a rôle which the professional philosophers once regarded as their own but now seem largely to have abandoned in favour of linguistics and logical analysis. This concern with literary myth-making is most obvious in certain novels themselves, but it is also directly reflected in the recent entry of the expression *roman-mythe* into the French critic's vocabulary. Critical interest in non-French authors like Melville, Dostoievsky, Kafka and Faulkner is stimulated and maintained by the discovery of certain central myths in their work. And it is noticeable that these authors have also been the subject of essays along the same lines by those very novelists in France—Malraux and Camus—to whose own work the expression *roman-mythe* is most frequently applied. It is, I think, this prevalence of the *roman-mythe* which enabled a young American critic to write a few years ago that 'the basic formal problem of modern literature . . . has been: how to bring Naturalism to terms with Symbolism.' *

At this point we may take stock and say that we have so far spoken of three distinct though connected attitudes: a readiness to interpret popular ideas and responses in terms of a myth-centred psychology; a renewed interest in classical mythology interpreted in contemporary terms; a desire to create in literature new myths embodying fundamental truths about human destiny. All three attitudes, in their different ways, reflect our obsession with myth-making. Yet we also have here something of a paradox. It is the paradox to which Kierkegaard referred with prophetic insight when he spoke of a scientific age concerned to produce myths although wanting to destroy all myths. The majority of the writers most active in creating new myths are also those who have explicitly rejected the traditional myths, particularly those associated with Christianity. It almost seems as though the old myths can only be rejected by being replaced by others. The reason for this may be, I suppose, that myth-making has a strong therapeutic effect and is a natural and spontaneous activity of the mind. It perhaps entails the projection of mental and emotional conflicts, within an individual or a group, which are thus reduced or even

* Nathan A. Scott, *Rehearsals of Discomposure*, London, Lehmann, 1952, p. 14.

exorcised. Such speculations as these, however, would lead us into realms far beyond the competence of the literary critic.

Although most critics are not qualified to pronounce on the psychological origins of myth-making they are bound to take notice of its ubiquitous existence in the world of letters. They will be struck by the many symbolical and allegorical works that not only seem to reflect certain general tendencies of the times but also provide an ideal vehicle for the philosophical interests of many modern writers. An interest in the *roman-mythe* is clear not only from Camus' critical writings but in his own practice as a novelist. I mainly confined myself, in Chapter 7, to the techniques used in *L'Étranger*, but this novel could clearly be interpreted also as a modern myth. Meursault ultimately emerges as a symbolical figure representing man's metaphysical status as an outsider, a being who does not feel he belongs—and who does not seem to belong—to the world in which he has been placed. Camus himself suggested something of the kind, though from a different angle, when he described Meursault as 'un Christ sordide'. Yet the fact remains that a myth is not explicitly created in this first novel. It is predominantly critical and negative in temper, and this is not an attitude that readily encourages myth-making. A myth, for Camus, seems to require a greater degree of affirmation than he allowed himself in *L'Étranger*. But in his second novel, *La Peste*, he does present a more positive attitude to human destiny. This novel is one of modest hope and determined endeavour in a way that *L'Étranger* was not, and in it Camus uses clear and unmistakable symbolism. Indeed, the whole conception and construction of *La Peste* make it one of the most impressive novels of recent times to which the term *roman-mythe* may be applied.

La Peste is an account of the fight against an imaginary epidemic —the 'plague' referred to in the title—which supposedly afflicted Oran sometime in the 1940s. Camus describes a particular event (the plague) in a geographical location (North Africa), but he handles his subject in such a way that he extends its meaning beyond the particular to the universal. He conveys a general picture of man's position in the universe, faced by the problem of evil and the necessity of suffering. In a less total fashion Camus also includes a series of indirect references to the German Occupation of France and so adds a second level of symbolical meaning to the novel. *La Peste* is thus an ambitious attempt to combine in one whole a literal and two metaphorical interpretations. In this way it contains a network of symbols—situations, characters and physical objects which, while being themselves, also represent other things beyond themselves.

So far I have spoken of *La Peste* as a *roman-mythe*. I have done so because this term is commonly applied to it in France and because it helps to place Camus' novel in the general context of modern myth-making. Yet my own impression is that the expression *roman-mythe*, like the word *mythe* itself, is often loosely and vaguely used by the French. At various times it has been applied to such very different novels as *Don Quixote, The Brothers Kara-mazov, Heart of Darkness, La Condition humaine* and *The Aerodrome*, not to mention both *L'Étranger* and *La Peste*. Used in this way a *roman-mythe* will sometimes mean an allegorical novel, sometimes a symbolist novel, sometimes any novel which adds a metaphysical dimension to the temporal events it describes. Such vagueness is better avoided; indeed it seems clear that the full significance of *La Peste*, at any rate, will be better understood by describing it more precisely. To begin with, it is not, strictly speaking, an allegorical novel. In an allegorical novel—*The Pilgrim's Progress*, for example—two levels of interpretation are continuously maintained throughout. But a reading of *La Peste* shows that its symbolism, though frequent, is of an intermittent kind. There are certainly many moments when its narrative calls for an added, metaphorical interpretation, but there are also stretches of narrative which, as far as I can see, are to be taken at a literal level only. At the other extreme of classification, *La Peste* is clearly something more than a directly realistic account of dramatic contemporary events to which metaphysical meanings are added. It is a different kind of novel from those of Malraux or Graham Greene. Camus is not writing as the witness of some contemporary happening, as a reporter on real situations in Europe or Africa or Mexico or the Far East. Instead he has deliberately created an imaginary situation, an epidemic in Oran. He has chosen a situation which is also a symbol. It allows him to give an impression of realism but it is also a neat prefigurement of his own desperate metaphysic. The plague provides him both with the closed universe of the absurd (the town of Oran cut off from contact with the outside world) and with the necessity for revolt (the efforts of Dr. Rieux and others to combat the plague and reduce its lethal effects). Perhaps it is not too great a generalization to say that whereas Malraux and Greene experience situations and then derive a philosophy from them, Camus, in *La Peste*, has reversed the process by imagining a series of events specifically designed to embody his prior metaphysic. The result is a more abstract novel, but one in which the literal and metaphorical levels are more closely combined.

In the light of these distinctions I propose to call *La Peste* a symbolist novel. By this I mean a novel in which the relationship between two or more levels of meaning is not so continuously sustained as in the allegory, yet is more complete and organic than in what might be called politico-metaphysical fiction. And such a symbolist novel, it should be noted, enables Camus to get the best of two worlds. In the pure allegory the literal level of meaning is often weak because of the constant strain of allegorical significance. Thus a book like *Gulliver's Travels* is enjoyed at the literal level mainly by children, whereas adults largely ignore this aspect and treat seriously only its metaphorical meaning. In the politico-metaphysical novel, on the other hand, the emphasis is quite different. Here the 'realistic' element is most powerful. The particular human drama described is of prime interest to most readers and possible metaphysical interpretations come rather as an afterthought. A symbolist novel like *La Peste* lies midway between these two types and possesses the best qualities of each. The close integration of both literal and metaphorical levels means that both are readily recognized by the reader and each is enjoyed for its own sake. The immediate story is not overstrained by the need for continuous allegorical reference. The interpretation of the symbol by the reader is not an unbroken process. Transition from one level to another is only called for intermittently and the non-literal aspect is all the more persuasive because it emerges at intervals, and not all the time, from a firmly and continuously realistic narrative.

I have said that *La Peste* is a typical example of an outstanding general feature in recent literature and thought. It is also worth pointing out, however, that this novel fits naturally into Camus' own ideal of fiction which I outlined in the opening pages of

Chapter 7. Camus claims that the novel has tended, throughout its history, either towards increased naturalism or greater formalism. Particularity and abstraction are the two poles by which it has been alternately attracted at different periods. But the novel has only been great, he claims, when it has been more or less equally attracted by both poles at once. Too ready a movement in either single direction has led to aesthetic heresy and a misunderstanding of the true nature of fiction. Camus thus claims that novels should take a middle path between the particular and the universal; that they will receive dimensional fullness only from a proper combination of both. Novels should hold the concrete and the abstract in a natural and closely knit proportion and balance. One would have to say, I think, that the symbolist novel is not the only way of obtaining this result, but it is also clear that the very nature of the symbol makes it one of the most obvious and natural means to such an end. The successful symbolist novel will combine the concrete and the abstract in an organically inevitable relationship. They will be as inseparable, and yet as distinguishable, as the flower and its scent or the memento and its associations. In this way the symbolist novel achieves that reconciliation of the singular and the universal desired by Hegel and described by Camus as the essential activity of art.

The symbolist novel, as we find it in *La Peste*, is not only consistent with Camus' interpretation of art but seems to be encouraged by his attitude to history. I have already pointed out Camus' anti-historicism in *L'Homme révolté* and his identification of himself with those whose problems are not solved either by Christ (Christianity) or Marx (history). Now in *La Peste* Camus is attempting to diagnose the human dilemma and offer some remedy for it. Yet his view of the nature of this dilemma is that it lies outside the resources of history. There is no temporal remedy that will meet the case. For this reason he avoids writing a novel which would seem to present the problem in purely temporal terms and offer a purely temporal solution. Instead, by means of a central and pervasive symbol, he is concerned to place the problem outside time. This is where he thinks the problem really belongs, and in *La Peste* he moves beyond the wastage of time to the conservation of the symbol. The plague, because it must first assume concrete and historical form, enables *La Peste* to be a philosophical novel and not simply a philosophical treatise. But since the plague is also a symbol possessing non-literal and non-temporal meaning, it allows this same novel to discuss the problem of evil and of man's estrangement in the universe in those non-historical terms which Camus requires.

One final word should be said concerning the critical approach to *La Peste* before coming to examine it in more detail. This is a matter on which Camus has expressed himself indirectly in his essay on Kafka (added to the later editions of *Le Mythe de Sisyphe*). His opening remark is that Kafka puts the reader under an obligation to read him twice. The nature of the symbolist novel requires two readings—one for each of the two levels of interpretation which even the simplest symbol contains. But one should add, I think, that a third reading is also necessary. Having responded as completely as possible to the literal and latent meanings of the symbol, the critic should then read the novel again so as to reconstitute it in its organic duality. Only in this way, and at this third reading, can one fully appreciate the richness of texture and the continuous interplay of the explicit and the implicit which are a fundamental part of the symbolist novel's effect on the reader. The real justification for taking the symbol apart and distinguishing its literal and non-literal aspects is the increased response to its recreated wholeness which such a procedure makes possible.

Camus then goes on to emphasize that the task of distinguishing between the literal and latent levels of interpretation is not an easy one. In particular, the ingenious critic may be tempted to find meanings or allusions which formed no part of the writer's own intention. I myself would say that it is permissible to find in a symbolist novel more than the author consciously intended— Melville was grateful to Hawthorne for doing so in the case of *Moby Dick*—but the conscientious critic must be uneasy unless some kind of limiting factor can be found. This kind of limiting factor probably escapes very clear definition and it is noticeable that Camus himself does not formulate one. Instead he suggests that if the method of approach is sound in emphasis the right amount of freedom in interpretation will follow from it. The nature of the critical approach should itself guarantee the operation of a suitable limit. Camus seems to suggest, in speaking of Kafka, that one should keep the literal interpretation of the story in the forefront of one's mind while realizing that it is also a symbol. This emphasis on the literal meaning helps to ensure that the gap is not too great between the explicit and implicit levels, and that the critic will not be tempted to strain the symbolism.

In the last analysis, however, the limit can never operate with precision. There must always be an ill-defined area where the appropriateness and validity of a particular interpretation will remain a matter for individual judgement. The symbolist novel will always have a fringe of uncertainty and an aura of imprecision. Yet in the work of art this uncertainty adds an extra dimension. It gives to the symbolist novel an imaginative margin which increases its artistic status and power. Some such idea seems to have been in Camus' own mind when he wrote of Kafka's work that its nature, and perhaps its greatness, is to offer us all interpretations and to confirm none.

Camus indicates the symbolical nature of *La Peste* on the title-page. He takes his epigraph from Defoe's preface to the third volume of *Robinson Crusoe:* '. . . it is as reasonable to represent one kind of imprisonment by another, as it is to represent anything that really exists by that which exists not'. He goes farther than Defoe, however. As I have already pointed out, he derives *two* figurative meanings from the symbol of the plague since there are clear and repeated allusions both to the German Occupation and to man's metaphysical dereliction in the world. Camus appears to have conceived his theme and his symbol originally in 1939, and this obviously means that he first thought of it in terms of the plague/problem of evil analogy only. But the writing of *La Peste* in its final form did not begin until 1944. By this time Camus' experience of the Occupation had strongly suggested a further analogy which the original image of the plague seemed capable of absorbing. No doubt this further level of meaning was also prompted, if only verbally, by the common French description of Hitler's armies as '*la peste* brune'. At all events it is not surprising that by 1944 the Occupation aspect had become of considerable importance in the novel. In a letter to Roland Barthes Camus himself has said that *La Peste* is, in a sense, more than a chronicle of the Resistance but that it is also certainly no less than this.*

Here, then, we have a symbolist novel which, through historical chance, possesses two major figurative interpretations. Later I shall have to discuss how far the plague is a satisfactory symbol at each of these two levels, but for the moment I only wish to emphasize its potential richness and scope. Sartre has rightly spoken of the way in which the plague-symbol gives organic unity to a plurality of critical and constructive themes, but its richness can also be seen from a slightly different angle. In *La Peste* we have an image which expands to universal significance through three stages. It speaks directly of individual life and indirectly of politics and metaphysics. Thus the three major areas of human experience are included—the personal, the social, the speculative—and all three are unified in the symbol of the plague. In this way Camus attempts, through his novel, to make contact with the whole experience of man, with the triple living and thinking of the reader.

At the literal level *La Peste* has very little plot. The narrative, which is absorbing for all that, simply follows the natural curve of the plague from its beginnings, through its period of lethal intensity, to its eventual disappearance. The plague is first indicated by the large number of rats lying dead in the houses and streets of Oran. Soon, human beings also begin to die, stricken by inflammatory swellings in the groin and armpit. When the number of deaths rises steeply the Government admits the fact of the plague, Oran is shut off from the outside world, various measures are taken and serums tried. For months the plague rages unabated, however, and no effective answer can be found. Eventually one person recovers despite having had the dreaded symptoms, and others gradually follow. In time the illness becomes much less common, the death-rate falls sharply, and finally the plague disappears in as apparently arbitrary a fashion as it first arrived. During the period of the plague, which is described with something approaching scientific detachment and exactness, the reactions of the inhabitants are also reported. The attitudes of some individuals, but mainly of the population as a whole—fear or

* See 'Lettre d'Albert Camus à Roland Barthes sur *La Peste*', *Club*, 21 (February 1955), p. 7.

indifference or escapism—are described. Lastly, the fight against the plague, the different attempts to overcome it by medicine or heroism or prayer, is studied in the principal characters, who include Dr. Rieux, Tarrou, Rambert, Grand and Father Paneloux. It is Dr. Rieux who tells the story, though this does not become clear until near the end of the book.

As regards this literal level—the story purely as a 'realistic' account of an epidemic—it is significant that Camus chooses to call *La Peste* a *chronique*, not a *roman*. Whereas, in *L'Étranger*, he used the method of direct presentation, he chooses here the vehicle of detached narration. The situation is reported on objectively in *La Peste*: it is not subjectively embodied and recreated as in *L'Étranger*. This desire for objectivity is stated at various times in the novel. We read, for example:

. . . in order to give nothing away, and especially not himself, the narrator has aimed at objectivity. His desire has been to change nothing by means of artistic devices, except where this has been necessary in the straightforward interests of a more or less coherent story.[1]

This objective narration, the method of the chronicle, serves an important purpose in the symbolist novel. Although in a sense it reinforces the authenticity of events at the literal level, it also holds the reader at some distance from these events. The reader, conscious of the presence of the objective narrator, the chronicler, is prevented from identifying himself fully with the characters and their situation. This detachment from reality, which exists side by side with acceptance of it, makes the reader potentially more receptive to the further implications of the symbol. It enables him to transfer his attention more easily from the literal to the figurative level. At the same time it means that the 'realism' can be thoroughly indulged in without the symbolical inferences being weakened. This strengthening of the straightforward 'story' aspect clearly makes for a better symbolist novel and even adds to the power of the symbol itself. And the two most common snares of the symbolist novel, obvious didacticism or excessive abstraction, are most likely to be avoided by the objective narrative method of the chronicle.

One of the main difficulties of the symbolist novel, at the realistic level, lies in the presentation of the characters. Characters such as

Rieux, Tarrou and Grand are by no means mere puppets voicing ideas, yet it remains true that we do not have a very clear picture of them. The chronicle method in *La Peste* holds us at a distance from them, and in general they do not have psychological density or completely convincing personalities. This point suggests two comments. Firstly, Camus only claims to have written a *chronique*, not a *roman*. He shows a careful discrimination in such matters reminiscent of Gide's distinctions, in his own work, between *roman, récit* and *sotie*. There is therefore some point in accepting *La Peste* for what it is. The presentation of character which it contains is entirely consistent with Camus' own classification of it as a literary form. To complain that the characters are psychologically flat and not sufficiently individualized is to ask for a different genre from that which Camus set out to give us. Secondly —and this is perhaps a more important point—all the major characters in *La Peste* do have strongly marked *moral* features. In their reactions to a sudden and overwhelming catastrophe, the plague, they are clearly defined and focused. They are presented to us in an extreme situation and it is with their behaviour in the face of this situation that Camus is concerned. Furthermore, the primary aim in *La Peste* is to portray a collective reaction to a collective problem. Private solutions of personal dilemmas are secondary— sometimes even irrelevant. And so Camus is concerned to give his main characters general moral features rather than individual psychological aspects. And this, one may add, is in keeping with his own statement, in which he echoes Malraux, that the emphasis in literature has shifted from psychology to metaphysics.*

Before leaving these matters of narrative method and characterization in *La Peste* one further feature should be mentioned. Camus tells his story through a first-person narrator who maintains a strict anonymity until the final chapter. He then reveals himself as Dr. Rieux, the chief character in the book. The narrative method here is largely the reverse of that in *L'Étranger*. Meursault revealed himself directly to the reader in recounting events towards which he felt a complete outsider. His way of telling his story emphasized his rôle as a victim. Conversely, Rieux conceals his identity from the reader while speaking of events in which he is deeply involved.

* 'L'objet de l'art, malgré les regrets des pasticheurs, s'est étendu de la psychologie à la condition de l'homme', *L'Homme révolté*, pp. 338–9.

His way of telling his story emphasizes his rôle as a witness, and he is as deeply committed in act as he is detached in narration. In this way Camus may be said to present Rieux's personal story impersonally. He avoids abstraction and maintains 'human interest' by using Rieux as narrator, but he makes him narrate in a way that ultimately assists the universalizing intention of the symbol. This universalizing intention appears in Rieux's explanation of his lengthy and strict anonymity:

When tempted to blend his own secret directly with the voices of a thousand plague victims he was stopped by the thought that each one of his sufferings was also experienced by the others and that this was an advantage in a world where suffering is so often solitary. Clearly he had to speak on behalf of everybody.[2]

The narrative effect obtained by Camus in *La Peste* is thus one which arouses the reader's interest by means of an individual who then directs it away from himself towards a representative group of human beings. Rieux is used as the narrator first to focus the reader's attention and then to diffuse it again. In this way Camus attempts to obtain that extension of interest beyond individual psychology to the general human condition which he holds to be a major feature of contemporary writing of the highest quality.

I now turn to the first of the two figurative levels of *La Peste*—the plague as a symbol of the Occupation. At this level there are many obvious analogies to be made. Among a large number of possible examples one may mention the confusion of public opinion and the feeling of stupefaction when the presence of the plague is finally accepted as a reality (p. 48); the rationing of food and petrol, the growing electricity cuts and the disappearance of most of the town's traffic (p. 94); the restrictive measures announced by the press and the increased police surveillance (p. 130); the growth of 'resistance' against the plague (p. 151); Cottard's 'black-market' activities (pp. 160–1); the mass burial of victims of the plague in open graves (p. 198); the isolation camps with their loud-speakers (p. 267); the growing hopes of liberation from the plague, the rejoicing at its disappearance, the later reprisals and the beating-up of Cottard (pp. 293, 298, 330–3).

The advantages of this symbolical treatment of the Occupation are no doubt obvious. Although the immediacy of the *témoignage* is lost, its temptations are also avoided. By rejecting a directly realistic account of the Occupation Camus also removes his narrative from the sphere of personal passion and private bias. Symbolic presentation enables him to avoid those contemporary pressures which have lessened the value of so many accounts of the Occupation and Liberation. The use of the symbol also enables him to increase the scope of his narrative so as to include all political tyrannies. At the first figurative level his symbol is an expanding one ranging outward in space and backward in time. From an epidemic in Oran it extends to the German Occupation of France, then of Western Europe, then to any dictatorship—Hitlerian or Stalinist—and finally it contains features common to the tyrannies of the past as well as of recent history. I think that a realization of this extension of the symbol lay behind some of the most intelligent, and most severe, criticism of *La Peste* by Marxists in France. And Camus seems to be referring to this fact when he says in the letter to Barthes mentioned above: 'No doubt this is why they reproach me—because *La Peste* can serve any resistance to any kind of tyranny'.[5]

Criticisms of another kind, however, can and should be made against the Occupation aspect of *La Peste*. In a way, of course, the symbol of the plague is an ideal image of the Occupation, yet in several important respects its validity breaks down. For example, the moral dilemmas of the Occupation are almost entirely absent from this symbolical representation. The difficult debates about ends and means, or the difficult responsibility of choosing to kill a German soldier thereby causing, perhaps, the deaths of a dozen French hostages—these are aspects which the symbol fails to cover. Within the context of the plague, at least as Camus presents it, right actions are clear once one has chosen to struggle against it. But in the case of the Occupation acute problems of action arose precisely because one had chosen to resist. Another inadequacy is the weakness of the plague as a symbol of man's inhumanity to man. There is a disturbing moral ambiguity present in such products of human agency as war, oppression and injustice, but this ambiguity is entirely absent in *La Peste*. By using the plague as his symbol, and by emphasizing its arbitrary nature, Camus places political evil in a phenomenon existing outside the scope of human responsibility. It appears to me that at this point Camus falls victim of the extreme humanist fallacy of a perfect, or per-fectible, human nature. He avoids facing the problem of the evil that results from human actions—presumably because this might lead him to a logical acceptance of some kind of deity. By using the symbol of the plague, however, he puts war and its attendant evils on a level with natural catastrophes such as earthquakes or avalanches—phenomena beyond the apparent responsibility of man. He equates war with the plague, evil with illness, and then looks round for humanist medicaments. One has to admit, of course, that this attitude to the Occupation is strictly in keeping with Camus' own metaphysical views. It is consistent with his sensitivity to human suffering and death, combined with his dis-belief in God. For my own part, however, I am unable to avoid the conviction that Camus' symbol of the plague is inadequate at the Occupation level. I find it appropriate in the context of suffer-ing but unsatisfactory before the fact of wrong-doing. It covers human wretchedness but ignores human wickedness. And so the whole picture of the Occupation in *La Peste* seems to me to have been morally simplified. There is never any question of the right things being done for the wrong reasons, of evil consequences following uncontrollably from virtuous motives, etc. The plague offers many circumstantial similarities to the Occupation, but it is powerless to convey a sense of its human agency and moral ambiguity.

Such features in this symbol, although they weaken its political interpretation, strengthen its metaphysical application. At this third level Camus is concerned with the problem of evil in the sense of suffering, not wrong-doing. For this purpose the plague is an admirable vehicle. It is arbitrary. Its appearance and disappear-ance are ultimately beyond the scope of human agency. It is terrible in its effects and little known in its origins. It is a familiar catas-trophe, yet an apparently unavoidable one. Among the many features of the plague, however, its spatially concentrated and temporally undifferentiated character makes it a particularly suit-able medium for the expression of Camus' metaphysical ideas. The town of Oran is sealed off on one side by the sea. On the other side, once the fact of the epidemic has been recognized and accepted, the gates are closed to prevent the spread of infection. This picture of Oran, isolated by geography and catastrophe, provides another version of that 'univers clos' which Camus finds in Lucretius, Sade, the Romantics, Nietzsche, Lautréamont, Rimbaud, the surrealists and various more recent writers. He discusses this question at the beginning of Part IV of *L'Homme révolté* and claims that metaphysical revolt has always found expression either in a special rhetoric or in the image of a closed universe. Within the limitation and concentration of the closed universe writers in metaphysical revolt have looked for the coherence and unity on which to base a new metaphysic. The plague thus has a spatially confined and unified setting whose very narrowness and concentration enable it to take on universal significance.

A similar effect is obtained by the temporal quality of the epidemic. For most of the duration of the plague time is experienced by the inhabitants of Oran as mere undifferentiated succession. Temporal relationships, or an interpretative historical pattern, are notably absent. The chronicle method of telling the story reinforces this impression of unmeasured time. There is movement and flow, but no explanation or evaluation. The result is a kind of ideal, abstract time which again strengthens the universal aspect of the symbol and makes its metaphysical application all the more natural and smooth.

La Peste, then, with its picture of the inhabitants of Oran cut off from the rest of the world and suffering and dying from the epidemic, is a picture of cosmic alienation, of that metaphysical absurdity of man's condition analysed in *Le Mythe de Sisyphe*. The feature of the absurd which is particularly emphasized in *La Peste*, and against which Camus revolts most strongly, is the problem of evil. As I have already suggested he uses the plague as a symbol of suffering, of that human wretchedness and pain which is a major aspect of the problem of evil. This is a subject which preoccupies Camus. There are repeated references to it in his writings. The following statement, made in the course of a talk given to the Dominicans of Latour-Maubourg in 1948, is a brief but typical formulation of his attitude : 'I share your horror of evil. But I do not share your optimism, and I continue to struggle against this universe in which children suffer and die.' [4] The problem of evil, in this sense, is particularly concentrated round two sermons preached by the Jesuit Father Paneloux. The first sermon, recalling in several ways the fiery rhetoric of another Jesuit Father in *A Portrait of the Artist as a Young Man,* is preached during the early days of the plague. Father Paneloux interprets the plague as being divine in origin and punitive in purpose, a fitting judgment on the sins of Oran. He emphasizes his point that evil as a method of punishment is an instrument for good.

In this first sermon we have a militant and bloodthirsty form of Christianity. Even allowing for a certain element of caricature Camus here presents an interpretation of the problem of evil which would still be capable of splitting Christians into two camps. Father Paneloux's hearers are similarly divided. Some accept his arguments as irrefutable and some are not convinced. Others, the *révoltés* among whom Camus himself would be numbered, derive from the spectacle of the plague a sense of being condemned to inconceivable imprisonment for an unknown crime. And Rieux, discussing the sermon some time later with Tarrou, says that though the plague may increase the moral stature of some, one would have to be mad, blind or a coward to be resigned to the misery and suffering which it brings. He believes he is on the right road in striving against the order of creation.

Father Paneloux's first sermon had been preached in April during the original onset of the plague. In the following six months the death-rate rises to terrible proportions. There then occurs the death of a child, the son of M. Othon, the examining magistrate, and this is described in detail by Camus. The scene is witnessed by both Rieux and Paneloux. As they go away together the latter admits that he has been as revolted as Rieux by the child's agony, but he suggests that they may both experience revulsion because their understanding cannot grasp the final meaning of suffering. When he adds that we perhaps ought to love that which exceeds our understanding Rieux replies vehemently in words similar to Camus' own above: 'No, Father . . . I have a different conception of love. And I shall refuse to the bitter end to love this scheme of things in which children are tortured'.[5]

Father Paneloux's second sermon on the plague is preached shortly after the death of Othon's son. It differs markedly from the earlier one in that he now speaks of 'we' rather than 'you'. There is much greater humility, and a certain hesitancy in his manner and phrasing. Although he still maintains that good finally comes out of evil he now says that this belief cannot be demonstrated rationally but must be accepted by faith. He goes on to distinguish—moved again by the death of Othon's child—between necessary suffering (e.g. Don Juan in Hell) and apparently unnecessary suffering (e.g. the child slowly and painfully killed by the plague). He also refuses as too facile the argument that earthly pain is compensated by eternal bliss. And so the problem of evil brings one to the cross-roads of complete faith or complete disbelief. Father Paneloux is not afraid to use the word 'fatalism' in connection with the attitude which he finally commends. But it must be an active fatalism which leaps into the heart of the unacceptable by an act of positive choice.

I have spent some time summarizing these two sermons, partly because they deal with a central theme in *La Peste*, but mainly to show how metaphysical—or theological—considerations can arise directly at the literal level. This latter feature also helps, I think, to make one accept more readily the broader metaphysical implications of the second figurative level. The direct metaphysics of the sermons prepares the reader's mind for the effort of grasping the indirect metaphysics of the novel as a whole. This is also further evidence of the close integration existing between the concrete and abstract aspects of the symbol. Many secondary symbols connected with the *univers clos* might also be mentioned—the sea, for example, or the window towards which Rieux turns at several crucial moments. But enough has perhaps been said to show what Camus' purpose is and how he sets out to achieve it. One should add, of course, that although the preceding analysis may have some purpose the symbol can only be finally judged as it comes through during a direct reading of the novel. During such a reading it operates either on all three levels at once, or by swift transitions from one to another. In this way the novel is provided with an admirable focus. The symbol of the plague combines everyday elements with political and metaphysical ones in a powerful and pervasive single image. Each level of presentation gains something by its simultaneous meaning at a different level. Not only do all the themes in the book issue from the dominant image of the plague; they meet in it again with renewed significance.

The Art of the Novel (II)

Camus' first novel, *L'Étranger,* was very much a 'contemporary' novel with its various and brilliant techniques, its resemblance to a type of recent American fiction, its detachment from conventional moral attitudes. It was sufficiently original and experimental to come close to being an anti-novel. The second novel, *La Peste,* was less obviously experimental in form. Its symbolic structure and intention suggested a turning back towards one of the earliest forms of prose romance—the allegory. I have already said it is not an allegory, but part of the reason for this is the fact that the allegory, in the early and strict sense of the term, is scarcely possible today as a serious and satisfactory form of fiction. At the same time *La Peste* did suggest a certain nostalgia for the formal devices of an earlier tradition. It is Camus' third novel, *La Chute,* which is most thoroughly traditional in form. From this point of view it comes nearest to the type of French novel which he himself most admires. It is the intimate story of an individual life told in the first person. This, together with its psychological insight and moral intentions, encourages one to put it into the category of *roman personnel* which persists with such vigour and success in France. The choice and treatment of subject in *La Chute* emphasize Camus' connection not only with the *roman personnel* but with the wider moralist tradition of French literature. To think of this tradition is to think of the seventeenth century and, sooner or later, of La Rochefoucauld's *Maximes.* La Rochefoucauld made his own particular contribution to the growth of the *roman personnel,* and Camus' link with the *Maximes* may be seen in the many striking aphorisms that enrich *La Chute.** Similarities to the same tradition in the eighteenth century are also apparent. An interesting parallel might be drawn, for example, with Diderot's *Le Neveu de Rameau*

* The following are examples :

(i) 'Quand on n'a pas de caractère, il faut bien se donner une méthode' (p. 16) ['If one lacks character one must provide oneself with a method'];

(ii) 'On ne vous pardonne, votre bonheur et vos succes que si vous consentez généreusement à les partager' (p. 94) ['Your happiness and your successes will not be forgiven by people unless you generously agree to share them'];

(iii) 'Voyez-vous, une personne de mon entourage divisait les êtres en trois catégories : ceux qui préfèrent n'avoir rien à cacher plutôt que d'être obligés de mentir, ceux qui préfèrent mentir plutôt que de n'avoir rien à cacher, et ceux enfin qui aiment en même temps le mensonge et le secret' (p. 139) ['Let me tell you that one of my acquaintances used to divide human beings into three categories : those who prefer to have nothing to hide rather than be obliged to tell lies, those who prefer to tell lies rather than have nothing to hide, and finally those who like both lies and secrecy'].

181

and its discussion—sometimes cynical, sometimes sentimental—of such topics as genius, bohemianism, the nature of happiness and the relativity of virtue. The attitude to life expressed in *La Chute* makes it an unusual and original novel, but the formal presentation of this attitude is much more conventional than in Camus' earlier fiction.

La Chute is an account by Jean-Baptiste Clamence of his life and ideas. This account is witty and cynical, egotistical but elusive, and is given to a chance acquaintance whose comments are sometimes indirectly suggested but never verbally reported. The conversation takes place in Amsterdam where Clamence frequents a cheap waterfront bar. At one time he had been a highly successful Parisian lawyer. He had defended with his oratorical gifts the poor, the victimized and the more romantic criminals. He had enjoyed the respect and admiration which his devotion to good deeds and charitable causes had aroused in the public. He was very much an 'insider' and a pillar of society. Then, without warning, he underwent an experience which stripped him of his moral comfort and self-esteem. As he was crossing the Seine late at night a young woman committed suicide by jumping from a bridge into the river. Although he heard the splash of her body and her despairing cry he failed to turn back and try to help. He simply 'passed by on the other side'. The memory of this moment of cowardice, kept alive by a mysterious laugh which he occasionally thought he could hear, now haunted Clamence. He gradually came to see his former good deeds as a mere sham indulged in for the sake of popular applause. He had utterly failed to do good when no potential witnesses against him were present. Overcome by a sense of moral bankruptcy he sought escape in various forms of debauchery. Eventually he gave up his career as a lawyer, exiled himself from Paris, and became what he calls a *juge-pénitent* in the 'Mexico City Bar' in Amsterdam. It is at this point that we first meet Clamence in *La Chute*, when his progress from professional lawyer to moral 'judge-penitent' is complete. His new occupation is to buttonhole strangers in the bar and confess his moral failure to them in such a way as to accuse them in turn of similar cowardice. His story of his own life becomes a mirror held up to their lives. This is what he means by being a 'judge-penitent' and his attempt to play this rôle with another stranger provides *La Chute* with its immediate subject-matter.

I have given this summary of the novel because, in contrast to *L'Étranger* and *La Peste*, its formal aspects are mostly quite ordinary whereas its content is often difficult to interpret with certainty. What I have said so far also suggests, I think, that *La Chute* differs from the earlier novels in other ways. Whereas both *L'Étranger* and *La Peste* were set in the sharply defined light and shade of North Africa, *La Chute* has for its background the damp mists and grey skies of Amsterdam. This change in physical location reflects a change in moral climate. The atmosphere which pervades the novel is one of guilt, uncertainty and ambiguity, whereas unequivocal innocence was the source of alienation in *L'Étranger* and of obstinate revolt in *La Peste*. *La Chute* is a more profoundly pessimistic novel than the two earlier ones. It appears to be the outcome of further brooding meditation on their subject-matter. And as its title suggests it questions that assumption of human innocence so noticeable in *L'Étranger* and *La Peste*. No doubt it is not intended to be a Christian novel, but it is clearly not positively and confidently non-Christian in the way the earlier novels were. The viewpoint of Clamence is very different from that expressed by Meursault to the prison chaplain. In emphasis at least it also differs from that of Tarrou who wanted to become 'un saint sans Dieu'.

If the purely formal qualities of *La Chute* are less striking than those of the previous novels, it still remains an impressive piece of writing. The ironical tone is well sustained throughout, and there are many penetrating observations about life in general and contemporary bourgeois society in particular. At times the humour takes on an almost nightmarish quality, as do phrasing and imagery. The brilliant flow of words, and the way these words are handled, contrasts strongly with the flat narration of Meursault's estrangement or the precisely objective formulation of Rieux's dogged hope. Camus shows himself here to be the master of a style which he raised to a pitch of frenzied monologue in a short story, 'Le Renégat', written in 1956, the same year as *La Chute*, and later collected with other short stories in *L'Exil et le royaume*. Clamence does not fall into a frenzy, but his humour and imagery sometimes have an almost surrealist quality and are only saved from an appearance of artificiality or mere virtuosity by the close adherence of his phrases to natural speech rhythms.

This striking style in *La Chute* is accompanied by one unusual narrative device. Camus makes Clamence carry on a conversation throughout the novel with an anonymous character whose speech is never directly reported. From this point of view *La Chute* resembles one of those telephone conversations, so familiar in the theatre, in which we hear only the words of one speaker and have to construct the missing half of the dialogue on this single basis. The novel's constant flow of talk is spoken dialogue reduced to the proportions of literary monologue. It is as though, in *Le Neveu de Rameau* for instance, all the 'moi' speeches had been removed and were yet clearly and naturally conveyed by careful re-phrasing of the 'lui' speeches. Of course the comments of Clamence's companion play a minor rôle, but it is still a considerable technical achievement to have prolonged this kind of writing throughout the length of a novel. At the same time Camus is not the sort of writer who would give himself this difficulty solely for the technical satisfaction of solving it. Its purpose is to be seen, I think, in relation to the main ideas of the book.

In the first place, this narrative method is related to that ambiguity of subject-matter already mentioned. The equivocation in Clamence's rôle as a 'judge-penitent', in his ethical ideas and his attitude to Christianity, is reinforced by the reader's reaction to the way he expresses his views. We have to accept the artifice of monologue masquerading as dialogue. This is how he tells his story, and we may even admire the skill with which he keeps it up. But there is also something unsettling and disturbing about such a narrative method. The use of truncated dialogue suggests, among other things, that something may be suppressed or distorted. This lack of straightforwardness in Clamence's way of telling his story becomes associated in the reader's mind with the ambiguities of the story itself. At this first and very general level narrative subject and narrative method form a related and unified whole.

Further examination of the story along these lines makes it clear, I think, that our dissatisfaction with Clamence as the narrator lies specifically in the egoism of his manner. His companion is never allowed to put a point of view directly. Clamence does this for him in an arbitrary way. As a result we are completely dependent on

Clamence's interpretation of his companion's remarks. Although this second character participates formally in the dialogue he is not really granted any existence at all. The attitude of Clamence corresponds in this respect to his own estimate of human nature. He says, for example, that men see only themselves in the faces of others and love only themselves. The monologue masquerading as dialogue is used to reinforce its author's views concerning the fundamental narcissism of human beings. Even speech directed towards some second person is primarily focused on the speaker himself. Later, Clamence makes this admission :

And so I could only live . . . on condition that all human beings in the world, or the greatest possible number, were turned towards me, eternally empty, deprived of an independent life, ready to answer my call at any moment, dedicated in fact to sterility . . .[6]

In this account of himself Clamence provides an incidental explanation of the rôle of his anonymous companion whose function in the novel is best defined in the negative terms of emptiness and sterility.

The whole 'confession' of Clamence now begins to have a very hollow sound. The presence of an unrecorded speaker turns what seemed like a series of private confidences into something approaching an interrogation (the aim, in fact, of a 'judge-penitent'). Thus the third purpose of this monologue masquerading as dialogue is to prepare us for Clamence's contention that communication in modern society has become increasingly authoritarian. The communiqué, he says, has ousted the dialogue. More particularly, this device enables Camus to condemn Clamence for the very fault which the latter finds in other people. In this way Camus shows that although he himself would probably approve a number of Clamence's strictures he would also apply them to Clamence himself. This kind of effect is usually obtained by the somewhat clumsy method of making the narrator condemn himself in an obvious way by his own statements (Gide does this with the pastor in *La Symphonie pastorale*, for example). Camus uses a more subtle way of obtaining his effect here by means of the completely one-sided dialogue.

To turn from these questions of technique to the outlook on life contained in *La Chute* is to enter a world of uncomfortable truths

and disturbing uncertainties. These are the things that Clamence
speaks of in the highly appropriate manner we have just discussed.
His emphasis on human duplicity is, of course, a common enough
idea. It is rather startling to find Camus expressing the idea with
such force and conviction, but in itself it fits in perfectly with the
cynicism displayed by Clamence towards himself as well as
towards people in general. At one time Clamence had believed in
the possible innocence of man. He speaks of his early attitude to
life in language that recalls the Camus of *Noces* and *L'Étranger*:
'I was in perfect harmony with life. I blended with its entire being
and avoided no part of its irony, its grandeur and its demands'.[7]

This picture of primal innocence and ideal adjustment was shat-
tered, however, by Clamence's experience of his own cowardice.
The compromising underside of each of his virtues became increasingly clear to him. His modesty had allowed him to shine, his
humility had helped him to succeed, his goodness had permitted
him to dominate. It was in himself that he first discovered 'la
duplicité profonde de la créature'. To find an element of self-
interest in morality is not necessarily, of course, to affirm the utter
uselessness of morality. But what does emerge from such an
experience is the presence of a disturbing ambiguity in human
conduct. This ambiguity gives rise to distrust, a distrust that
envelops both man's capacity to fulfil his ideals and even the very
existence of these ideals themselves. Doubt is thus woven into the
fabric of all existence. Clamence says that the world is ambiguous
in its essence.*

It is this kind of attitude, so widely and intensely felt at the
present time, which has justified young French writers like
Nathalie Sarraute in speaking of 'the age of suspicion'. It is of
course true that Saint Paul emphasized human ambiguity of this
kind 1900 years ago, but he offered a solution which is now
unacceptable to many of those who give most serious thought to the
matter. Camus sums up the predominant contemporary attitude
when he makes Clamence say that to cease to be an object of doubt
would itself mean ceasing to exist at all. When existence is ambiguous and uncertain to this extent the idea of innocence cannot
easily be accepted. All men seem compromised and guilty in some
measure. This might well seem to bring the wheel back full circle

* cf. *La Chute*, p. 131: 'L'ordre du monde aussi est ambigu'.

to Christianity, but Clamence appears to avoid this possible conclusion by asserting that even Christ was not without guilt. He was
after all the cause, however indirect or unwitting, of the massacre
of the innocents. While he was taken to the safety of Egypt the
young children of Judea perished at the hands of Herod's soldiers.
When he grew up, Clamence says, he must have been haunted by
the knowledge of his *crime innocent*.

It is against this background of ambiguity that one must interpret
the fall which is the central symbol of the novel and which gives
it its title. There are, admittedly, straightforward Christian
parallels in *La Chute*. There are references to the Eden in which
Clamence lived before his own fall. His very name, Jean-Baptiste
Clamence, suggests John the Baptist, the *vox clamentis in deserto*.
He refers to himself as a prophet preaching in the desert of stone,
mist and stagnant water which is Amsterdam. But this biblical
symbolism does not embody Christian convictions. The Christian
doctrine of redemption, which goes hand in hand with the
Christian doctrine of the fall, is explicitly rejected. There is a sense
in which Camus means by the fall human fallibility, but this
fallibility is not original sin. It is, rather, human guilt experienced
without reference to any law; human guilt rendered all the more
acute because there is no available standard of innocence. Clamence
says that the worst human torment is to be judged without reference to laws and that this is precisely our torment.

The connection between ambiguity and the fall now becomes
clearer. The nature of ambiguity is its lack of a single and certain
point of reference. The nature of falling is loss of stability and
failure to grasp and hold some permanent object. Ambiguity and
falling are aspects of the same reality in *La Chute*. Man is seen
more as continually falling than fallen.* And this falling is without beginning or end—like the fall into a bottomless void which is
a familiar kind of nightmare. There are no certainties except the
certainty of falling. There is no rest, only a continual slithering
movement—'How can I explain it? Things kept slipping. Yes,
everything slipped past me'.⁸ Constant talking is one of the few

* There are interesting comparisons to be made between this idea and the
relationship of ambiguity (die Zweideutigkeit) to downfall (das Verfallen) in
Heidegger's *Sein und Zeit*. Camus is certainly familiar with Heidegger's thought
though not a disciple of Heidegger in the way Sartre seems to be. A related conception of universal falling is found in Rilke's short poem, *Herbst*.

ways of even seeming to arrest the process of falling, and no doubt this is the main psychological reason for Clamence's voluble monologue. Talking becomes an absolute necessity for him. Yet this is no permanent solution. Even oratory cannot hide the truth for long. Despite his admission of moral cowardice Clamence had at first managed to judge others by saying in effect: 'I am in a hopeless situation, but so are you, so are we all.' In this way he regained some assurance and moral comfort. But in the end even this expedient of becoming a 'judge-penitent' fails Clamence. Not the least of the novel's many ironies is the fact that by assuming this rôle he becomes much more odious than he had been earlier. In the very last pages of *La Chute* Clamence himself appears to realize something of the kind. He speaks of himself as a false prophet and his final words express a cynical despair: 'It is too late now. It will always be too late—fortunately!' [9]

$\mathcal{9}$ THE DRAMA

Le seul vrai théâtre est ce miroir de la vie où chaque
homme vient se contempler, contempler son époque,
et se forme dans le même temps une image universelle
de l'espèce.

Francis Ambrière

The last years of the Occupation and the immediate post-Liberation period were a rich and exciting time in the French theatre. The drama in France displayed a freshness and vitality which made it pre-eminent in Europe, perhaps in the world. Not only did Anouilh confirm his pre-war promise and Sartre emerge as a skilful and original playwright, but many other writers, previously known chiefly or solely as novelists, were at least temporarily attracted by the possibilities of the stage. A number of these writers gave to the public plays of great interest—Bernanos' *Dialogues des carmélites*, Mauriac's *Les Mal-Aimés*, Simone de Beauvoir's *Les Bouches inutiles,* Montherlant's *Le Maître de Santiago*. A little later Julien Green wrote *Sud* and *L'Ennemi*. It is the same period that witnessed the striking productions at the Marigny by Jean-Louis Barrault (particularly his revivals of some of Claudel's pre-war plays) and the many enterprising activities of such *metteurs en scène* as André Barsacq, Jacques Hébertot, Jean Marchat and Marcel Herrand. New reputations were made on the stage itself—one thinks of Maria Casarès, Gérard Philipe, Serge Reggiani—and other signs of vitality included the remarkable success of Jean Vilar's Théâtre National Populaire and the founding of the 'centres dramatiques' based on such provincial towns as Toulouse, Strasbourg and Saint-Étienne.

One of the most striking features of the post-war French drama has been its concern with the human condition, with man's place and purpose in the universe. There are many possible ways of putting such a subject on the stage, however, and theatre audiences have vehemently discussed such different plays as Anouilh's *Antigone*, Sartre's *Huis clos*, Thierry Maulnier's *Le Profanateur* or André Obey's *Lazare*. To this list might be added the plays of Camus. I spoke in Chapter 1 of Camus' enthusiasm for the theatre and of the wide experience which he gained with the Théâtre de l'Équipe in Algiers. Since the war he has gone on to make a distinctive contribution to the French drama. It is true that his second play, *Le Malentendu*, had a mixed reception when first produced, though its revival within a year was much more successful. It is also true that his third play, *L'État de siège,* was a bold experiment that failed. But his first and fourth plays, *Caligula* and *Les Justes*, were widely praised as soon as they were performed. In these two plays particularly Camus displayed very considerable dramatic talent and indeed *Les Justes* is regarded by many as being on a level with the finest achievements of Anouilh and Sartre.

Like the other dramatists mentioned above Camus has treated the theatre as a medium for serious statements about human life in some of its most general aspects. Leading writers for the post-war French stage have all been concerned to reflect in their work the moral dilemmas and philosophical inquiries of the day. The 'serious' French drama has been distinguished by its attempt to dissect contemporary unrest and, in many cases, to prescribe remedies for it. This general invasion of the theatre by metaphysics has been encouraged, I think, by the predominance of various 'existential' philosophies and attitudes, whether these be Christian or atheistic. A widespread distrust of abstract logic and a repeated insistence on the primacy of direct human experience have caused various writers with philosophical interests to regard the theatre as an ideal vehicle for a particular kind of philosophizing. Gabriel Marcel, for example, has described his plays as containing his philosophical thought in what he calls its 'virgin state'. Later he adds that 'the rôle of the drama, at a certain level, seems to be to place us at a point of vantage at which truth is made concrete to us, far above any level of abstract definitions'.* Again one may say that Marcel's philosophy, Sartre's atheistic existentialism and Camus' doctrine of revolt against the absurd all have in common noticeable features of tension and drama. In different though related ways they emphasize conflict, choice, unrest, responsibility.

* G. Marcel, *The Mystery of Being* (Vol. I), London, Harvill Press, 1950, p. 58.

They also find it desirable to demonstrate or exemplify this view of the human condition in order to discuss it, and the drama has proved a forceful and economical means of carrying out both operations.

Such a predominantly philosophical attitude to the function of the drama has given it some distinctive features. The general proposition that existence precedes essence, for example, has resulted in many plays in which the *situation* confronting the characters receives much fuller treatment than those characters' *psychological* aspects. Sartre was referring to Anouilh, Camus and Simone de Beauvoir, as well as to himself, when he wrote:

What is universal to their way of thinking is not nature but the situation in which man finds himself; that is, not the sum total of his psychological traits but the limits which enclose him on all sides . . . . As a successor to the theatre of characters we want to have a theatre of situation . . . . The people in our plays will be distinct from one another—not as a coward is from a miser or a miser from a brave man, but rather as actions are divergent or clashing, as right may conflict with right.*

This last sentence hints at another feature of many recent French plays—their concern with ethical conflict and choice. They often contain situations of intense moral ambiguity, as in *Les Mains sales* or *Les Justes*. Frequently the situations in question are of a type least adequately provided for by traditional moral teaching. Their solution requires a wisdom that begins beyond the point where moral systems end. In other words they attempt to create a new and more adequate ethic in the light of contemporary experience and altered philosophical ideas. This aim, in its turn, has introduced a didactic element into many plays and resulted in a 'theatre of ideas'. This kind of drama has not usually been popular in England. Indeed, there is probably some truth in the claim that English theatre audiences tend to remember what they *see* and French audiences what they *hear*. But these recent French plays have mostly been well received in England because they also possess an excellent sense of the theatre and because the moral issues behind their didacticism are the source of intense dramatic conflict. A theatre of ideas has proved acceptable when supported by sufficient skill and sufficiently important subject-matter.

* Article by Sartre translated under the title 'Forgers of myths' in *Theatre Arts*, June 1946.

Albert Camus

It would be misleading, of course, to suggest that such play-wrights as Sartre, Anouilh, Montherlant, Camus, Marcel and others have a close enough similarity to constitute a distinct school or movement. They resemble one another in so far as they write philosophical plays reflecting the darker doubts and more uncertain aspirations of their day, but they do this in separate and individual ways. No doubt Camus was expressing a view shared by the others when he insisted that the drama must draw its strength first and foremost from the significance of its subject-matter. He believes that a living theatre can only retain its vitality by discussing serious themes and portraying fundamental emotions. But the choice of themes and the manner in which they are developed on the stage varies with each particular dramatist. Camus himself, as we have already seen, is a particularly independent thinker and writer, and his aims in his plays have distinctive features of their own.

In a note included in the programme for his stage adaptation of Faulkner's *Requiem for a Nun* Camus says that his interest in the theatre is confined to two things: the creation of a modern form of tragedy and the technical problems of the stage. These two points of interest bulk large in his own dramatic output and indeed the success or failure of individual plays depends very largely on the extent to which he has solved the problems arising from them. His main aim as a dramatist is to create what he calls 'une tragédie en veston' or tragedy in lounge suits.* Because our age has its own form of tragedy this tragedy should be embodied in a specifically contemporary dramatic form by living playwrights. Works like *Le Mythe de Sisyphe* and *L'Homme révolté* show that Camus sees contemporary tragedy as ultimately metaphysical in nature and this view has had a very noticeable effect on his own plays. Difficult situations, as Sartre has said, have an important part in them, and Camus usually pays more attention to the philosophical implications of these situations than to the psychology of the characters

* According to Marc Blanquet in *Opéra,* 12 September 1945, Camus told him: 'The public is tired of the Atridae, of adaptations from antiquity, of that modern tragic sense which, alas, is all too rarely present in ancient myths however generously they may be stuffed with anachronisms. A great modern form of the tragic must and will be born . . . certainly I shall not achieve this; perhaps none of our contemporaries will . . . . But this does not lessen our duty to assist in the work of clearance which is now necessary so as to prepare the ground for it. We must use our limited means to hasten its arrival.'

who experience them. One of his main problems as a dramatist has therefore been to portray individualized and convincing people while exploring metaphysical dilemmas. In this respect his plays have had to reach a compromise between his own intellectual interests and the familiar expectations of theatre audiences. Sometimes the compromise has been very successful, but not always so. There has occasionally been much justification in the complaint that certain characters are the mouthpieces of abstract ideas and not convincing human individuals.

It should be added, I think, that some of the characters in Camus' plays are also remote from ordinary members of the audience in so far as they are *hommes révoltés*. They do not always experience a tragic destiny in a passive way and sometimes, as in the different cases of Caligula and Martha, they actively provoke it. Because they are obsessed by the desire for truth, or feel betrayed by existence, their lucidity and tenacity prompt them to act with an inhuman singleness of purpose or to bring about situations that will reveal the desperateness of their condition. As a result some of these characters are near to being monsters, judged by ordinary standards, and repel the desire for emotional involvement and identification which most audiences feel. Thus various characters are not only insufficiently individualized and humanized; they also seem psychologically remote. They appear to be eccentrics or monsters and the tragedy in which they are involved becomes a matter for intellectual apprehension, not emotional experience. This intellectual presentation of tragedy brings to mind Greek tragic drama. The plays of Aeschylus and Sophocles are more studies of metaphysical dilemmas than of tragically flawed characters in, for example, the Shakespearian sense. In the Greek theatre, of course, the chorus played a part in bridging the gap between the audience and the play by helping to make clear the metaphysical implications of the action. In plays like *Caligula* and *L'État de siège* we find that certain groups of characters have a similar function. We have already seen, however, that Camus himself rejects any direct or detailed borrowing from ancient drama. He avoids the widespread French fashion, in Anouilh, Cocteau and others, of using 'modernized' classical myths as a means of introducing a tragic metaphysic into the contemporary theatre. He believes that modern tragedy should be independent and distinctive. This attitude gives rise in its turn to problems of tonality and language. Legendary heroes and heroines are sufficiently remote for us to accept easily enough a somewhat artificial rhetoric on their part. Indeed we sometimes regard this as the authentic tone of tragedy. But contemporary characters in a contemporary play are similar to ourselves in appearance and speak to us in our own times about our own times. In these circumstances they must address us in something nearer to our own vocabulary. They cannot speak like Antigone or Orpheus. The problem is therefore to devise a language for them which will be simple enough to be natural yet elevated enough to achieve tragic power. Camus finds a near approach to his ideal in Faulkner's *Requiem for a Nun*, and his own method of solving the problem has been to adopt a style of speech for most of his characters which is literary in tone without being too far removed from spoken language. This is his compromise between naturalness and tragic elevation. He also seems to strengthen the device, in *Le Malentendu* at least, by making the opening dialogues almost completely naturalistic and then, as the play develops, raising the tone of the language so that the characters gradually achieve an almost mythic status of their own through the way in which they express themselves.

It seems most sensible to discuss Camus' plays in the order in which he wrote them. I shall therefore begin with some comments on *Caligula*. Although *Caligula* reached the Parisian stage fifteen months after *Le Malentendu* its composition preceded that of the latter by five years. It was completed in 1938, published in 1944 and performed in September 1945. Paul Œttly produced it at the Hébertot with Gérard Philipe in the title part.

Caligula has a straightforward historical basis. Its subject is the third of the twelve Caesars described by Suetonius. Caius Caesar Caligula came to power in A.D. 37 at the age of 25, and reigned for four years until his assassination in A.D. 41. For the first eight months of his reign he proved a relatively enlightened and generous ruler. He largely reversed the policy of Tiberius and made a series of concessions by freeing state prisoners, bringing about progressive changes in the judicial system, etc. During this same period, however, he conceived an incestuous love for his sister Drusilla and announced his intention of marrying her. Then

Drusilla suddenly died and almost overnight Caligula's character seemed to change completely. He abruptly became a monster of vice and cruelty. Suetonius speaks of him as being 'rather a monster than a man'. He killed, tortured or condemned his subjects until some members of his court rebelled openly and assassinated him. In his play Camus draws directly from Suetonius. *Le Figaro* of 25 September 1945 quotes him as saying that he invented nothing, added nothing, but accepted the account of Caligula given by Suetonius—'un journaliste qui savait voir'. Thus one finds, both in Suetonius and in Camus' play, references to Caligula's restlessness and insomnia, his apparent madness, his grimacing in front of the mirror, his wooing of the moon. The same is true of many other details including his murder of his mistress, Caesonia, his orders to arrange a famine in the land, his scheme to open brothels as a source of income for himself. Two of the most dramatically effective scenes in the play are also derived from Suetonius: the worship of Caligula dressed up as Venus in Act III, sc. i, and his 'poetic contest' on the subject of death in Act IV, sc. xi. Although he took so many facts from Suetonius Camus naturally interpreted them in a way that suited his own ideas at the time the play was written. *Caligula* belongs to the period in which he was most acutely aware of the absurd. In an article previously mentioned Marc Blanquet reports him as saying:

I have been all the way with the character I chose as my subject and could not do otherwise despite the moral lesson which, I think, emerges from the play. This is that one cannot be free by being against other people.[1]

The case history of Caligula is associated by Camus with the absurd. The play opens a day or two after the death of Drusilla and this event makes Caligula really conscious of the absurd for the first time. It appears, however, that Drusilla's death in itself has upset him less than the features of the human condition which it indicates. It has revealed to him, he tells Helicon, that 'men die and are not happy' (*Caligula*, I, v). The death and despair of human beings constitute his discovery of the absurd. Having become aware of the absurd in this way Caligula both accepts its inevitability and rebels against it. Although he really regards it as an inescapable reality he also tries to evade its consequences for himself by intensifying those consequences for other people. He wants to enter what he himself describes as the realm of the impossible. This is why he desires the moon:

This world as it is is not to be endured. Therefore I need the moon, or happiness, or immortality, something which is mad perhaps, but which does not belong to this world.[2]

Caligula thus exemplifies one form of revolt against the absurd, a form which Camus soon rejected. Caligula adds after the remark just quoted that the seemingly impossible may perhaps be obtained if one is logical to the utmost limits. In the context of the absurd this all-embracing logic means reducing everything to the same level of unimportance and turning upside down most conventions and sanctions. The logic of the absurd makes the greatness of Rome and Caesonia's arthritis equally unimportant. This logic also brings complete freedom to the individual who wields power and authority. Furthermore it tells him that all human beings are condemned to death so that whether they die sooner or later matters little. It is this kind of logic that Caligula has bitterly decided to follow to its conclusion and this decision sets the main action of the play in motion. Caligula institutes a cruel and capricious reign of terror among his subjects. It has the threefold purpose of accepting the fact of the absurd, making a personal protest against it by bringing it out into the open, forcing others to recognize the truth Caligula has discovered. As Act I comes to an end he beats furiously on a gong and shouts to Caesonia:

Life, Caesonia, life is the opposite of love. It is I who tell you so and it is I who invite you to an unsurpassed celebration, to a public trial, to the finest of all spectacles. And I need people, spectators, victims, the guilty. Bring in the guilty. I need the guilty. All of them are guilty. I want the condemned to be brought in . . . . Judges, witnesses, the accused, all of them condemned in advance![3]

The remaining three acts of the play show the effects of Caligula's decision. He imposes arbitrary suffering. At a whim he kills individuals or has them killed. His cruelty is appalling in its consequences, though one can at least admire the way in which he exposes the shallowness, the mediocrity, the hypocrisy of many of his subjects. At one point, in the course of some comments on his own cruelty, he says to Scipio:

The rivalry of the gods has its irritating side for a man who loves power. I have suppressed it. I have proved to these illusory gods that, provided a man has the will, he can carry on their ridiculous trade without prior training.

SCIPIO : That is blasphemy, Caius.

CALIGULA : No Scipio, it is lucidity. I have simply realized that there is only one way of being equal with the gods. It is enough to be as cruel as they are.[4]

Statements like these make it clear that Caligula is a certain kind of *révolté*, but by his rebellion against the absurd he only intensifies it. The motives of his revolt—a desire for lucidity and a readiness to act in accordance with the truth he finds—would have Camus' approval, but the methods of his revolt are utterly wrong. Caligula himself begins to realize this towards the end of the play. Having strangled Caesonia, he mutters in Act IV, sc. xii : 'yet murder is no solution'. In the next scene, which is also the last, he condemns his actions as a whole. Not only does he decide that murder is no solution; he adds : 'I have not taken the right road, I have achieved nothing. Mine is not the right kind of freedom.'[5] Camus' own comment on Caligula's mistake is contained in a note included in the programme for the Hébertot production :

. . . if his integrity consists in his denial of the gods, his fault is to be found in his denial of men. One cannot destroy everything without destroying oneself. This is why Caligula depopulates the world around him and then, in keeping with his own logic, does what is necessary to arm against himself those who will ultimately kill him. Caligula's story is that of a high-minded type of suicide. It is an account of the most human and most tragic of mistakes. Caligula is faithless towards humanity in order to keep faith with himself. He consents to die, having learnt that no man can save himself alone and that one cannot be free by working against mankind. But at least he will have rescued some souls, including his own and that of his friend Scipio, from the dreamless sleep of mediocrity.

One of the other main characters in the play, Cherea, makes this last point. He says that Caligula forces people to think by making them insecure, by jolting them out of the rut, and this is really why he arouses their hatred. He shatters their easy assumptions and makes them face unpalatable truths. This is the aspect of Caligula's behaviour which Camus admires, and Cherea understands it. It is also understood by Scipio. Caligula says that Scipio is pure in the realm of good as he himself is pure in the realm of evil. This enables Scipio to understand the ideals pursued—and also perverted—by Caligula. One can say, in fact, that four different attitudes to Caligula's behaviour are indicated in the play. The patricians generally are too sunk in mediocrity to understand him. The outraged attitude they display centres round their own unimportant lives and their private wealth. Caesonia does not understand him either, though she uneasily accepts his actions. By accepting his logic she seals her own fate since this very logic finally requires her to become one of Caligula's victims. An attitude of comprehension is found is Cherea and Scipio. Camus thus uses them in part at least, to explain more fully to the audience the apparently outrageous and demented activities of Caligula. To some extent they act as a chorus, as in ancient tragedy, since they reveal the real nature of Caligula's revolt and indicate two different attitudes to it based on a proper understanding of its metaphysical nature. Cherea understands it and rejects it utterly. He is convinced that Caligula must be removed and he works for this end. Scipio also understands Caligula's reaction to the absurd but in his case understanding prevents him from joining the assassins. He says to Cherea: '. . . I cannot be against him. If I killed him my heart, at least, would still be on his side.'[6] When pressed further by Cherea he adds: 'The same flame consumes our hearts . . . . My misfortune is that I can see reason in every attitude.'[7] Cherea now considers that Scipio has been completely corrupted by Caligula's logic. He has accepted abstract logic rather than practical reasonableness because of the depths of his own despair. Cherea regards it as the worst of all Caligula's crimes to have wrought this transformation in the purity of Scipio. He leaves Scipio in order to make final preparations for the assassination of Caligula.

Readers of *L'Homme révolté* will find *Caligula* particularly interesting because it contains an imaginative projection of various ideas more fully explained and discussed in the later essay. For the audiences of 1945, however, especially those unacquainted with Camus' other writings on the absurd, the play was perhaps chiefly interesting as a kind of political morality. Several of the first critical notices made this point by speaking of similarities between the megalomania of Caligula and of Hitler, between Caligula's attitude of mind and that revealed by some Nazi theorists, between Caligula's actions and those of Hitler, between Caligula's suicidal death and Hitler's self-immolation in the Berlin bunker. These are genuine aspects of the play of course, and they contributed to its first success. *Caligula* contains various ideas also discussed in *Lettres à un ami allemand*. But a more important aspect of the play remains. How good a play is *Caligula* in itself, independent of its apparent topicality in 1945 or its special interest now for those who know Camus' other writings well? I think the answer should be that it is a good play, for several reasons. For instance, the subject-matter itself clearly provides Camus with a wealth of material. This material is dramatic, spectacular, and it moves steadily and inevitably towards a climax. Camus, by having such material at his disposal, was therefore able to adopt the natural order of his subject while retaining tenseness and dramatic density. In the case of *Le Malentendu* one may feel that a rather limited amount of dramatic material is being artificially, if cleverly, expanded for the purposes of a full-length play. This is not so in *Caligula* which is free from wordy *longueurs*. At the same time it has been suggested that the play is unsatisfactory after the first act. From then on we have a series of situations logically derived from Caligula's earlier decision to try to achieve the impossible. The result, it is argued, is a sequence of tableaux which are striking enough in themselves but lack real dramatic connection with one another. In a sense this is undoubtedly true, and it may appear to be a serious criticism of *Caligula* as a drama for the stage. My own feeling is, however, that the cumulative effect of these tableaux and their rise towards a climax ensures their effect in the theatre. In addition, the fact that they all have a direct logical link with Caligula's first decision gives them a collective necessity and preserves their dramatic unity.

This unity is also strengthened by the domineering and neurotic figure of Caligula himself. The play is organized around him. He gives it a dramatic centre and dramatic impact. His personality holds the attention of the audience. He is repellent and yet fascinating, a tyrant and also a victim, a madman whose logic nevertheless cuts cleanly through the muddle-headedness and hypocrisy of many of his subjects. Camus also makes dramatically effective use of his tempestuous beating on the gong and his repeated self-scrutiny in the mirror. This latter device has obvious symbolical as well as direct meaning, and this indicates another source of strength in the play. The character of Caligula allows the play to appeal to the audience on two distinct levels. For those who do not grasp the philosophical ideas fully, or who find them too abstract to hold their attention, the play can still appeal as an unusual and powerful psychological study. Caligula himself is no mere abstraction; his very inhumanity is humanized. This also means that for those who accept more readily the metaphysical nature of Caligula's revolt it has a double interest. The success the play enjoyed on its first performance is partly due, I think, to this unified duality which allowed Camus to give psychological body to his admittedly didactic intentions. Some critics, it must be added, found the play too abstract on its first performance in spite of everything. One said it was philosophy, not theatre, and another described it as being literature but not drama. Most of the leading critics were enthusiastic, however, and several claimed *Caligula* to be the most impressive new play to have reached the Parisian stage since before the war.

Near the beginning of the second part of *L'Étranger*, while Meursault is awaiting his trial, he finds a piece of newspaper that is yellow with age and has stuck to the underside of his mattress in the prison cell. On examining the scrap of paper he finds that it contains a news item reporting an unusually macabre tragedy. A man had left his village, apparently somewhere in Czechoslovakia, and gone abroad to make his fortune. He was successful, became rich, and after twenty-five years returned to the place of his birth accompanied by his wife and child. His mother and sister now ran a small hotel in the village. The son decided that for fun he would put up at this hotel as an ordinary guest without revealing his identity. He left his wife and child behind at another inn. His mother failed to recognize him as her son and during the night she and her daughter killed him, took his money and threw his body into the river. Next morning his wife arrived and his identity was revealed. Thereupon the mother hung herself and the sister threw herself into a well. Commenting on this story Meursault says that in one way he finds it improbable and in another quite natural.

He adds that the son was himself guilty in so far as 'one should not play tricks'.

In *Le Malentendu* Camus again takes up this *fait-divers* and with a few very minor changes makes it the subject of a tragedy in three acts. This is his second play, though his first to be performed in Paris. It was written in 1943 and produced by Marcel Herrand at the Mathurins in June 1944. Herrand himself played Jan, the son; the parts of Jan's mother and sister, 'la mère' and Martha, were interpreted by Marie Kalff and Maria Casarès respectively.

I have already said that the material used in *Le Malentendu* is perhaps somewhat slight for a three-act play. It should also be pointed out, however, that the nature of this material is such as to contain several advantages for the purpose of dramatic presentation. To begin with, it offers a unified plot that builds up to a tragic climax. The story has a formal simplicity and directness which allows Camus to observe the unities of time, place and action still much admired in the French theatre. There are no side-issues to detract from the progressive unfolding of the final tragedy. Everything contributes to the climax so that the plot gains in coherence and singleness of purpose as a result. Another noticeable feature is the way in which this climax is related to the preceding events by a series of closely knit occurrences. This introduces into the plot an element of tragic inevitability giving added impact to it. Camus has blunted the impact, according to some critics, by moving too slowly through the phases of inevitability to the dénouement, but this is not a criticism made by most people who have seen the play on the stage. My own view is that the nature of the subject-matter requires a relatively slow dramatic pace. As Camus interprets his material it produces a drama of hesitation and misunderstanding, and the various moments of hesitation contribute to the play's tension. The misunderstanding referred to in the title of the play is a third outstanding feature of the original story. It depends, in fact, on a central failure of recognition. This means that the material offers many opportunities for dramatic irony and Camus handles this theatrical device very effectively in the play. Finally, because of a misunderstanding in this sense, the characters in the story are the unwitting victims of a fate whose operation is clear from an early stage to those who read about it. This situation is of the essence of one kind of tragedy in the theatre and gives further dramatic impact to the play.

Such considerations as these confirm the view that in *Le Malentendu* Camus chose material containing promising dramatic possibilities. It is also true that his feeling for the theatre prompted him to use these possibilities to advantage in the play itself. And yet, despite such apparent advantages, *Le Malentendu* was not well received. Camus even went so far as to call it a failure.* It is also noticeable that the most friendly disposed critics found fault with the play, though some still insisted that it gave evidence of Camus' future promise as a dramatist. It is not altogether easy to give precise reasons for the failure of *Le Malentendu* to please the theatre-going public, but I think two features of the play were mainly responsible. In the first place, although the original material was straightforward in a certain sense, the interpretation put on it by Camus in his concern with the absurd was unusual and not widely understood. *Le Malentendu* therefore presented difficulties of interpretation to audiences unfamiliar with Camus' ideas in general. Secondly, this preoccupation with a philosophical attitude weakened the dramatic appeal of the original material in a fundamental way. The story used by Camus seems to demand that the playwright concern himself with intricate psychological explanations and moral discussions. If the average audience is to accept this drama of fratricide and suicide it must see the main characters as human beings and gradually be led to understand why they acted in the way they did. But Camus deliberately depersonalized the main characters and treated the situation not in psychological but in philosophical terms. Therefore it was difficult for an audience to appreciate *Le Malentendu* because it was being asked to accept the metaphysical interpretation of a situation which it could not accept in straightforward human terms in the first place. I think these two difficulties are mainly responsible for the cool reception given to *Le Malentendu*, and they must now be considered more closely by a more detailed examination of the play.

Le Malentendu is primarily a portrait of several characters caught up in the absurdity of existence. The incoherence of the

---

* '. . . the truth of the matter is that *Le Malentendu*, though it drew quite large audiences, was rejected by the majority of these audiences. This is what is called, in plain terms, a failure' (*Le Figaro*, 15–16 October, 1944).

world is referred to on various occasions, particularly in the third act. In the first scene of this act the mother speaks of 'this earth where nothing is certain' and adds that 'the world itself is not rational'. At the very end of the play awareness of the absurd is presented as the reason for Martha's acceptance of crime and lack of remorse. Earlier it had been the reason for her desire to escape to a distant and sunny country close to the sea. In the closing moments of the play, speaking of the brother she has murdered, she says to his distraught wife, Maria:

You must understand that there is neither homeland nor peace for him or for us, either in life or in death. One cannot regard as one's homeland, can one, this obscure world deprived of light. . . .[8]

Almost immediately afterwards she adds:

Pray to your God that he may make you like stone. This is his private form of happiness, the only true happiness. Be like him, make yourself deaf to all cries, be like the stone while there is still time.[9]

Martha's behaviour thus bears a close resemblance to that of Caligula. She attempts a violent and murderous revolt against the absurd. As in the case of Caligula, however, she sees in the end the sterility of this kind of revolt. She had thought that she and her mother were inseparably united by the crimes they had committed together, yet her mother, on discovering Jan's true identity, rejected her daughter and took her own life. Therefore Martha says: 'Crime is also a form of solitude, even if a thousand people commit it together. It is just that I should die alone after having lived and killed alone.' [10] In this last sentence Martha refers to her own resolution to commit suicide—an action that recalls the 'high-minded' suicide of Caligula.

The awareness of solitude shown by Martha is another aspect of her feeling for the absurd. In fact, *Le Malentendu* is very much a drama of human separation and exile. The theme of loneliness takes many forms and is particularly obvious in the case of both Martha and Jan. She meets solitude in the course of destroying life; he finds himself equally alone in the way he chooses to affirm life. He must leave his wife behind him in the attempt to make contact with his mother and sister, yet when the time comes he cannot find the formula that would establish this contact.

Albert Camus

Martha and Jan differ greatly, of course, in the way each is related to the absurd. It is Martha's sharp awareness of it that brings it into prominence in her life; it is Jan's unawareness of it that makes it manifest in his. Martha sees absurdity as the essential fact of existence and she bases her actions on its ineradicable nature 'life is more cruel than we are' (I, i). Jan takes the opposite point of view—'I have confidence in the things that are' (I, iii)—and becomes an unwitting vehicle through which the absurd works. He seeks happiness through confidence in existence rather than revolt against it. Despite this confidence, however, he is still something of an outsider. Indeed he is an outsider rather than the prodigal son which some critics have claimed him to be. He returns to the lives of his mother and sister as a stranger. His overriding desire is to be spontaneously recognized, to be given his true identity, to be accepted as a member of his family. His fundamental mistake is to indulge his phantasy, to act irresponsibly in the desperate and serious situation that is life overshadowed by the absurd. A whim prevents him from speaking the one vital sentence and the result is death—death for himself, his mother and his sister, and suffering for his wife, Maria. On this point Camus has claimed that the play, despite its obvious pessimism, also points to a relative optimism. If Jan had revealed his identity the tragedy could have been avoided. In one sense this is true, and Jan's obstinate refusal to take the obvious course may be regarded as a weakness in the play's structure. But Camus makes the point in order to salvage the optimistic interpretation which says, in effect, that a man can save himself and others, even in an absurd world, by exercising sincerity and speaking with simple directness to those with whom he comes in contact. This is no serious solution of the absurd. At best it is an idea prompted by objections to the depressing aspects of the play. It is hardly consistent with what Camus has written elsewhere about the absurd, nor does it seem justified by the emphasis on individual solitude and exile in *Le Malentendu* itself. There is truth in the view that this play of separation and failure to communicate appears as a tragedy of lost opportunities. But the absurd is more complete and insuperable than such a view might suggest. It works at times through an ironical reversal of values and can turn even genuine communication into fatal channels. Martha is characterized above all by an almost inhuman harshness, yet Jan actually seals his own fate by managing to arouse the small human residue in her nature. Martha explains the point to her mother:

In the end you persuaded me to share your doubt. But he spoke to me of the country to which my thoughts are turned and because he was able to move me provided me with weapons against himself. That is how innocence is rewarded.[11]

It is at moments such as this that the play really descends into the depths of pessimism. And it is difficult to reconcile them even with the indirect optimism that Camus claims for it.

One may say then that within the wider context of Camus' doctrine of the absurd *Le Malentendu* is clearly comprehensible, if very disquieting. But this philosophical meaning does not develop naturally from the realistic aspect as it did in the case of *Caligula*. The naturalistic and symbolic interpretations are not closely integrated; indeed there are occasions when certain remarks or reactions by the characters make little or no sense at an ordinary human level. Jan's meditation in the hotel bedroom (II, ii) is a case in point. His fear of everlasting solitude and his anxiety lest there be no reply to his call are expressed in the midst of repeated entries into his room, both before and after these thoughts, by Martha and by his mother. At a naturalistic level his remarks therefore seem unmotivated and unjustified. They only make sense when given a metaphysical interpretation. Again, unlike *Caligula*, *Le Malentendu* contains no explanatory 'chorus' guiding the audience towards an understanding of its philosophical implications. Maria might possibly have fulfilled this rôle. In fact she does give Martha an opportunity of coming near to an explanation of these matters in the final moments. But Maria is primarily outraged and uncomprehending (it is possible to see some kind of parallel with the biblical Martha and Mary here). She is the one genuine human being in the play. This very fact, however causes her to emerge rather as the mouthpiece of those who remain baffled by the abstract asperities of *Le Malentendu*. Far from making events more understandable she presumably voiced and confirmed the puzzlement experienced by audiences who first saw the play in 1944.

These features of the play are among the factors that made its central meaning elusive on the stage. In addition, the dichotomy already mentioned between the literal and philosophical levels added to the difficulty by making the main characters unacceptable as credible human figures. It is understandable, of course, that these characters should be stylized to some extent. This fits in with Camus' own ideas about the creation of a modern 'tragédie en veston'. But the stylization is imposed on characters who, because of the situation in which they are placed, must first convince us of their human probability before going on to represent philosophical attitudes. This is precisely what they fail to do. One banal but, I think, justifiable objection arises from the fact that Martha and her mother are not only excessively articulate for two peasant women but engage in surprisingly abstract or disconcertingly enigmatic discussions which are meant to arise naturally from their actions. The things they say at some length are not satisfactorily related to the emotions they would surely experience if they really were human beings. It is not their cruelty which disturbs one most. It is their complete lack of recognizable human attributes, whether these be vices or virtues. Martha, in particular, appears to be devoid of all human responses and entirely empty, except for her logically inconsistent desire to escape from the absurd—which she holds to be inescapable—to a far-off country of sunshine and plenty. The inhuman indifference of Martha and her mother, combined with the obstinate obtuseness of Jan which sometimes has to be 'managed' in an obvious way, leads to several dramatic weaknesses in the play. It means, for instance, that the formal heroine of the play, Martha, is an unsympathetic figure who experiences no sense of guilt at any point and who commits suicide through rage, not remorse. Furthermore, given her imperviousness to feeling, there seems to be nothing in her character to explain this final act and no reason for acting as she did. Again, the central situation—the murder of a man by his mother and sister—loses much of its dramatic impact because, in accordance with the absurd, it is carried out in indifference, having been set in motion by a capricious combination of chance and habit. The murder appears at no point as being due to a fatal clash of real characters. Indeed, the tragedy in *Le Malentendu* is one of banality, indifference and human emptiness. A rather similar account of an emotional void was most successfully treated by Camus in his novel, *L'Étranger*, but this type of hollow, absurdist character is not a success on the stage. The whole atmosphere of *Le Malentendu*, couched as it is in chill and severe dialogue, makes it a play that can be read with much interest but which fails to communicate itself adequately in the theatre. I say that it can be read with much interest because I am bound to confess to a liking for the play despite its demonstrable faults. Its very severity and human remoteness seem to me to give it a certain tragic grandeur. On the other hand, such qualities have told against it in the theatre. One must admit, with whatever reluctance, that Camus' preoccupation with the absurd led him, in this instance, to interpret promising dramatic material in such a way as to deprive it of its dramatic strength. The philosophical attitude behind the play, which requires that the characters should fail to communicate and to understand each other, also leads ultimately to a breakdown in communication and understanding between these same characters and their audience.

We have seen that *Caligula* and *Le Malentendu* are both dramas of the absurd. Camus' two later plays, *L'État de siège* and *Les Justes*, reflect his subsequent preoccupation with the idea of revolt. The power of revolt over the absurd, particularly over its political and social forms, is the central theme of *L'État de siège*. The play deals with the eventual powerlessness of political dictatorship and bureaucratic frenzy before an attitude of humane and courageous rebellion. The efficacy of revolt is mentioned several times. Even the dictator's secretary admits its strength when she says:

As far back as I can remember it has always proved enough that a man should conquer his fear, and rebel, for their machinery to begin to creak. I do not say that it stops functioning; this is by no means so. But at any rate it creaks, and sometimes it ends by being really jammed.[12]

One may say as a general comment on *L'État de siège* that, whereas *Le Malentendu* recalled *L'Étranger*, this third play suggests aspects both of *La Peste* and *L'Homme révolté*. It employs the same central symbol as *La Peste*—that of a plague striking down the inhabitants of a town—while the objects of its satire include some of the features of political life most strongly criticized in *L'Homme révolté*.

The action of the play may be briefly described as follows. The plague, embodied in a sinister human dictator, comes to the Spanish town of Cadiz. The Plague/dictator is accompanied by a female secretary who keeps a list of the town's inhabitants in a notebook. She can infect individuals with the epidemic and she can also kill them outright by striking their names off the list with her pencil. The Plague himself institutes a reign of terror which he reinforces by a series of administrative measures. These involve all the worst features of bureaucracy and are largely carried out by a drunken nihilist appropriately named Nada. A chorus of ordinary citizens expresses confusion, anger and fear at various points in the play. A young man, Diego, is in love with Victoria, the daughter of a judge, and he gradually emerges as the hero. In the end he accepts death and renounces life with Victoria, but by his action, compounded of courage and sacrifice, he frees the town of Cadiz from the Plague.

It seems clear that *L'État de siège* is Camus' most ambitious play. He has created a modern myth and put into it the essence of his analysis and criticism of contemporary society. He has also used it to indicate, in imaginative terms, some general idea of the solution he proposes to the problems he has raised. The play is, in fact, an artistic projection of some of his most fundamental attitudes, and some indication of the care Camus lavished upon it may be gained from his year's collaboration with Barrault before it was completed and from the fact that he says he wrote as many as five or six versions of parts of the text during rehearsals. *L'État de siège* is an ambitious theatrical venture in another sense. It attempts to use all the various possibilities of the stage. Not only does it contain a variety of dramatic styles such as lyricism, satire, tragedy, burlesque; in addition the stage directions indicate the use of mime, of complicated movements by the chorus, of ingenious lighting effects. All this took place, in Barrault's production, against a background of striking music by Honegger and a most imaginative décor devised by Balthus, the former surrealist and close friend of Joan Miró. As a result, the visual and aural aspects of the production were among its most memorable features. When the play was first produced at the Marigny in October 1948 it was also provided with a star-studded cast. This included Barrault himself as Diego, Maria Casarès as Victoria, Pierre Bertin as the Plague, Madeleine Renaud as his secretary, Pierre Brasseur as Nada. Such distinguished members of the Marigny company as Simone Valère and Jean Desailly accepted parts in the chorus. This last feature was of particular satisfaction both to Barrault and Camus. The former held it to be a measure of the strength and cohesion of his company, while Camus regarded it as a renewed approach to that experiment in 'collective theatre' which he attempted in Algiers twelve years earlier with *La Révolte dans les Asturies*.

As in the case of *Le Malentendu*, Camus' subject in *L'État de siège* possesses interest and importance. What one assumes to have been his intentions in writing this play also show a good deal of imagination and spirit. Yet in spite of these advantages, and in spite of the assistance of Balthus and Honegger, the play proved a more complete failure than *Le Malentendu*. Because of this fact one is bound to say, I think, that the point of critical interest, where *L'État de siège* is concerned, has now mainly become identified with the attempt to understand clearly the reasons for its failure. Many of the critical notices which followed the early performances put the blame squarely on Barrault's shoulders. It was frequently asserted that Barrault had exercised an unfortunate influence on Camus and had persuaded him to succumb to the idea of 'total theatre' with its indiscriminate mixing of theatrical styles, its accent on mime and 'choreography', its disproportionate emphasis on the décor and the incidental music. In *Témoignage chrétien* for 5 November 1948, Jean Mauduit went so far as to say : 'Barrault has devoured Camus'. Camus has at no time minimized his debt to Barrault. He readily acknowledges it in his preface to the published play. It is also clear, however, that he accepts, with characteristic fairness and loyalty, full responsibility for whatever faults and weaknesses the play may possess. Indeed, one would imagine that his own stated interest in the technical aspects of production made him a willing and even an enthusiastic collaborator with Barrault in this connection. I myself think it a mistake to attribute the failure of *L'État de siège* to its producer. The chief reasons for this failure are to be found in the play itself, not in the manner of its presentation. Even if the loose construction and disjointed rhythm are partly a result of Barrault's requirements, it is also true that more radical faults exist within the play as a play. These faults must be attributed to Camus.

Le Malentendu presented the absurd as an integral part of all existence. The central theme of the play was a metaphysical one and a degree of stylization both of the characters and their speech became necessary. In the case of *L'État de siège*, however, Camus turns to a much more concrete aspect of the absurd—its incorporation into social and political action. The absurd now appears more as the source of a particular kind of human folly, and its expression in social and political terms becomes the object of Camus' satirical attacks. And yet, despite this less abstract conception of absurdism, the stylization in the play is much more thorough-going than in *Le Malentendu*. There seems to be a certain contradiction and a certain inappropriateness here. It is true, of course, that successful political or social allegories have been written, but in modern times at least these have been mainly critical in their attitude. Now the main dramatic feature of *L'État de siège* is the heroic emergence of Diego and his victory over the Plague. Through Diego Camus is presenting the audience with a solution to the problems he raises and the evils he exposes. But Diego is little more than a cipher in a highly stylized drama. He may point to a solution expressed in terms of revolt and non-acceptance, but this solution—and indeed the whole positive side of the play—loses most of its force through being given such abstract expression. We saw, in the case of *L'Homme révolté*, that the conception of revolt has its very unsatisfactory features even when discussed in direct and practical terms. Here, in *L'État de siège*, it is reduced to the kind of abstract bombast that Camus so rightly attacks on other occasions. One is unimpressed, if not irritated, by statements like the following made by Diego.

> Oh holy revolt, living refusal and glory of the people, give to these gagged citizens the strength of thy cry! [13]

This contrast between the practical subject-matter of the play and its abstract treatment results in an unsuccessful compromise. *L'État de siège* becomes a hybrid creation suggesting at times a contemporary social drama and at other times a medieval morality. Both features are often combined in the same scene and the effect of this on the characters is particularly unfortunate. Although many of them have individual names and take part in all-too-familiar situations of oppression and violence, they remain ciphers standing for abstractly conceived ideas such as nihilism, legality, the absurd, revolt, romantic love, etc. This is particularly noticeable in the love scenes between Diego and Victoria. Victoria lacks the warmth and human appeal even of Maria in *Le Malentendu*, and the following kind of dialogue between lovers is banal and unconvincing:

DIEGO: They have forbidden love! Oh, I shall miss you with my whole being!

VICTORIA: No! No! I beg you! I know what they want. They arrange everything so as to make love impossible. But I shall be stronger than they are.

DIEGO: I am not stronger. This is a defeat which I am not prepared to share with you.

VICTORIA: I am strong-willed! I acknowledge only my love for you! Nothing frightens me any longer. If the heavens were to fall I should cry aloud my happiness as they crushed me, so long as I was holding your hand.

. . . .

DIEGO: But there is pain in these heavens which press down upon us!

VICTORIA: I am too busy bearing the weight of my love! I shall not burden myself with the world's pain in addition! That is a man's task, one of those vain, sterile, obstinate tasks which you men undertake in order to avoid the only struggle that would be really difficult, the only victory of which you could be proud.

. . . .

DIEGO: How beautiful you are and how I would love you if only I were not afraid!

VICTORIA: How unimportant your fear would be if only you wanted to love me!

DIEGO: I do love you. But I do not know which of us is right.[14]

Exchanges such as these belong neither to naturalistic speech nor to poetic stylization. Their stiffness and obvious rhetoric remind one rather of the worst passages of dialogue in Hugo's plays. Victoria and Diego make parallel speeches. Their speeches fail to make contact. They lack conviction as they lack poetry.

One of the most dominant figures in the play is Nada. He is completely without belief and displays an ironical sense of humour. He is aware of the absurd but finds escape, in drink, from the consequences of his realism. In general he connives at the absurd and says: 'it is better to be an accomplice of the heavens rather than their victim' (p. 23).

His nihilism places Nada beyond the power of the Plague to destroy him. It is the same nihilism that prompts him to become the dictator's tool. He proves to be the perfect state functionary, applying laws and regulations whose ridiculousness is quite apparent to him. At the actual performance of *L'État de siège* I found, curiously enough, that Nada came nearest to being a character with human features. A re-reading of the play hardly confirms this impression, however, and I imagine that the original experience was chiefly due to Brasseur's special gift for infusing life into the part.

Another fault in the play, related to that just discussed, arises again from the conflict between Camus' universalizing intention and his desire to make as immediate an impact as possible. In an article published in *Le Monde* on 27 October 1948, Henry Magnan reported him as saying that he wanted to express in *L'État de siège* certain ideas which it was not possible to formulate with direct precision in his novel. Camus has rightly insisted that *L'État de siège* is not simply a stage adaptation of *La Peste* but an attempt to profit from the special opportunities provided by the theatre for a direct exchange of ideas between the playwright and his audience. One result of this is that the plague remained an epidemic in *La Peste*, seen only indirectly through its effect on human beings, whereas it becomes a character, the Plague, in *L'État de siège* and is given a Himmler-like appearance. Indeed, in the Marigny production, Pierre Bertin wore the unmistakable field-grey uniform and rimless spectacles. The secretary, too, wore a grey dress recalling those of the so-called 'souris grises' during the German Occupation. When one adds to this the Spanish setting of the play and also its thinly veiled portrayal of aspects of Stalinism it will be seen that this particularization of the plague becomes confused and fragmentary. Camus' stated intention, included in his reply to the criticisms of Gabriel Marcel, was to write a play that would be an attack on totalitarianism in general. This no doubt explains the variety of political references, but I think it is unsuccessful and harms the play. The right way to achieve general validity was surely not to fill the play with oblique references to Hitler, Franco and Stalin, but to use a general form of criticism corresponding to the generalized object of that criticism. Too much half-hearted particularity is included within the abstract framework of the play. Instead of raising one general and dominant contemporary reference to the status of a modern myth Camus weakened the mythic power of *L'État de siège* by reducing it to a jumble of loosely related contemporary allusions.

These allusions, as Camus handles them, constitute a further weakness of the play. They too often give surprisingly banal and obvious expression to what remains an essentially admirable and humane attitude. The dialogue between the Governor of Cadiz and the Plague, when the former surrenders power and authority to the latter, is a case in point. As a satirical account of a political event it is obvious to the point of childishness. The same is true, I think, of Nada's attempted explanation of how opposition votes are discounted. The other main theme, bureaucracy, sometimes receives similar treatment. There is something very commonplace in such devices as thirteen copies of the fisherman's certificate of existence—one for himself and twelve to ensure smooth administrative functioning. Even the following kind of satire is very familiar in the anti-government songs of the Parisian *chansonniers*:

NADA: It's very simple! Table number 108. The memorandum on the readjustment of interprofessional and other wages involves cancellation of the basic wage and unconditional freeing of the sliding scales which are thus permitted to attain the maximum wage which has still to be decided. These scales, less the increases fictitiously granted in table number 107, will however continue to be calculated, apart from the conditions properly known as conditions and terms of reclassification, in accordance with the previously cancelled basic wage.[15]

It would not be fair to leave the impression that no good word can be said for *L'État de siège*. Perhaps its best aspect apart from the actual subject, is provided by the chorus. The speeches of the chorus have a lyrical pathos which often succeeds very well in conveying the rôle of the ordinary citizens of Cadiz as the suffering victims of calamity. One can also admire some of the dramatic devices used. Although the play seemed noisy and agitated on the stage to the point of confusion, the repeated use of the air-raid siren sound was effective. Dramatic tension was also generated by the gradual closing, in turn, of the six gates of the town. Yet despite details like these, and despite the genuine liveliness and wit of some of the satire, *L'État de siège* fails in the end. Camus described it to one critic (Claude Outie of *L'Aurore*) as an attempt to emulate the Elizabethan theatre, but the result of this ambition is a plurality of dramatic styles and periods, ranging from the morality play to the *chansonnier* joke, which leave it without coherence of form or subject.

Camus' career as a dramatist may appear at this point to be one of steady decline. It seems to descend from the success of *Caligula*, through the partial failure of *Le Malentendu*, to the more radical rejection of *L'État de siège* by critics and public alike. In judging Camus' fundamental ability as a playwright, however, one should not allow the genuine dramatic talent displayed in *Caligula* to be obscured by the mistakes or shortcomings of the other two plays. It is true that such shortcomings cannot simply be glossed over, but it is equally true that weaknesses can arise from a variety of causes. My own view is that where Camus' plays have failed they have mainly done so because of the originality and ambition of his dramatic purpose. His failures have been due more to an inadequate control of his dramatic gifts than to any lack of ability as a playwright. When his plays have failed, their failure should be seen in the context of what he undertook to do. His own conception of the scope and purpose of the drama is enlightening in this respect. He describes the drama as the most difficult literary form because he sees it as concerned to communicate, in an original way, lofty ideas that must be accepted by an audience in which imbeciles and intelligent people sit side by side. For such an enterprise to be successful an unusually high degree of skill is required. Measured by this standard both *Le Malentendu* and *L'État de siège* are failures, but adverse criticism of *Le Malentendu* still leaves intact its adventurous approach to the theatre, while even *L'État de siège* reminds us that Camus has something of importance to say and that the theatre could be an ideal medium for many of his ideas. In these circumstances it is not so surprising that Camus' least successful play, *L'État de siège*, should have been followed in a year by what is generally considered to be his greatest dramatic achievement to date, *Les Justes*. On this occasion the subject fitted in perfectly both with Camus' general attitude to life and with his ideas on the nature and aims of the drama. Indeed, it not only permitted a harmonious relationship between his ideas and his dramatic talent, but enabled these two elements to strengthen one another and combine to produce a powerful theatrical experience. Many people regard *Les Justes* not only as his finest play but as one of the most impressive dramas to reach the post-war French stage.

Les Justes was first performed in Paris at the Hébertot in December 1949. The production was by Paul Œttley, the décor by the young painter, G. de Rosnay. The leading parts of Kaliaev and Dora Doulebov were played by Serge Reggiani and Maria Casarès. The action of the play takes place in Moscow in 1905. Its central incident is the assassination of the Grand-Duke Serge, the Czar's uncle, by a student named Ivan Kaliaev. The latter belonged to a group of idealistic terrorists led by Boris Savinkov and including among its most prominent members Voinarovski, Sasonov and Dora Brilliant. These are, in fact, the 'meurtriers délicats' about whom Camus wrote with admiration in *L'Homme révolté*. As one might expect, several characters in the play are modelled on actual historical figures: Dora Doulebov on Dora Brilliant, Boris Annenkov on Boris Savinkov, Alexis Voinov on Voinarovski. As a particular tribute to Kaliaev Camus retained his historical name in the play. It is clear, too, that Camus has drawn on the available writings of the group, including Savinkov's memoirs, and that other historical sources were used in *Les Justes*. Indeed, he claimed historical veracity for the whole play in a short article published by *Combat* on 12 December 1949:

However strange some situations in this play may appear they are nevertheless historically true. . . . All my characters really existed and behaved in the way I describe. I have simply tried to give probability to what was already true.

When the play opens Stepan Fedorov has just returned from prison and is discussing with Annenkov, Dora and Kaliaev the projected assassination of the Grand-Duke. During the conversation a fundamental difference of attitude develops between Stepan and Kaliaev. Stepan's bitter experiences in prison cause him to feel deep hatred for the aristocratic rulers of Russia and he is ready to destroy them by any available means. He distrusts and even despises the idealism behind Kaliaev's acceptance of the rôle of terrorist. We have here, in fact, that conflict between ideals and efficacity which runs through the whole history of the revolutionary movement as Camus discussed it in *L'Homme révolté*. Kaliaev is supported by Dora and Annenkov in his determination to maintain the purity of their ideals and to prevent their degeneration into the terms of Stepan's attitude. These idealistic terrorists think of their movement as constituting an order of chivalry. This leads to Kaliaev's preoccupation with suicide which is incomprehensible to Stepan. Kaliaev, and later Dora, considers that only his own death can redeem the death of others brought about in the service of his ideal. He belongs to a group of revolutionaries who view their enterprise as a crusade which is also a martyrdom. The first act ends with a conversation between Dora and Kaliaev during which doubts arise concerning the latter's capacity to assassinate the Grand-Duke. Kaliaev is confident, however, and welcomes the news that the Grand-Duke will visit the theatre on the following day. This means that the time and place of the assassination are definitely fixed at last.

It is clear from this account that the first act is without significant action. Nevertheless, it contains an atmosphere of genuine dramatic tension, and this tension is built up in three ways. Firstly there is the drama of approaching action. The conversation is dominated by the nearness of the attempt to throw a bomb at the Grand-Duke's carriage. This imminent event, the climax of weeks of planning, has its inevitable effect on the nerves of the main characters. Camus skilfully communicates their anxiety and concern to the audience. Secondly, an atmosphere of danger pervades the act since the possibility of discovery or betrayal is continually present. From this point of view the meeting that we witness takes place in a set of conditions further overshadowed by uneasy suspense. Thirdly, several facts which emerge, from the speeches of both Stepan and Dora, cast doubt on Kaliaev's ability to carry out the deed. This doubt as to how he will acquit himself is another contributory factor to the general tension. Nor does his own confidence reassure us completely, particularly since it appears to depend on his deceiving himself with words. Thus when Dora points out that the Grand-Duke remains a human being, that their eyes may meet and he will then be unable to throw the bomb, Kaliaev replies: 'I am not killing him. I am killing a despotic government'.[16]

One is incidentally rei inded here of the killing of Jaurès by Villain. Villain confessed that the day before the assassination in the Rue du Croissant Jaurès passed within a couple of yards of him but he could not bring himself to fire a shot. The assassination of Jaurès was in fact preceded by one unsuccessful attempt because, according to Villain, the glances of the two men met and he saw such serenity and goodness in Jaurès' eyes that he found assassination impossible on that occasion.

A situation similar to this and to that imagined by Dora occurs off-stage during the early part of the second act. Kaliaev fails to throw the bomb on finding that the Grand-Duke is accompanied by two children, his niece and nephew. The Grand-Duchess was also present in the carriage, although Kaliaev did not see her at the time. He says of the incident:

Everything happened too quickly. Those two serious little faces and that terrible weight in my hand. It's at them I would have had to throw it. Like this. Straight at them. Oh no! I couldn't do it.[17]

This incident inevitably brings to a head the conflict between Kaliaev and Stepan described in the previous act. This is a concrete case which serves to accentuate their differences. In answer to a question from Dora, Stepan asserts that he would deliberately kill a child if the revolutionary organization required him to do so. Kaliaev holds such an attitude to be completely dishonourable. He adds passionately that the day the revolution becomes divorced from a sense of honour he will quit the organization. Stepan, on the contrary, regards honour as a luxury which only those in royal carriages can afford. He is prepared to commit any deed which he believes will contribute to the eventual reign of justice. Kaliaev rejects such an attitude because it subordinates morality to alleged efficacity and is prepared to increase the sum of injustice here and now in the name of an uncertain justice placed in the future. Thus the initial drama of the second act, the drama of Kaliaev's failure to carry out the assassination, is followed by a tense moral conflict between Stepan and the other members of the group. This conflict is embodied in some excellent dialogue that is vivid and moving, particularly because it allows Camus to write with passion on a subject about which he feels deeply.

In the third act we return, two days later, to the tension of waiting which precedes the second attempt on the Grand-Duke's life. After Kaliaev's first failure and the debate which followed it we now have further evidence, from a different angle, of the fundamental purity and nobility of these idealistic terrorists. This is seen in Voinov's loss of nerve which in no way diminishes his revolutionary fervour or his loyalty. Indeed, it is he who describes the organization as an order of chivalry. But he also adds: 'I wasn't made for terrorism' (p. 91) just as Kaliaev says later to the Grand-Duchess: 'I wasn't made for killing' (p. 147). The leader, Annenkov, accepts Voinov's position with considerable understanding. We are reminded that he too, like Kaliaev and Dora, entered the revolutionary movement out of a sense of moral duty which cannot wholly remove his nostalgia for the happy, carefree existence he led before his dedication to terrorism. As the act progresses these human qualities existing behind the severe rôles adopted by the characters become even more evident. The struggle experienced by Dora and Kaliaev between their love and their revolutionary responsibilities is embodied in some moving dialogue which further brings these characters to life. In fact, this central act is primarily important in increasing our knowledge of the characters as ordinary human beings immediately prior to the assassination to which their lives are dedicated. The assassination itself, the killing of the Grand-Duke, takes place off-stage in the closing moments of the act. On this second occasion Kaliaev carries out the deed. Thus this event renews the dramatic tension of the act, the more so because its significance and interest are both further heightened by the additional insight gained just beforehand into the minds of these terrorists as a group and into the mind of Kaliaev in particular.

The successful assassination at the end of the third act appears to be the obvious dramatic climax of the whole play. By placing this event at such a point, while extending the play much farther, Camus clearly presents himself with the problem of retaining the interest of his audience for a further two acts. In the fourth act he succeeds admirably in his object and does so mainly by means of three dramatic situations which develop one after the other in Kaliaev's cell. Another prisoner, Foka, is brought along by a warder to clean out this cell. The ensuing conversation between Kaliaev and the proletarian Foka shows the dishearteningly wide gap between the idealistic conceptions of the terrorists and those of the common people whom they aim to serve. This is a possibility which had already been mentioned by Dora in the previous act and is not a particularly original idea in itself. Nevertheless it possesses a certain impact in the context of the play, and the whole scene is raised to a high dramatic level when Foka reveals that he is also the prison hangman. Immediately after this revelation Skuratov, the head of police, enters the cell. This results in another dramatic situation during which Skuratov employs a good deal of subtlety, and a calculated amount of frankness, in an unsuccessful attempt to make Kaliaev betray his comrades. He is clearly playing on Kaliaev's doubts, and probably recalling to his mind the arguments with Stepan, when he says: 'One begins by seeking justice and ends with a police organization.'[18] A new emotional climax is reached with Kaliaev's third visitor—the Grand-Duchess herself. Skuratov came with a proposal for political pardon, the Grand-Duchess now arrives bringing Christian forgiveness as her special gift. Kaliaev refuses her help and her prayers. In this fourth act Kaliaev is thus faced by three kinds of temptation: the temptation to despair, the temptation to betray his friends, the temptation to renounce his own ideals. He successfully resists temptation in these three forms, yet he yields to a different temptation in the process. This is seen, I think, in his desperate desire to achieve a kind of martyrdom. In order to justify to himself the killing of the Grand-Duke he insists on sacrificing his own life. The temptation in this case is a particular kind of 'superior suicide' which is the desire to redeem his life by ending it. It is a temptation which he cannot resist, nor does he want to resist it. The fourth act thus comes as no anti-climax after the assassination. On the contrary it contains some highly dramatic material which, at the same time, enhances the nobility and purity of Kaliaev.

The fifth act is necessary to the play because of the account which it contains of Kaliaev's fearless death on the gallows. It also allows Camus to add further important details to his portraits of the other characters. Dora, in particular, emerges as a dominant figure and obtains Annenkov's consent that she should be the first to throw the next bomb. This is her solution now that she cannot have Kaliaev's love, just as it was his solution to the conflict between his conscience and his political actions. A realization, however, that

Albert Camus

neither has found a real answer to these problems is suggested by Dora's words: 'It's so much easier to die from one's inner conflicts than to live with them.' [19]

The emphasis on a solution which makes things easier to bear is repeated in the final words of the play which Dora addresses to the dead Kaliaev: 'Janek! A chill night and the same rope! Everything will be easier now.' [20]

I have given this fairly full account of *Les Justes* in order to try to convey something of the atmosphere and quality of the play. A proper appreciation of its qualities, of course, can only be arrived at by seeing it performed on the stage. In its dramatic appeal and moral strength *Les Justes* is, in some degree, a modern successor to the Cornelian tradition of the seventeenth-century French theatre. Honour, nobility and the moral conscience combine in a moving struggle to realize high human ideals. It is also true, however, that a humanity pervades Camus' play which is scarcely present in the plays of Corneille. Camus' characters are scrupulous, they are hypersensitive, they experience doubts and fears. This prevents them from becoming merely abstract expressions of the author's moral exaltation. They are subject to human frailty but also possess such courage and will-power that they achieve superhuman feats while still remaining human beings. It is in *Les Justes* most of all that Camus the moralist and Camus the dramatist combine to produce a spectacle that is noble without humbug and moving without sentimentality. This play amply confirms one's earlier impression that its author will appeal primarily to those whose theatre-going has not dulled their ability to appreciate the efforts of a fresh dramatic mind working to relate moral illumination and intellectual power.

10 CONCLUSION

Plus encore que le style, le rythme même de notre civilisation est basé sur l'honorabilité de la rebellion. On dirait que pour nous la valeur de l'indvidu se mesure à la somme de ses désaccords avec les choses.

E.-M. CIORAN

Il faut être de son temps.

DAUMIER

The examination of Camus' work contained in the preceding chapters will have emphasized the fact that it expresses a distinctive moral and intellectual attitude. Camus has given it a noticeably individual resonance which, at one level, sets him apart from his contemporaries. At another level, however, these novels, plays and essays reflect those more general tendencies in modern writing which the French include under the heading of *littérature problématique*. The viewpoint which they contain is personal, but it is Camus' personal response to certain widespread features of his times. His writings on the absurd, for instance, belong to a wider world in which the sense of incoherence has grown rapidly more acute. The author of *L'Étranger* and *Le Mythe de Sisyphe* bears witness to an age marked by increasing division, conflict, violence and the failure to communicate adequately. A lack of common standards or agreed values has given rise to the disquiet and the calling in question which characterize *l'homme absurde*. Writers we think of as distinctively modern—Malraux, Sartre, Bernanos, Greene, Faulkner, Kafka, Jünger, etc.—have all made their particular contribution to 'problematical' literature and in doing so have expressed something similar to Camus' feeling of insecurity and his search for meaning in experience.

This general attitude of disquiet and interrogation has brought with it a rebelliousness which is another characteristic of much recent writing. The emphasis on the absurdity or incoherence of existence has entailed a rejection of those explanatory and unifying absolutes which a more self-confident age was ready to affirm. This is the general revolt in literature—a rejection of traditional forms, attitudes and content—which was briefly discussed in the introductory chapter. There are thus two distinct stages or aspects of this contemporary revolt. What might be termed 'implicit revolt' accompanies the affirmation of incoherence; this affirmation is then followed by a more obvious rebelliousness which we may call 'explicit revolt'. The two major themes in Camus' work—*l'absurde* and *la révolte*—emphasize this dual rebellion particularly clearly. From this point of view he is an exemplary contemporary and his influence and relevance at the present time explain themselves. But Camus is also a man of the south, a mediterranean. His allegiance is given primarily to certain values associated with the ancient world, particularly with Greece. This is a feature of his thought which makes it distinctive and individual. It also goes far to explain, I think, both the strength and the weakness of his views on revolt.

The strength of Camus' position is clear. By adhering to what he calls *la pensée de midi* or *la pensée solaire* (man as man's chief concern; the ideal of moderation; stoicism; a trust in nature rather than history, etc.) he gives a positive character to his revolt. What he offers is not nihilism—indeed, as we have seen, he sometimes criticizes contemporary nihilism severely—but revolt in the name of values and ideals on which Europe seems to have turned its back. The values in whose name he rebels are essentially humane ones. Their influence controls his revolt and gives it an impressive dignity and moral force. At the same time, however, these features also have their disadvantages. For example, it is clear that Camus' revolt is one of replacement, not total rejection. He rejects one set of absolutes only to replace them by another. This fact commends him to the more cautious, but for some of his fellow-rebels it blunts the edge of his rebellion, making it little more than an apparently progressive attitude concealing an essentially traditionalist point of view. For others Camus is ultimately an absolutist, an essentialist rather than an existentialist, in the sphere of morals. This is why his political quarrel with Sartre must be reduced in the end to one of moral attitudes. Camus is a static moralist. Despite absurdism and revolt he puts his confidence in certain previously established ideals. Sartre is a dynamic moralist. He is concerned to create a new and constantly evolving ethic in the course of his revolt against the absurd. Finally, this general conflict in Camus between revolution and conservation produces specific contradictions in his intellectual position. It explains some of the main objections made earlier to his ideals: the fact that his awareness of the *absurd* prompts him to assert *significance*; the fact that his will to *revolt* leads him to advocate *moderation*. It also explains his attacks on efficacy in politics and the atmosphere of noble impracticality that many attribute to his political position. Furthermore, this conflict lies behind the difference in quality between his essays on ideas and his imaginative works. The preceding chapters make it clear, I think, that Camus' achievement as a novelist and playwright is very high indeed and markedly superior to his moral and political philosophizing. The obvious sincerity and literary skill of *Le Mythe de Sisyphe* and *L'Homme révolté* should not blind one to their intellectual shortcomings. They both adopt extreme starting-points which, in the end, they cannot logically maintain. It is true, of course, that the novels and plays are also organized around these same extreme positions. Nevertheless, in the imaginative and artistic projection of his ideas Camus is able to profit from the advantages of a strong emotional impact without having to set out in any detail its logical or practical consequences. In other words this division in Camus' thought, while it weakens his main works of argument and exposition, leaves his imaginative writings relatively unscathed.

I have described this general conflict in Camus as being one between conservation and revolt, or between stability and change. In its most essential form, however, it is perhaps first and foremost a conflict between moderation and extremism. The Greek ideal of moderation is firmly ingrained in his nature and from this point of view his gaze seems mainly fixed on the past. But he is also very responsive to the extremist present from which this moderate past is viewed. The attitude and atmosphere which he brings to his writing find a ready echo in the experience of many of his readers. And yet it would be misleading, I think, to see this conflict between moderation and extremism in purely temporal terms. To do so would be to miss the real nature of his distinctiveness among his contemporaries. In other words he is not simply attempting to put the clock back, nor is he merely a writer who strives to understand the present in order that the past wisdom which he offers can be made more palatable to it. The uniqueness of Camus' position lies rather in the fact that he is a North African in the closest possible touch with present-day Europe. As one who grew up in Algeria he has a keen sense of the continuing vitality of what may roughly be called 'the Greek view of life'. But as a Frenchman living in Paris since the early 1940s he is also sharply aware of European intellectual dilemmas. Thus the conflict which characterizes his mind is as much geographical as temporal, allowing him to combine commitment and objectivity in a quite unusual way. It is this dualism which has been the main impulse behind his writing, just as his writing has largely been an attempt to resolve its persistent tension.

Camus himself is fully aware of this feature of his own mind. He referred to it at some length in the interview with Nicola Chiaromonte mentioned in the introductory chapter. This struggle between moderation and extremism has led him most often to adopt a *neither/nor* position. It has made his arguments mainly defensive in character in so far as he attempts to protect certain values against the extremes of nihilism. But Camus only takes up this stand after having himself experienced the temptation of nihilism. He represents his age by virtue of the conflict between belief and scepticism which has gone on, and to some extent still goes on, in his own mind. The geographical dualism referred to above has enabled him both to assess the problems of his contemporaries with some objectivity and to experience them with authenticity. He is both a spokesman and a symptom of his times. Thus by typifying his age in this particular way he has reflected its intellectual habits, dramatized its political experiences and laid bare some of the main sources of its moral unrest. It is for these reasons that he is regarded as an important writer by his contemporaries. For many of them he is also a great writer because of the artistry and technical skill he has shown as a novelist and dramatist who is deeply concerned to understand man's nature and his place in the world.

APPENDIX

1 Le vrai désespoir est agonie, tombeau ou abîme. S'il parle, s'il raisonne, s'il écrit surtout, aussitôt le frère nous tend la main, l'arbre est justifié, l'amour naît. Une littérature désespérée est une contradiction dans les termes.

Bien entendu, un certain optimisme n'est pas mon fait. J'ai grandi, avec tous les hommes de mon âge, aux tambours de la première guerre et notre histoire, depuis, n'a cessé d'être meurtre, injustice ou violence. Mais le vrai pessimisme, qui se rencontre, consiste à renchérir sur tant de cruauté et d'infamie. Je n'ai jamais cessé, pour ma part, de lutter contre ce déshonneur et je ne hais que les cruels. Au plus noir de notre nihilisme, j'ai cherché seulement des raisons de dépasser ce nihilisme (*L'Été*, pp. 135–6).

2 Jailli de l'inconnu; plus de passé, plus de modèle, rien sur quoi m'appuyer . . . O Créon . . . c'est un appel à la vaillance que de ne connaître ses parents (Gide, *Œdipe*).

3 Le matérialisme le plus répugnant n'est pas celui qu'on croit, mais bien celui qui veut nous faire passer des idées mortes pour des réalités vivantes et détourner sur des mythes stériles l'attention obstinée et lucide que nous portons à ce qui en nous doit mourir pour toujours (*Noces*, p. 79).

4 Je pense à un enfant qui vécut dans un quartier pauvre. Ce quartier, cette maison ! Il n'y avait qu'un étage et les escaliers n'étaient pas éclairés. Maintenant encore, après de longues années, il pourrait y retourner en pleine nuit. Il sait qu'il grimperait l'escalier à toute vitesse sans trébucher une seule fois. Son corps même est imprégné de cette maison. Ses jambes conservent en elles la mesure exacte de la hauteur des marches. Sa main, l'horreur instinctive, jamais vaincue, de la rampe d'escalier. Et c'était à cause des cafards (*L'Envers et l'endroit* (original ed.), p. 25).

5 Notre plus grande occupation était, et est restée longtemps pour moi, le sport. C'est là que j'ai pris mes seules leçons de morale . . . (Part of letter from Camus to P. Néraud de Boisdeffre quoted in latter's *Métamorphoses de la littérature*, II, p. 272).

6 Je n'ai vraiment été sincère et enthousiaste qu'au temps où je faisais du sport, et, au régiment, quand je jouais dans les pièces que nous représentions pour notre plaisir . . . . Maintenant encore, les

225

matches du dimanche, dans un stade plein à craquer, et le théâtre, que j'ai aimé avec une passion sans égale, sont les seuls endroits au monde où je me sente innocent (*La Chute*, pp. 102–3).

7 Un Théâtre du Travail s'organise à Alger grâce à un effort collectif et désintéressé. Ce théâtre a conscience de la valeur artistique propre à toute littérature de masse, veut démontrer que l'art peut gagner quelquefois à sortir de sa tour d'ivoire et croit que le sens de la beauté est inséparable d'un certain sens de l'humanité .... Son effort est de restituer quelques valeurs humaines et non d'apporter de nouveaux thèmes de pensée (Quoted by G. Brée in 'Introduction to Albert Camus', *French Studies*, IV, 1, (Jan. 1950), p. 34).

8 ... sa mort, loin de me rendre meilleur, comme il est dit dans les livres consolants, a rendu ma révolte plus aveugle. Ce que je puis dire de plus élevé en sa faveur c'est qu'il ne m'aurait pas suivi dans cette révolte (R. Leynaud, *Poésies posthumes* (préface d'Albert Camus), p. 17).

CHAPTER 2 : *The Quest for Happiness*

1 La Grèce c'est l'ombre et la lumière. Nous savons bien, n'est-ce pas, nous autres hommes du Sud, que le soleil a sa face noire (*Les Nouvelles littéraires*, 10 May 1951).

2 Quand il m'arrive de chercher ce qu'il y a en moi de fondamental, c'est le goût du bonheur que j'y trouve . . . . Au centre de mon œuvre, il y a un soleil invincible (Ibid.).

3 Dieu ne lui servait de rien, qu'à l'ôter aux hommes et la rendre seule. Elle ne voulait pas quitter les hommes (*L'Envers et l'endroit*, (original ed.), p. 12).

4 Une femme qu'on abandonne pour aller au cinéma, un vieil homme qu'on n'écoute plus, une mort qui ne rachète rien et puis de l'autre côté toute la lumière du monde. Qu'est-ce que ça fait si on accepte tout? Il s'agit de trois destins semblables et pourtant différents. La mort pour tous, mais à chacun sa mort. Après tout, le soleil nous chauffe quand même les os (Ibid., p. 20).

5 Puisque cette heure est comme un intervalle entre oui et non, je laisse pour d'autres heures l'espoir ou le dégoût de vivre . . . (Ibid., p. 31).

6 Que me faisait de revivre en mon âme, et sans yeux pour voir Vicence, sans mains pour toucher les raisins de Vicence, sans peau pour sentir la caresse de la nuit sur la route du Monte Berico à la villa Valmarana? (Ibid., p. 49).

7 Il n'y a pas d'amour de vivre sans désespoir de vivre (Ibid., p. 58).

8 Si j'écoute l'ironie, tapie au fond des choses, elle se découvre lente-

ment. Clignant son œil petit et clair : 'Vivez comme si . . .,' dit-elle. Malgré bien des recherches, c'est là toute ma science (Ibid., p. 67).

9 Le bourreau étrangla le Cardinal Carrafa avec un cordon de soie qui se rompit : il fallut y revenir deux fois. Le Cardinal regarda le bourreau sans daigner prononcer un mot (Epigraph to *Noces*).

10 . . . s'il y a un péché contre la vie, ce n'est peut-être pas tant d'en désespérer que d'espérer une autre vie, et se dérober à l'implacable grandeur de celle-ci (*Noces*, p. 63).

11 . . . je suis ce vent et dans le vent, ces colonnes et cet arc, ces dalles qui sentent chaud et ces montagnes pâles autour de la ville déserte (Ibid., p. 33).

12 Entre ce ciel et ces visages tournés vers lui, rien où accrocher une mythologie, une littérature, une éthique ou une religion, mais des pierres, la chair, des étoiles et ces vérités que la main peut toucher (Ibid., p. 60).

13 Si je refuse obstinément tous les 'plus tard' du monde, c'est qu'il s'agit aussi bien de ne pas renoncer à ma richesse présente. Il ne me plaît pas de croire que la mort ouvre sur une autre vie. Elle est pour moi une porte fermée . . . . Tout ce qu'on me propose s'efforce de décharger l'homme du poids de sa propre vie (Ibid., p. 34).

14 Ce peuple tout entier jeté dans son présent vit sans mythes, sans consolations (Ibid., p. 59).

15 Même si je la souhaite, qu'ai-je à faire d'une vérité qui ne doive pas pourrir? Elle n'est pas à ma mesure. Et l'aimer serait un faux-semblant (Ibid., p. 90).

16 . . . comment consacrer l'accord de l'amour et de la révolte? La terre ! Dans ce grand temple déserté par les dieux, toutes mes idoles ont des pieds d'argile (Ibid., p. 92).

CHAPTER 3 : *The Nature of the Absurd*

1 Je disais que le monde est absurde et j'allais trop vite. Ce monde en lui-même n'est pas raisonnable, c'est tout ce qu'on en peut dire. Mais ce qui est absurde, c'est la confrontation de cet irrationnel et de ce désir éperdu de clarté dont l'appel résonne au plus profond de l'homme. L'absurde dépend autant de l'homme que du monde (*Le Mythe de Sisyphe*, p. 37).

2 Si j'étais arbre parmi les arbres, chat parmi les animaux, cette vie aurait un sens ou plutôt ce problème n'en aurait point car je ferais partie de ce monde (Ibid., p. 74).

3 Tout ce qui détruit, escamote ou subtilise ces exigences (et en premier lieu le consentement qui détruit le divorce) ruine l'absurde et dévalorise l'attitude qu'on peut alors proposer (Ibid., p. 50).

Albert Camus

4 Le corps, la tendresse, la création, l'action, la noblesse humaine, reprendront alors leur place dans ce monde insensé. L'homme y retrouvera enfin le vin de l'absurde et le pain de l'indifférence dont il nourrit sa grandeur (Ibid., p. 75).

5 J'ai choisi la justice . . . pour rester fidèle à la terre. Je continue à croire que ce monde n'a pas de sens supérieur. Mais je sais que quelque chose en lui a du sens et c'est l'homme, parce qu'il est le seul être à exiger d'en avoir. Ce monde a du moins la vérité de l'homme et notre tâche est de lui donner ses raisons contre le destin lui-même (*Lettres à un ami allemand*, pp. 72–3).

CHAPTER 4: *The Emergence of Revolt*

1 On voudrait lui faire reconnaître sa culpabilité. Lui se sent innocent. A vrai dire il ne sent que cela, son innocence irréparable (*Le Mythe de Sisyphe*, pp. 75–6).

2 Justement, c'est le seul péché dont l'homme absurde puisse sentir qu'il fait à la fois sa culpabilité et son innocence. On lui propose un dénouement où toutes les contradictions passées ne sont plus que des jeux polémiques. Mais ce n'est pas ainsi qu'il les a ressenties. Il faut garder leur vérité qui est de ne point être satisfaites (Ibid., p. 71).

3 L'absurde est sa tension la plus extrême, celle qu'il maintient constamment d'un effort solitaire, car il sait que dans cette conscience et dans cette révolte au jour le jour, il témoigne de sa seule vérité qui est le défi. Ceci est une première conséquence (Ibid., pp. 78–9).

4 . . . si l'absurde annihile toutes mes chances de liberté éternelle, il me rend et exalte au contraire ma liberté d'action. Cette privation d'espoir et d'avenir signifie un accroissement dans la disponibilité de l'homme (Ibid., p. 80).

5 . . . la mort et l'absurde sont ici les principes de la seule liberté raisonnable: celle qu'un cœur humain peut éprouver et vivre. Ceci est une deuxième conséquence (Ibid., p. 83).

6 Le présent et la succession des présents devant une âme sans cesse consciente, c'est l'idéal de l'homme absurde. Mais le mot idéal ici garde un son faux. Ce n'est pas même sa vocation, mais seulement la troisième conséquence de son raisonnement (Ibid., p. 88).

7 Cette vie le comble, rien n'est pire que de la perdre. Ce fou est un grand sage (Ibid., p. 99).

8 . . . c'est son art . . . de feindre absolument, d'entrer le plus avant possible dans des vies qui ne sont pas les siennes (Ibid., p. 110).

9 Il faut qu'en trois heures il éprouve et exprime tout un destin exceptionnel. Cela s'appelle se perdre pour se retrouver. Dans ces

trois heures, il va jusqu'au bout du chemin sans issue que l'homme du parterre met toute sa vie à parcourir (Ibid., p. 110).

10 Entre l'histoire et l'éternel, j'ai choisi l'histoire parce que j'aime les certitudes (Ibid., p. 118).

11 . . . en face de la contradiction essentielle, je soutiens mon humaine contradiction. J'installe ma lucidité au milieu de ce qui la nie. J'exalte l'homme devant ce qui l'écrase et ma liberté, ma révolte et ma passion se rejoignent alors dans cette tension, cette clairvoyance et cette répétition démesurée (Ibid., p. 120).

CHAPTER 5 : *The Theory of Revolt*

1 Quand j'analysais le sentiment de l'absurde dans *Le Mythe de Sisyphe,* j'étais à la recherche d'une méthode et non d'une doctrine. Je pratiquais le doute méthodique. Je cherchais à faire cette 'table rase' à partir de laquelle on peut commencer à construire (*Les Nouvelles littéraires,* 10 May 1951).

2 Apparemment négative, puisqu'elle ne crée rien, la révolte est profondément positive puisqu'elle révèle ce qui, en l'homme, est toujours à défendre (*L'Homme révolté,* p. 32).

3 Le soulèvement contre la condition s'ordonne en une expédition démesurée contre le ciel pour en ramener un roi prisonnier dont on prononcera la déchéance d'abord, la condamnation à mort ensuite (Ibid., p. 41).

4 . . . ces frénétiques voulaient une 'révolution quelconque', n'importe quoi qui les sortît du monde de boutiquiers et de compromis où ils étaient forcés de vivre (Ibid., p. 122).

5 La vérité, la raison et la justice se sont brusquement incarnées dans le devenir du monde. Mais, en les jetant dans une accélération perpétuelle, l'idéologie allemande confondait leur être avec leur mouvement et fixait l'achèvement de cet être à la fin du devenir historique, s'il en était une (Ibid., p. 169).

6 Leur victoire exténuée a été finalement trahie. Mais par leur sacrifice, et jusque dans leurs négations les plus extrêmes, ils ont donné corps à une valeur, ou une vertu nouvelle, qui n'a pas fini, même aujourd'hui, de faire face à la tyrannie et d'aider à la vraie libération (Ibid., p. 188).

7 L'avenir est la seule transcendance des hommes sans dieu (Ibid., p. 207).

8 S'ils ont vécu dans la terreur . . . ils n'ont jamais cessé d'y être déchirés (Ibid., p. 208).

9 Kaliayev a douté jusqu'à la fin et ce doute ne l'a pas empêché d'agir; c'est en cela qu'il est l'image la plus pure de la révolte (Ibid., p. 216).

10 La revendication de la révolte est l'unité, la revendication de la révolution historique la totalité. La première part du non appuyé sur un oui, la seconde part de la négation absolue et se condamne à toutes les servitudes pour fabriquer un oui rejeté à l'extrémité des temps. L'une est créatrice, l'autre nihiliste (Ibid., p. 308).

11 Le révolté exige sans doute une certaine liberté pour lui-même; mais en aucun cas, s'il est conséquent, le droit de détruire l'être et la liberté de l'autre. Il n'humilie personne. La liberté qu'il réclame, il la revendique pour tous; celle qu'il refuse, il l'interdit à tous. Il n'est pas seulement esclave contre maître, mais aussi homme contre le monde du maître et de l'esclave (Ibid., p. 351).

12 . . . les rêves allemands et la tradition méditerranéenne, les violences de l'éternelle adolescence et la force virile, la nostalgie, exaspérée par la connaissance et les livres, et le courage durci et éclairé dans la course de la vie; l'histoire enfin et la nature (Ibid., p. 369).

Chapter 6: *The Practice of Revolt*

1 Vous avez été pour nous—demain vous pouvez l'être encore—l'admirable conjonction d'une personne, d'une action et d'une œuvre. C'était en 45: on découvrait Camus, le résistant, comme on avait découvert Camus, l'auteur de *l'Étranger* . . . vous résumiez en vous les conflits de l'époque, et vous les dépassiez par votre ardeur à les vivre. Vous étiez une *personne*, la plus complexe et la plus riche . . . (*Les Temps modernes*, Aug. 1952).

2 Vous vous êtes choisi et créé tel que vous êtes en méditant sur les malheurs et les inquiétudes qui étaient votre lot personnel et la solution que vous leur avez donné, c'est une amère sagesse qui s'efforce de nier le temps (Ibid.).

3 Vous blâmez le prolétariat européen parce qu'il n'a pas publiquement marqué de réprobation aux Soviets, mais vous blâmez aussi les gouvernements de l'Europe parce qu'ils font admettre l'Espagne à l'Unesco; dans ce cas, je ne vois qu'une solution pour vous: les îles Galapagos (Ibid.).

4 Si l'homme n'a pas de fin qu'on puisse élire en règle de valeur, comment l'histoire aurait-elle un sens dès maintenant perceptible? Si elle en a un, pourquoi l'homme n'en ferait-il sa fin? Et s'il le fait, comment serait-il dans la terrible et incessante liberté dont vous parlez? (Ibid.).

5 L'homme se fait historique pour poursuivre l'éternel et découvre des valeurs universelles dans l'action concrète qu'il mène en vue d'un résultat particulier (Ibid.).

6 . . . ce n'est pas le combat qui fait de nous des artistes, mais l'art qui nous contraint à être des combattants (*Actuelles*, p. 264).

7 La justice est à la fois une idée et une chaleur de l'âme. Sachons la prendre dans ce qu'elle a d'humain, sans la transformer en cette terrible passion abstraite qui a mutilé tant d'hommes (Ibid., p. 41).

8 Notre monde n'a pas besoin d'âmes tièdes. Il a besoin de cœurs brûlants qui sachent faire à la modération sa juste place (Ibid., p. 69).

9 Le démocrate, après tout, est celui qui admet qu'un adversaire peut avoir raison, qui le laisse donc s'exprimer et qui accepte de réfléchir à ses arguments (Ibid., p. 125).

10 Nous savons aujourd'hui qu'il n'y a plus d'îles et que les frontières sont vaines. Nous savons que dans un monde en accélération constante, où l'Atlantique se traverse en moins d'une journée, où Moscou parle à Washington en quelques heures, nous sommes forcés à la solidarité ou à la complicité, suivant le cas (Ibid., p. 160).

11 . . . aucun problème économique, si secondaire apparaisse-t-il, ne peut se régler aujourd'hui en dehors de la solidarité des nations. Le pain de l'Europe est à Buenos-Ayres, et les machines-outils de Sibérie sont fabriquées à Detroit. Aujourd'hui, la tragédie est collective (Ibid., p. 161).

12 Qu'est-ce que la démocratie nationale ou internationale? C'est une forme de société où la loi est au-dessus des gouvernants, cette loi étant l'expression de la volonté de tous, représentée par un corps législatif. Est-ce là ce qu'on essaie de fonder aujourd'hui? On nous prépare, en effet, une loi internationale. Mais cette loi est faite ou défaite par des gouvernements, c'est-à-dire par l'exécutif. Nous sommes donc en régime de dictature internationale. La seule façon d'en sortir est de mettre la loi internationale au-dessus des gouvernements, donc de faire cette loi, donc de disposer d'un parlement, donc de constituer ce parlement au moyen d'élections mondiales auxquelles participeront tous les peuples. Et puisque nous n'avons pas ce parlement, le seul moyen est de résister à cette dictature internationale sur un plan international et selon des moyens qui ne contrediront pas la fin poursuivie (Ibid., p. 164).

13 . . . il ne s'agit pas ici de plaider pour un sentimentalisme ridicule qui mêlerait toutes les races dans la même confusion attendrie. Les hommes ne se ressemblent pas, il est vrai, et je sais bien quelle profondeur de traditions me sépare d'un Africain ou d'un musulman. Mais je sais bien aussi ce qui m'unit à eux et qu'il est quelque chose en chacun d'eux que je ne puis mépriser sans me ravaler moi-même (Ibid., p. 130).

14 . . . vous acceptez de faire silence sur une terreur pour mieux en combattre une autre. Nous sommes quelques-uns qui ne voulons faire silence sur rien (Ibid., p. 248).

15 Mais même en tant que marchandage, il ne peut se justifier. Peut-être enrichera-t-il pour finir quelques marchands de primeurs, mais il ne sert aucun pays et aucune cause, il dessert seulement les quelques raisons que les hommes d'Europe peuvent encore avoir de lutter (*Actuelles II*, pp. 143–4).

CHAPTER 7 : *The Art of the Novel (I)*

1 Le roman naît en même temps que l'esprit de révolte et il traduit, sur le plan esthétique, la même ambition (*L'Homme révolté*, p. 320).

2 Quand la stylisation est exagérée et se laisse voir, l'œuvre est une nostalgie pure : l'unité qu'elle tente de conquérir est étrangère au concret. Quand la réalité est livrée au contraire à l'état brut et la stylisation insignifiante, le concret est offert sans unité. Le grand art, le style, le vrai visage de la révolte, sont entre ces deux hérésies (Ibid., pp. 335–6).

3 Créer ou ne pas créer, cela ne change rien (*Le Mythe de Sisyphe*, p. 134).

4 Le roman fabrique du destin sur mesure. C'est ainsi qu'il concurrence la création et qu'il triomphe, provisoirement, de la mort (*L'Homme révolté*, pp. 326–7).

5 Aujourd'hui, maman est morte. Ou peut-être hier, je ne sais pas. J'ai reçu un télégramme de l'asile : "Mère décédée. Enterrement demain. Sentiments distingués". Cela ne veut rien dire. C'était peut-être hier (*L'Étranger*, p. 9).

6 . . . (le) divorce entre l'homme et sa vie, l'acteur et son décor . . . (*Le Mythe de Sisyphe*, p. 18).

7 J'ai pensé que c'était dimanche et cela m'a ennuyé : je n'aime pas le dimanche (*L'Étranger*, p. 33).

8 En généralisant ce procédé, on aboutirait à un univers d'automates et d'instincts. Ce serait un appauvrissement considérable. C'est pourquoi, tout en rendant au roman américain ce qui lui revient, je donnerais cent Hemingways pour un Stendhal ou un Benjamin Constant. Et je regrette l'influence de cette littérature sur beaucoup de jeunes auteurs (*Les Nouvelles littéraires*, 15 Nov. 1945).

CHAPTER 8 : *The Art of the Novel (II)*

1 . . . pour ne rien trahir et surtout pour ne pas se trahir lui-même, le narrateur a tendu à l'objectivité. Il n'a presque rien voulu modifier

par les effets de l'art, sauf en ce qui concerne les besoins élémentaires d'une relation à peu près cohérente (*La Peste*, pp. 200–1).

2 Quand il se trouvait tenté de mêler directement sa confidence aux mille voix des pestiférés, il était arrêté par la pensée qu'il n'y avait pas une de ses souffrances qui ne fût en même temps celle des autres et que dans un monde où la douleur est si souvent solitaire, cela était un avantage. Décidément, il devait parler pour tous (Ibid., p. 330).

3 Sans doute est-ce là ce qu'on me reproche, que *La Peste* puisse servir à toutes les résistances contre toutes les tyrannies (*Club*, 21 (Feb. 1955), p. 7).

4 Je partage avec vous la même horreur du mal. Mais je ne partage pas votre espoir et je continue à lutter contre cet univers où des enfants souffrent et meurent (*Actuelles*, p. 213).

5 Non, mon Père . . . Je me fais une autre idée de l'amour. Et je refuserai jusqu'à la mort d'aimer cette création où des enfants sont torturés (*La Peste*, p. 240).

6 Je ne pouvais donc vivre . . . qu'à la condition que, sur toute la terre, tous les êtres, ou le plus grand nombre possible, fussent tournés vers moi, éternellement vacants, privés de vie indépendante, prêts à répondre à mon appel à n'importe quel moment, voués enfin à la stérilité . . . (*La Chute*, p. 80).

7 Mon accord avec la vie était total, j'adhérais à ce qu'elle était, du haut en bas, sans rien refuser de ses ironies, de sa grandeur, ni de ses servitudes (Ibid., p. 35).

8 Comment vous dire? Ça glissait. Oui, tout glissait sur moi (Ibid., p. 59).

9 Il est trop tard, maintenant, il sera toujours trop tard. Heureusement! (Ibid., p. 170).

Chapter 9: *The Drama*

1 J'ai été jusqu'au bout du caractère que je m'étais choisi pour sujet et ne pouvais agir différemment en dépit de la morale qui sera, je crois, celle de la pièce, à savoir: qu'on ne peut pas être libre contre les autres (*Opéra*, 12 Sept. 1945).

2 Ce monde, tel qu'il est fait, n'est pas supportable. J'ai donc besoin de la lune, ou du bonheur, ou de l'immortalité, de quelque chose qui soit dément peut-être, mais qui ne soit pas de ce monde. (*Caligula*, I, v).

3 Vivre Cæsonia, vivre, c'est le contraire d'aimer. C'est moi qui te le dis et c'est moi qui t'invite à une fête sans mesure, à un procès général, au plus beau des spectacles. Et il me faut du monde, des

spectateurs, des victimes et des coupables. Faites entrer les coupables.
Il me faut des coupables. Et ils le sont tous. Je veux qu'on fasse
entrer les condamnés à mort . . . Juges, témoins, accusés, tous condamnés d'avance! (Ibid., I, xii).

4 Pour un homme qui aime le pouvoir, la rivalité des dieux a quelque
chose d'agaçant. J'ai supprimé cela. J'ai prouvé à ces dieux illusoires
qu'un homme, s'il en a la volonté, peut exercer, sans apprentissage,
leur métier ridicule.

SCIPION: C'est cela le blasphème, Caïus.

CALIGULA: Non, Scipion, c'est de la clairvoyance. J'ai simplement compris qu'il n'y a qu'une façon de s'égaler aux dieux: il suffit d'être
aussi cruel qu'eux (Ibid., III, ii).

5 Je n'ai pas pris la voie qu'il fallait, je n'aboutis à rien. Ma liberté
n'est pas la bonne (Ibid., IV, xiii).

6 . . . je ne puis être contre lui. Si je le tuais, mon cœur du moins
serait avec lui (Ibid., IV, i).

7 La même flamme nous brûle le cœur . . . Mon malheur est de tout
comprendre (Ibid., IV, i).

8 Comprenez que ni pour lui ni pour nous, ni dans la vie ni dans la
mort, il n'est de patrie ni de paix. Car on ne peut appeler patrie,
n'est-ce pas, cette terre épaisse, privée de lumière . . . (*Le Malentendu*, III, iii).

9 Priez votre Dieu qu'il vous fasse semblable à la pierre. C'est le
bonheur qu'il prend pour lui, c'est le seul vrai bonheur. Faites
comme lui, rendez-vous sourde à tous les cris, rejoignez la pierre
pendant qu'il en est temps (Ibid., III, iii).

10 Le crime aussi est une solitude, même si on se met à mille pour
l'accomplir. Et il est juste que je meure seule, après avoir vécu et
tué seule (Ibid., III, iii).

11 Vous aviez fini par me faire entrer dans votre doute. Mais il m'a
parlé des pays que j'attends et, pour avoir su me toucher, il m'a
donné des armes contre lui. C'est ainsi que l'innocence est récom-
pensée (Ibid., II, viii).

12 Du plus loin que je me souvienne, il a toujours suffi qu'un homme
surmonte sa peur et se révolte pour que leur machine commence à
grincer. Je ne dis pas qu'elle s'arrête, il s'en faut. Mais enfin, elle
grince et, quelquefois, elle finit vraiment par se gripper (*L'État de
siège*, p. 178).*

13 O sainte révolte, refus vivant, honneur du peuple, donne à ces
bâillonnés la force de ton cri! (Ibid., p. 184).

* I have used page references as *L'État de siège* is not divided into acts and scenes.

14 DIEGO : Ils ont interdit l'amour ! Ah ! Je te regrette de toutes mes forces !

VICTORIA : Non ! Non ! Je t'en supplie ! J'ai compris ce qu'ils veulent. Ils arrangent toutes choses pour que l'amour soit impossible. Mais je serais la plus forte.

DIEGO : Je ne suis pas le plus fort. Et ce n'est pas une défaite que je voulais partager avec toi !

VICTORIA : Je suis entière ! Je ne connais que mon amour ! Rien ne me fait plus peur et quand le ciel croulerait, je m'abîmerais en criant mon bonheur si seulement je tenais ta main.

.   .   .   .

DIEGO : Mais la douleur est dans ce ciel qui pèse sur nous !

VICTORIA : J'ai trop à faire pour porter mon amour ! Je ne vais pas encore me charger de la douleur du monde ! C'est une tâche d'homme, cela, une de ces tâches, vaines, stériles, entêtées, que vous en reprenez pour vous détourner du seul combat qui serait vraiment difficile, de la seule victoire dont vous pourriez être fiers.

.   .   .   .

DIEGO : Que tu es belle et que je t'aimerais si seulement je ne craignais pas !

VICTORIA : Que tu craindrais peu si seulement tu voulais m'aimer !

DIEGO : Je t'aime. Mais je ne sais qui a raison. (Ibid., pp. 157–60).

15 C'est très simple ! Barème numéro 108. L'arrêté de revalorisation des salaires interprofessionnels et subséquents porte suppression du salaire de base et libération inconditionnelle des échelons mobiles qui reçoivent ainsi licence de rejoindre un salaire maximum qui reste à prévoir. Les échelons, soustraction faite des majorations consenties fictivement par le barème numéro 107, continueront cependant d'être calculés, en dehors des modalités proprement dites de reclassement, sur le salaire de base précédemment supprimé (Ibid., pp. 122–3).

16 Ce n'est pas lui que je tue. Je tue le despotisme (*Les Justes*, p. 47).*

17 Tout s'est passé trop vite. Ces deux petits visages sérieux et dans ma main, ce poids terrible. C'est sur eux qu'il fallait le lancer. Ainsi. Tout droit. Oh, non ! Je n'ai pas pu (Ibid., pp. 64–5).

* I have used page references again as the five acts of *Les Justes* are not sub-divided into scenes.

18 On commence par vouloir la justice et on finit par organiser une police (Ibid., pp. 129-30).

19 C'est tellement plus facile de mourir de ses contradictions que de les vivre (Ibid., p. 169).

20 Yanek! Une nuit froide, et la même corde! Tout sera plus facile maintenant (Ibid., p. 183).

BIBLIOGRAPHY

I. Works by Camus

Novels:

L'Étranger, Paris, Gallimard, 1942 (written 1939–41).
La Peste, Paris, Gallimard, 1947 (written 1944–7).
La Chute, Paris, Gallimard, 1956.

Short stories:

L'Exil et le royaume, Paris, Gallimard, 1957 (two of these stories, 'La Femme adultère' and 'L'Esprit confus', were published earlier, in 1954 and 1956 respectively).

Plays:

La Révolte dans les Asturies (essai de création collective, dédié aux victimes de répression), Algiers, Charlot, 1936.
Le Malentendu, suivi de Caligula, Paris, Gallimard, 1944 (*Caligula* was actually written in 1938).
L'État de siège, Paris, Gallimard, 1948.
Les Justes, Paris, Gallimard, 1950.

Lyrical essays:

L'Envers et l'endroit, Algiers, Charlot, 1937 (a new edition, with a preface by Camus himself, was published by Gallimard in 1958).
Noces, Algiers, Charlot, 1939 (subsequently published by Gallimard in 'Les Essais' series in 1947).
L'Été, Paris, Gallimard, 1954 (contains several important essays written much earlier and published separately, e.g., 'Le Prométhée aux enfers', 1947; 'L'Exil d'Hélène', 1948; 'Le Minotaure ou la halte d'Oran', 1950).

Essays in moral and political philosophy:

Le Mythe de Sisyphe, Paris, Gallimard, 1942 (written 1940).
Lettres à un ami allemand, Paris, Gallimard, 1945 (the first two of these four letters were published in 1943 and 1944 respectively).
L'Homme révolté, Paris, Gallimard, 1951 (written 1947–51).

Albert Camus

Collected political journalism, speeches, interviews, etc. :

Actuelles, chroniques 1944–1948, Paris, Gallimard, 1950.

Actuelles II, chroniques 1948–1953, Paris, Gallimard, 1953 (apart from interviews published in these two books the following should also be noted : with J. Delpech in *Les Nouvelles littéraires*, 15 Nov. 1945; in *Servir* (Lausanne), Dec. 1945; with N. Chiaromonte in *Partisan Review*, Oct. 1948; with G. d'Aubarède in *Les Nouvelles littéraires,* 10 May 1951; with P. Berger in *La Gazette des lettres*, 15 Feb. 1952; in *La Gazette de Lausanne*, 28 March 1954; in *Encounter*, April 1957).

Other books :

L'Art, Brussels/Paris, Dutilleul (Coll. Métamorphose), 1955.

Discours de Suède, Paris, Gallimard, 1958 (Nobel Prize speech and speech delivered at Upsala University on 14 December 1957).

Collaboration with other writers :

J. Prévost (ed), *Problèmes du roman*, special no. of *Confluences* for July/Aug. 1943 (articles on novel by Valéry, Arland, Cocteau, Prévost etc., including one by Camus entitled 'L'Intelligence et l'échafaud').

Hommage à André Gide, Paris, Nouvelle Revue Française, 1951 (includes article by Camus entitled 'Rencontres avec André Gide').

Désert vivant: images en couleurs de Walt Disney, Paris, Société française du livre, 1954 (includes articles by Camus, Marcel Aymé and others).

A. Koestler and A. Camus, *Réflexions sur la peine capitale*, Paris, Calmann-Lévy, 1957.

Translations and adaptations :

James Thurber, *La dernière fleur (The Lost Flower)*, Paris, Gallimard, 1952. Traduit par Albert Camus.

Calderón, *La dévotion à la croix (La devoción de la Cruz)*, Paris, Gallimard, 1953. Texte français d'Albert Camus.

Pierre de Larivey, *Les Esprits*, Paris, Gallimard, 1953. Adaptation d'Albert Camus.

Dino Buzzati, *Un Cas intéressant (Un caso clinico)*, Paris, L'Avant-scène, 1955. Adaptation française d'Albert Camus.

William Faulkner, *Requiem pour une nonne (Requiem for a Nun)*, Paris, Gallimard, 1956. Adaptation d'Albert Camus.

Lope de Vega, *Le Chevalier d'Olmedo (El caballero de Olmedo)*, Paris, Gallimard, 1957. Texte français d'Albert Camus.

Introductions, prefaces and prefatory letters:

Chamfort, *Maximes et anecdotes*, Monaco, Dac, 1944.
A. Salvet, *Le Combat silencieux*, Paris, Le Portulan, 1945.
P. E. Clairin, *Dix estampes originales*, Paris, Rombaldi, 1946.
R. Leynaud, *Poésies posthumes*, Paris, Gallimard, 1947.
J. Méry, *Laissez passer mon peuple*, Paris, Seuil, 1947.
J. Héon-Canonne, *Devant la mort*, Angers, Siraudeau, 1951.
D. Mauroc, *Contre-amour*, Paris, Editions de Minuit, 1952.
Oscar Wilde, *La Ballade de la geôle de Reading*, Paris, Falaize, 1952.
L. Guilloux, *La Maison du peuple, suivi de Compagnons*, Paris, Grasset, 1953.
A. Rosmer, *Moscou sous Lénine; les origines du communisme*, Paris, P. Horay, 1953.
K. F. Bieber, *L'Allemagne vue par les écrivains de la Résistance française*, Geneva/Lille, Droz/Giard, 1954.
C. Targuebayre, *Cordes-en-Albigeois*, Toulouse, Privat, 1954.
Roger Martin du Gard, *Œuvres complètes*, Paris, Gallimard (Bibliothèque de la Pléiade), 1955. 2 vols.

Uncollected articles:

'Portrait d'un élu', *Cahiers du Sud*, xix, 255 (April 1943), pp. 306–11.
'Sur une philosophie de l'expression', *Poésie 44, 17* (Dec. 1943/Feb. 1944), pp. 15–23.
'Une macumba au Brésil', *Biblio*, xix, 9 (Nov. 1951), pp. 5–7.
'Lettre à l'UNESCO', *Simoun*, i, 4 (Sept. 1952), pp. 10–12.
'Lettre à Roland Barthes sur *La Peste*', *Club*, 21 (Feb. 1955), p. 7.
'Le Parti de la liberté: hommage à Salvador de Madariaga', *Monde Nouveau*, 110/111 (April/May 1957), pp. 1–9.
(Also articles on current political questions published from time to time in *L'Express*).

II. BOOKS AND ARTICLES ON CAMUS

The following full-length studies of Camus have been published:

L. Thoorens, *A la rencontre d'Albert Camus*, Brussels/Paris, La Sixaine, 1946.
R. de Luppé, *Albert Camus*, Paris, Éd. du Temps Présent, 1951. Republished in Paris by Les Éditions Universitaires, 1952.
R. Quilliot, *La Mer et les prisons. Essai sur Albert Camus*, Paris, Gallimard, 1956.
A. Maquet, *Albert Camus ou l'invincible été*, Paris, Debresse, 1956.
P. Thody, *Albert Camus: a study of his work*, London, Hamish Hamilton, 1957.

Albert Camus

T. Hanna, *The Thought and Art of Albert Camus*, Chicago, Regnery, 1958.

Chapters on Camus are included in the following books:

M. Blanchot, *Faux pas*, Paris, Gallimard, 1943.

A. Curtis, *New Developments in the French Theatre*, London, Curtain Press, 1948.

R.-M. Albérès, *Le Révolte des écrivains d'aujourd' hui*, Paris, Corrêa, 1949.

—— *Les Hommes traqués*, Paris, La Nouvelle Édition, 1953.

A. Rousseaux, *Littérature du XXe siècle* (Vol. III), Paris, Albin Michel, 1949.

P.-H. Simon, *L'Homme en procès*, Neuchâtel, La Baconnière, 1950.

—— *Les Témoins de l'homme: de Proust à Camus*, Paris, A. Colin, 1951.

—— *L'Esprit et l'histoire*, Paris, A. Colin, 1954.

P. Néraud de Boisdeffre, *Métamorphoses de la littérature* (Vol. II), Paris, Alsatia, 1951.

B. d'Astorg, *Aspects de la littérature européenne depuis 1945*, Paris, Seuil, 1952.

R. Kanters, *Des Écrivains et des hommes*, Paris, Julliard, 1952.

M. Nadeau, *Littérature présente*, Paris, Corrêa, 1952.

C. Mœller, *Littérature du XXe siècle et christianisme* (Vol. I: *Silence de Dieu*), Tournai/Paris, Casterman, 1953.

C. Mauriac, *Hommes et idées d'aujourd'hui*, Paris, Albin Michel, 1953.

E. Mounier, *L'Espoir des désespérés*, Paris, Seuil, 1953.

P. Brodin, *Présences contemporaines* (Vol. I), Paris, Debresse, 1955.

H. Peyre, *The Contemporary French Novel*, New York, Oxford University Press, 1955.

H. Perruchot, *La Haine des masques*, Paris, La Table Ronde, 1955.

G. Brée and M. Guiton, *An Age of Fiction: the French novel from Gide to Camus*, London, Chatto & Windus, 1958.

Hundreds of articles have already appeared on various aspects of Camus' work. The list which follows is restricted to a few articles which I consider to be of particular interest and importance. Admirably full bibliographies will be found in M. L. Drevet, *Bibliographie de la littérature française (1940–1949)*, Geneva/Lille, Droz/Giard, 1954 and D. W. Alden (general ed.), *Bibliography of critical and biographical references for the study of contemporary French literature*, New York, Stechert-Hafner, 1949 onwards (publ. annually):

H. Hell, 'Deux récits', *Fontaine*, No. 23 (July 1942), pp. 352–5.

Bibliography

J.-P. Sartre, 'Explication de *l'Etranger*', *Cahiers du Sud*, XXX (Feb. 1943), pp. 189–206.

J. Grenier, 'Une œuvre, un homme', *Cahiers du Sud*, XXX (Feb. 1943), pp. 224–8.

J. du Rostu, 'Un Pascal sans Christ, Albert Camus', *Etudes*, ccxlvii (Oct. 1945 and Nov. 1945), pp. 48–65 and 165–77.

A. J. Ayer, 'Albert Camus', *Horizon*, XIII, No. 75 (March 1946), pp. 155–68.

G. Teuler, 'Sur trois œuvres d'Albert Camus', *Revue de la Méditerranée*, III, No. 12 (March/April 1946), pp. 197–211.

G. Blin, 'Albert Camus et l'idée de révolte', *Fontaine*, No. 53 (June 1946), pp. 109–17.

R. Bespaloff, 'Réflexions sur l'esprit de la tragédie', *Deucalion*, No. 2 (1947), pp. 171–93.

G. Picon, 'Remarques sur *la Peste* d'Albert Camus', *Fontaine*, No. 61 (Sept. 1947), pp. 453–60.

M. Mohrt, 'Ethic and poetry in the work of Camus', *Yale French Studies*, I, No. 1 (Spring/Summer 1948), pp. 113–18.

W. M. Frohock, 'Camus: Image, influence and sensibility', *Yale French Studies*, II, No. 2 (Fall 1949), pp. 91–9.

J. Guiguet, 'Deux romans existentialistes: *La Nausée* et *L'Étranger*', *French Review*, XXIII, 2 (Dec. 1949), pp. 86–91.

R. Bespaloff, 'Le monde du condamné à mort', *Esprit*, XVIII (Jan. 1950), pp. 1–26.

G. Bataille, 'Le temps de la révolte', *Critique*, Nos. 55 and 56 (Dec. 1951 and Jan. 1952), pp. 1019–27 and 29–41.

A. Blanchet, ''L'Homme révolté' d'Albert Camus', *Études*, CCLXXII (Jan. 1952), pp. 48–60.

M. Moré, 'Les Racines métaphysiques de la révolte', *Dieu vivant* (1952), pp. 35–59.

A. Béguin, 'Albert Camus, la révolte et le bonheur', *Esprit*, XX (April 1952), pp. 736–46.

R. Dadoun, 'Albert Camus le méditerranéen. Le rêve de lumière et le complexe du clos-obscur', *Simoun*, 3 (June 1952), pp. 42–7.

P. Colin, 'Athéisme et révolte chez Camus', *La Vie intellectuelle*, VII (July 1952), pp. 30–51.

K. Lanser, ''Albert Camus', *Kenyon Review*, XIV, 4 (1952), pp. 562–78.

C. Buroca, 'Rencontres de deux points de vue: réflexions sur l'art chez Camus et chez Malraux', *Simoun*, 8 (1953), pp. 116–19.

C. A. Viggiani, 'Camus' *L'Étranger*', *PMLA*, LXXI, 5 (Dec. 1956), pp. 865–87.

INDEX

Index

Index

Index